WHY US

A fresh, honest look at the subject of infertility which shows how simple self-help measures can commonly work wonders, and gives reassurance and invaluable practical advice.

Andrew Stanway M.B., M.R.C.P., was a medical registrar at a London teaching hospital until twelve years ago. He now lectures, broadcasts, writes and makes films on medical topics, both for the medical profession and for the general public.

He has written many books including titles on nutrition and child care. *Breast is Best,* written jointly with his wife, has become a worldwide best seller. He is married with three children and lives in Surrey where he has a practice dealing with marital and psychosexual problems.

By the same author
ALTERNATIVE MEDICINE (Pelican)
THE BABY AND CHILD BOOK (Pan)
THE BOOTS BOOK OF FIRST AID
THE BREAST BOOK (Granada)
BREAST IS BEST (Pan)
CHOICES IN CHILDBIRTH (Pan)
THE COMPLETE BOOK OF LOVE AND SEX (Century)
A DICTIONARY OF OPERATIONS (Granada)
A GUIDE TO BIOCHEMIC TISSUE SALTS (Van Dyke)
OVERCOMING DEPRESSION (Hamlyn)
THE PEARS ENCYCLOPAEDIA OF CHILD HEALTH (Pelham)
TAKING THE ROUGH WITH THE SMOOTH (Pan)
TRACE ELEMENTS – A NEW CHAPTER IN NUTRITION (Van Dyke)

WHY US?

A common-sense guide for the childless

by

Dr Andrew Stanway

THORSONS PUBLISHERS LIMITED
Wellingborough, Northamptonshire

First published 1980
Second edition, completely revised and reset, 1984

© DR ANDREW STANWAY 1984

This book is sold subject to the condition that it shall not, by way of trade or otherwise, be lent, re-sold, hired out, or otherwise circulated without the publisher's prior consent in any form of binding or cover other than that in which it is published and without a similar condition including this condition being imposed on the subsequent purchaser.

British Library Cataloguing in Publication Data

Stanway, Andrew
  Why us? — 2nd edn
  1. Infertility
  I. Title
  616.6'9206   RC889

ISBN 0-7225-0952-9

Printed and bound in Great Britain

Acknowledgements

I should like to thank the following who have helped me with this book: The Association of British Adoption and Fostering Agencies; Dr J. D. Bromhall, Oxford University; Dr P. Cauthery; The Chief Rabbi's Office; The Ciba Foundation; Judith Lane and her colleagues at Oxford whose tape-recorded discussions with infertile couples helped me enormously; Peter Houghton and the National Association for the Childless; The National Foster Care Association; all the patients who have so freely talked to me about their problems; and especially John Newton, Professor of Obstetrics and Gynaecology at the Queen Elizabeth Medical Centre, University of Birmingham and editor of the international medical journal *Clinical Reproduction and Fertility*, whose help, encouragement and comments on the final typescript were so valuable.

Finally, I should like to thank Mr Elliot Philipp M.A., F.R.C.S., F.R.C.O.G. for kindly reviewing the book in this, the second edition, and for making many useful suggestions which bring it right up to date.

CONTENTS

	Page
Foreword	9
Introduction	11

Chapter
1. The Basic Equipment and How it Works ... 23
2. Helping Yourselves ... 41
3. Female Infertility and its Treatment ... 58
4. Male Infertility and its Treatment ... 81
5. Sorting Out the Causes ... 98
6. All in the Mind? ... 141
7. Miscarriage ... 150
8. The Impact on the Couple ... 162
9. Artificial Insemination (AI) ... 172
10. What If All Else Fails? ... 185
11. The Future ... 200
    Glossary ... 209
    Useful Addresses ... 218
    Index ... 219

Foreword

At last we have a book on this subject for the general reader, full of up-to-date facts. So often in the past books dealing with infertility have considered only one partner or one aspect of the problem, and have not usually mentioned the simple, practical 'self-help' that informed couples can use that so often results in pregnancy.

Why Us? contains easily understood chapters on the male and female causes of infertility, an excellent discussion on 'sorting out the causes', and advice on what a couple can expect from infertility investigations. Andrew Stanway has also included valuable information on the psychological aspects of infertility and the effects of childlessness on the couple involved. He discusses the alternatives to having your own child in 'What if all else fails?'

Altogether this excellent book is a must for all couples having problems with fertility, and one that all doctors who are interested in this subject should read as well.

John Newton
Professor of Obstetrics and Gynaecology,
University of Birmingham

Introduction

'Why on earth write a book about *that*?' 'Surely you could use your time better writing a book to help people who are really ill?' 'Anyway, there are far too many children already, so how can you possibly justify helping people to have more?' 'They ought to be grateful; I spend all my time trying to *stop* having them.'

These are just some of the remarks made to me while I was writing this book. Many highly intelligent, thinking people were incredulous that there was a need for such a book and often felt that the potential readers just ought to pull themselves together and get on with their lives. Anyway, there couldn't be that many of them, so why bother? Never in my fourteen years of writing about medicine for the public have I come across a subject that is so important to the sufferers yet is so ill-understood by the rest of society. This, together with time spent with couples who needed information and support, led me to write this book.

Clearly a subject as important as infertility could occupy a volume at least twice this size with considerations of the myths and taboos, the cultural importance of children, reasons for and against having children, people's motivations for wanting children and so on. The list of possibilities is endless, but my experience of infertile couples is that they want practical help rather than academic dissertations, so it is a practical book that I have written.

What is infertility?

Infertility can be primary or secondary. Primary infertility is arbitrarily defined as the inability to achieve a pregnancy after a year of unprotected, unlimited intercourse, or the inability to carry a pregnancy to birth. Secondary infertility is the term applied to those women who have conceived before but cannot conceive again. This is often called second pregnancy infertility. Sterility is a term meaning permanent and incurable infertility, and the term sub-fertile is sometimes used of people who are infertile but who don't seem to have a serious medical problem. This latter is not a good term and is probably used to give hope or to spare the feelings of certain infertile people.

How common is it?

There have been many surveys of primary infertility rates and figures between 11 and 22 per cent have been quoted. It is generally accepted that about 15 per cent of the adult population in the childbearing age group is primarily infertile. In the UK there are 16 million people between the ages of twenty and forty (which can be reasonably assumed to be the childbearing years). If 15 per cent of these are primarily infertile, this gives 2.4 million affected people. Add to this the proportion of secondarily infertile couples who never seek medical help and the number of infertile people in the UK soon reaches the three million mark. That's a lot of people, all of whom have been through or are going through a major life crisis – their inability to have their own children. The amount of heartache and suffering that this causes is enormous and involves not only the couples themselves but often their parents too – another four people per couple. Yet for all this, because of the nature of the subject, many couples have been inclined until recent times to keep their infertility to themselves. This is why most of us would say, if asked, that we don't know any infertile couples. We do, in fact, but they just don't go around talking about it.

As if all this isn't a bad enough picture, there is good evidence that the infertility rate is on the increase and that with the children born in the baby boom of the sixties coming up to childbearing age we're in for a massive increase in the absolute numbers of infertile people.

Is infertility becoming more common?

Infertility is becoming more common for several reasons. First, many couples are electing to stay childfree until their late twenties and early thirties and by this age fertility is beginning to diminish. Maximum fertility in the West seems to be at about the age of eighteen to twenty, and after that fertility rates decline. Well over 30 per cent of married women between the ages of forty and forty-four are infertile, and over this age the figure is strikingly higher. One UK survey found that three-quarters of mothers having a baby when they were thirty or more had been having unprotected intercourse for more than two years before they conceived.

Second, venereal diseases are now the fastest-growing epidemic diseases in the world and the growth figures are especially high and alarming among teenagers. A substantial proportion of girls with gonorrhoea have no symptoms and by the time they know something is wrong, the damage has been done. Gonorrhoea is probably the second biggest single cause of infertility after ovulation disorders, and is growing fast to become the number one cause of infertility.

Third, prolonged use of the Pill can cause a slow return of periods after cessation of the drug in about 2 per cent of women. This might seem a very small proportion indeed, but there are $3\frac{1}{2}$ million women on the Pill at any one time in the UK, so this adds up to a large number of individuals. The IUD is more popular now than it has been for many years and has been shown to delay conception for a short while after its removal. Older women especially seem to fare badly when it comes to conceiving after the removal of an IUD. Additionally, therapeutic abortions can be followed by infection and damage to the cervix in a small proportion of cases, and more abortions are being done every year so the number of women affected by these, admittedly uncommon, side effects is building up. Reliable statistics on the effect of abortions on subsequent fertility are hard to come by though, because women often deny having had abortions. One Yugoslavian study found that 63 per cent of known first-pregnancy aborters denied the abortion at an interview. The infertility rate after medically-induced abortions is probably about 1-2 per cent according to several surveys that followed women for several years *after* their abortions.

Fourth, our exposure to drugs, environmental pollutants and food additives is also rising and any or all of these may play a part in infertility as may specific nutrient lack. (For a discussion of the role of zinc deficiency, for example, see page 92.) Increasing numbers of drugs used quite legitimately in medicine are being found to affect sperm production adversely, and more people are abusing marijuana and hard drugs than ever before. These are known to reduce fertility by a variety of mechanisms, as does alcohol.

So all in all the actual numbers of infertile people in the UK and indeed in the West as a whole will quite probably rise to over 20 per cent in the next decade or two. An American professor of sociology and demographic studies writing in the magazine *Scientific American* provides evidence that the populations of East and West Germany, Austria and Luxembourg have already gone beyond zero population growth and that by the year 2015 both the US and the USSR will be recording more deaths than births. He, and others, foresee a time soon when Western governments will have to pay couples to have children.

What can be done?

Infertility is a frustrating and difficult condition to treat from a doctor's point of view. Emotions run high, the infertile couple naturally wants miracles, the level of information the average couple has is extremely low and their expectations paradoxically high and, when all is said and done, the best of modern medicine can only produce a pregnancy in just over half of all those who seek help even though a cause can be found in about 90 per cent of couples. However, having treatment is still much better than doing nothing, because among couples who have been infertile for a year or more, the chances of a pregnancy occuring 'out of the blue' are about 5 per cent.

Even after adoption, artificial insemination and all the medical world can offer, something like 40 per cent of all infertile couples come to the point where nothing can be done and they have to come to terms with childlessness. I firmly believe that if only people in and around the medical profession 'came clean' early on in the relationship and told the infertile couple that they have a 60-40 chance of sucess it could well defuse the tension of expectation from day one and so help the couple more. Most couples I've listened to honestly believed that with modern technological medicine anything was possible and that it was simply a matter of time before the doctors overcame their infertility. This leads to false hopes being raised at every test and treatment attempt. Of course, we should all be optimistic, especially as new treatments are being discovered all the time, but let's also be realistic.

Is infertility a real medical problem?

Quite often couples I've talked to about their infertility, especially before they embark on the medical road, seem apologetic for bothering the medical profession. Sometimes they feel that they're being impatient and should really have waited longer before putting the matter in the hands of the medical world and others feel guilty at taking up the doctor's time which could, they reason, be better spent in caring for the sick.

Let me put their minds at rest on both of these scores. First, if you've been trying seriously to have a baby for a year or more, with reasonably frequent intercourse and no contraception, no doctor will feel that you're wasting his time by seeing him too soon. If after two or three months you haven't conceived and go panicking to the doctor you certainly are expecting too much, but all he'll do is to suggest you try for longer (unless you're well into your thirties, in which case he'll probably refer you to a specialist).

On the second point, don't simply think of doctors as being there to cure people of dreadful diseases. This simply isn't the case. The vast majority of those going to their general practitioners are not seriously ill. In fact a very substantial proportion have nothing physically wrong with them at all and simply need reassurance, a shoulder to cry on, marital guidance or even just a sympathetic listener. No one will blame you for seeking medical help for infertility, especially if it has begun to worry you and upset your life. If doctors only treated cancers, heart attacks and other 'real' diseases they'd be idle most of the time. The 'not bothering the doctor' couples are especially found among those who are secondarily infertile. They feel, wrongly in my opinion, that because they have had one child already the doctor might tell them to count their blessings and not bother themselves further. No good doctor should say this and there is no reason why you should not seek help if you can't have a second baby just as quickly as if it were your first.

The only proviso I would put on seeking medical help for infertility is that if you are doing so to try to mend a broken or shaky marriage, it's probably a mistake – there is no evidence that having a baby mends marriages and the possibility that you'll end up with a baby *and* a broken marriage should be carefully weighed before you seek this way out of your problem. Of course the best thing to do is to get professional help for your marital problems.

If ever you ask yourself whether infertility is really a medical problem, just remember that with medical help your chances of success are raised tenfold compared with doing nothing – and that's a level of odds that few other people going to doctors can expect.

People's reactions

People's reactions to the childless are very varied but by and large the images they have are highly stereotyped. Many people think that the infertile are at best sad and lonely and at worst pathetic and bitter. The childless couple is often seen as having a dull, lifeless home, full of material things to compensate for the lack of children. The woman is depicted as hard and career-minded or alternatively pathetic and devoted to animals. The man is portrayed as cold and sexless with possibly even a touch of homosexuality. This pathetic pair, it is assumed, look after each other like some kind of juvenile Darby and Joan.

These images, just like most other stereotypes, are unfair to the vast majority of involuntarily childless couples and are probably typical of very few indeed. Unfortunately, living with other people's preconceptions of what being involuntarily childless is like, is a major part of the problem.

By the time you've bought this book you may have decided (possibly wrongly) that you're infertile and may also have decided whether or not to tell people about it. Many women discuss this subject with their closest friends and others tell their mothers. From my experience most couples don't broadcast their problem and often keep it a secret between themselves. By the time you've read this you'll have been through all the 'innocent' remarks and probing about when you're going to start a family, and you'll know just how unkind and hurtful these can be. It's to save themselves from these often well-meaning but in practice hurtful remarks that so many couples withdraw into themselves and keep their infertility a secret. I was with a woman recently who had confided in her dearest friend only to be told 'Well, you can always get a dog – they're wonderful company'. This kind of remark is easily made and was of no importance whatsoever to the person who made it, who simply thought she was being helpful. But to the infertile woman herself it was a deeply painful comment that sent her away in tears. As she said later, 'Would she like to have a dog in exchange for one of her children? How can she equate a dog with the child I so want?'

Unfortunately, the results of coming out with your problem can be just as unpleasant because you open yourself up to people's pity and no one wants to feel pitiable, especially when he's in the prime of life, healthy and has everything going for him. Real understanding and sympathy are, of course, helpful but it's terribly difficult to get these from people who don't understand the problem. A book my wife and I wrote on breast feeding exposed exactly comparable problems. We found that women who wanted to breast feed experienced considerable sadness when they failed to do so, and that this was not understood either by those who wanted to bottle feed or by those who breast fed easily. In these deep rooted personal matters it is perhaps asking too much of our friends and relatives really to understand. So my advice is to be highly selective about who you share your problems with. Don't be secretive, but be careful. The girl with four children who 'fell out of the sky' could be the last person to confide in because she probably won't know what you're going on about and anyway spends most of her time worrying about preventing number five.

Probably the best people to help are those who have experienced a similar problem themselves. Such people are to be found in self-help groups. Whatever a sophisticated clinic can offer, it cannot offer the time to chat around the subject that most couples need. One of the commonest complaints I hear is that the professionals simply don't have enough time and this is usually true. Ideally, each new couple at an infertility clinic should be able to spend an hour or so discussing their problem and all its ramifications with someone who knows, cares and is neutral, but this can only rarely be achieved in practice. A few of the more forward-looking centres are encouraging self-help counsellors to work alongside the professionals in their clinics and this is proving extremely valuable. After all, the majority of doctors have no personal experience of infertility and can only regard it in a technical and scientific way, however sympathetic they may feel.

This brings me to the doctors you'll meet. Most of them will have chosen to involve themselves in this field and are therefore genuinely interested in it. Most of them will be aware of all the problems you're going through and will certainly do all they can to help explain things to you. Don't be afraid to ask them what you want to know. By the time you first go to a specialist clinic you'll already have been through the mill socially and personally and will already have a lot of questions to ask. After all, it's not like getting appendicitis and turning up in hospital for the doctor to remove your appendix. The doctors who involve themselves in this area of medicine are generally exceptionally caring and sympathetic but they can't read your mind or answer questions you don't ask. Make a note of all the things you want to know before your first visit to the specialist clinic and when the doctor has asked all of his questions, ask yours. He won't think this is rude and will welcome the opportunity to learn what is most troubling you. Infertility and its management isn't like the 'treatment' of many other conditions. With infertility you enter into a teamwork situation with your clinic – it's you two and them working together towards a common goal. Your co-operation will be needed and expected, and you must be ready to be more than a passive 'patient' who just lets the medical investigations and treatment wash over you.

What childless people say

While I was researching this book, listening to infertile couples, their counsellors and medical advisers, a great many of them made remarks (which were often cries from the heart) which seemed to crystallize the nature of the problems infertile couples have. Many outsiders who have never been involved with infertility cannot understand what all the fuss is about – I hope the next few pages will enlighten them. I also hope they'll help the many infertile couples who feel so alone with their problem to realize that there are millions of others in the same predicament and that they are *not* alone with their feelings.

'I feel that we are being denied a basic human right, not necessarily by society but by Nature.'

'I can't stand seeing other girls with babies. I even got to the stage of thinking of stealing one but my husband said if I did it would only be harder as it would have to go back to its real mum ...please try to help.'

'I keep on telling my husband we should have sex more often...but I do realize my husband is not a machine...this is not doing our marriage any good.'

'She has tried Valium but is afraid of becoming addicted...she needs some form of treatment for the nerve trouble she experiences. The gynaecologist is more concerned with her physical condition but emotionally she is very upset.'

'Our emotions are really taking a battering...how does one go about ceasing to try too hard? It is difficult to be rational when deep down I feel obsessed by my own childlessness and having had an abortion eight years ago doesn't help.'

'We would do anything for this longed-for child but we are at a loss to know where to go for help...I know I get depressed and tense but how can I combat that?'

'Sadly, I am one of the women you'll know so well...I never stop counting the days to my next period, hopeful, "fertile" days. I sometimes drive myself crazy...two days late and my personality changes – everyone is marvellous...then the despair comes with the period. As soon as the worst is over, I'm planning next month, what I'll do and when, obsessive I know but I cannot help it.'

'I am going to kill myself. How I hate my barren, stagnant, wasted, useless body.'

'I am waiting for a divorce after an infertile marriage, the problems of which I faced alone, as my husband refused help and refused to help me.'

'We went to see if AIH or AID were possible...this was very depressing...the attitude of the doctors was offhand, almost distant. Our problem seems never ending...if we knew the medical facts...then if nothing could be done...we could at least carry on with our lives in peace.'

'We thought about AID but everyone makes it out to be almost criminal.'

'I strongly advise any wife of a sterile man, who longs for a child to have one. BY FAIR MEANS OR FOUL, DO IT NOW. Don't believe "they" will discover something tomorrow to help you. They will not. It's up to you to help yourself.'

'As a sub-fertile man in London one might expect to find some form of NHS provision but all I can find are clinics run as off-shoots of urology and endocrinology departments and few doctors with real concern for the overall problem.'

'I remember sitting out there alone (in the waiting area) and thinking that no one else can feel as bad about this as I do – it's a great release of tension to talk.'

'The worst problem is the name of it – "The Infertility Clinic" – I felt I was signing up for a leprosy colony or something.'

'It's a lot easier to talk to girls here who you know are in the same position rather than to friends about it.'

'It's the sort of problem you think only happens to other people – it's such a fundamental part of life.'

'If only people knew that everyone feels as badly. You can come here (to the clinic) for months and feel completely isolated, even though we're all sitting around trying to put a good face on it.'

'You get the feeling when they come to see you that they think it's your fault, your not wanting children, there's something odd about you – and you try to explain that you can't have children for some reason or another but you're not quite sure what the reason is.'

'I find that when we go somewhere where there are little children or babies, people say "she will play with them" and you can see them thinking "let her nurse the baby as she may not be able to have her own" and I feel like throwing it back at them.'

'My husband comes from a large family and they've all got children. Their attitude is to get married and have children and they think it's terrible we haven't got any – but I would never tell them. One or two of my friends at work know because I keep coming up (to the hospital) and you can't keep making excuses.'

'The most innocent remarks people make can be absolutely devastating at the time – for years I pretended I didn't want children – it was a form of self-protection.'

'I used to find I'd go into town and buy all sorts of things I didn't want and we couldn't afford – it was a sort of compensation. This was before I met anyone else in the same position – I felt I was going round the bend.'

'I go upstairs and weep about nothing in particular – if the potatoes boil over or something.'

'I feel I think about it all the time although I work full-time – I don't think there's an hour in the day goes by when I don't think about it. I kid myself it's not so important because I've got a husband and we love each other, we've got a nice home and all these animals, so we don't really need a baby – and I know damned well I'm lying.'

'You want to know which way your life is going – are you going to be a wife and mother or are you going to be a career woman.'

'The longer the treatment goes on the more demoralized you become – you feel a terrible failure – everyone around you is having kids – after a while they stop mentioning the subject.'

'This is what I've got more than anything – a tremendous sense of failure – towards my husband too – because it's me. Society has this pressure on you too, firstly to get married and then have children, especially if career-wise you're not going very far.'

'You just don't know whether it'll be next month or in five years, so it's difficult to plan anything.'

'My only fear is, like getting older all the time, that it gets more difficult to have one – you get that fear that the older you are the less chance you're going to have. Yes, that's when the panic sets in.'

'Once or twice friends have said "I'll lend you my husband" or "you should get a change". Friends are full of good advice. There's the feeling that you don't know how to have intercourse properly either, and that's very hurtful.'

'We have a fairly busy social life because if I sit at home I get more and more depressed and withdrawn.'

'My three closest friends all got pregnant one after the other and one of them didn't tell me until it showed, and then she sent her husband round to break the news. She was the one I felt I could always talk to and I felt she'd betrayed me.'

'My friend was upset that she'd fallen pregnant and didn't want one and I was upset that she was pregnant and didn't want one and I did. All the time she was pregnant it was really difficult – we had to work at being friends.'

'My husband says I'm not interested in him at all – just using him as a stallion almost. We want a baby because we're so happy together but it's not helping us to continue to be happy together – going through all this – yet I haven't reached the stage where I could accept the fact of not having a child at all.'

'It makes intercourse a cold experience – my husband complained I was only interested when my temperature went up.'

'I remember saying to my husband – "you can't be tired –

I've had my injections!"'

'It's like a vicious circle – on the one hand they say "relax, forget all about it" – but how can you when every time you think "perhaps this is it" and you rush to see if the temperature is doing anything?'

Conclusions

Infertility is a difficult condition to experience. There's nothing to show for it, you get little sympathy from those who have children and don't see the problem, and even less from those who choose to remain childfree and envy you. Because life has become more controllable and we now have almost 100 per cent effective contraception, society believes that doctors should be able to 'cure' 100 per cent of infertile couples, but this isn't so. In Western countries where many people plan their families as a chef plans a menu and in which children have become controlled commodities, you're in the awkward position of being unable to plan your life at all and this makes you feel even more unusual than you already do. Social pressures and religious and mythological beliefs all form part of the backdrop against which you have to bear your burden, and all the time society is changing its views on marriage, childbearing and family life. You've chosen to have children and you have been 'cheated'. Perhaps this is the first time in your life that you've come up against an immovable barrier and such a barrier is inevitably frustrating and even painful.

None of this is easy and it's for this reason that I decided to write this book. Unlike most books that have been written on this subject I have not written it from a doctor's standpoint. I first talked to infertile couples and their counsellors and found out what they most wanted to know, and then built a book around those needs. I hope I've succeeded.

CHAPTER 1

The Basic Equipment and How it Works

Surprising though it may seem, many people are ignorant or badly informed about their reproductive organs. A basic knowledge is however, an essential background to understand infertility.

Every infertility clinic has its share of stories which prove time and again that there are many who don't know some of the most basic things about their reproductive organs and that very often it's intelligent, middle-class people who are the most ignorant.

At a time when everyone is supposed to be so enlightened sexually it makes it even more difficult for those with doubts to come out with them for fear of seeming completely backward at worst or simply 'not with it' at best. A small proportion of couples attending infertility clinics haven't been having intercourse properly – they haven't got the basic plumbing sorted out and soon conceive when they were put right. Some couples are keen enough to do the right thing but, through ignorance, never quite achieve it. A girl of twenty-three attended an infertility clinic because she hadn't got pregnant after four years of regular intercourse. When she was examined, her urinary passage (urethra) was found to be grossly distended where her husband had been using it instead of the vagina. A man and his wife, both aged twenty-six, had been attempting to use the navel as a vagina because, they reasoned (wrongly), as children come out that way, they must get in that way too. So the stories go on. Even doctors and nurses are not immune to such problems, surprising though it may seem. Nonconsummated marriages are uncommon in the general population but are not so among the so-called infertile. Virgin wives clearly cannot conceive and need help.

So while many people are busy experimenting with sex aids, unusual love-making positions and all that the 'enlightened eighties' expects of young couples, a substantial number haven't even got past the starter's gun. Many of these attend an infertility clinic as their first port of call, simply because in spite of doing everything right (in their eyes) the woman is not getting pregnant. I hope this next section will help. Don't get the idea though that infertility is a sexual dysfunction in the majority of cases. Most infertile couples are having intercourse perfectly normally, albeit too infrequently in many cases. This chapter isn't aimed at those readers who have gross areas of ignorance or misunderstanding, rather it tries to give a factual backdrop to how the reproductive system works.

The female reproductive system and how it works

The *vulva* is the external and easily visible portion of a woman's sex organs and consists of several parts. The external genitals of a woman are very unobtrusive compared with a man's and when the woman has her legs together there is almost nothing to see. A mound of fat covers the pubic bone of the pelvis and this is in turn covered by an inverted triangle of hair. When a woman opens her legs the first parts that are most obvious are the large lips (labia majora). These are simply folds of skin which close over the inner and smaller lips (labia minora). These smaller lips unite above the clitoris, a highly sensitive organ made like a miniature penis. This book is not a sex manual so we cannot go into the great detail here about the sexual function of any part of the reproductive organs but because reproduction is intimately bound up with sexuality in man, a few points are worth considering as we go along.

The function of the *clitoris* has been much debated over the centuries and, as is so often the case, the ancient Greeks got it right when they called it a clitoris (from the Greek word for a 'key') because they thought that it was the key to a woman's sexual satisfaction. While some women can and do have

THE BASIC EQUIPMENT AND HOW IT WORKS

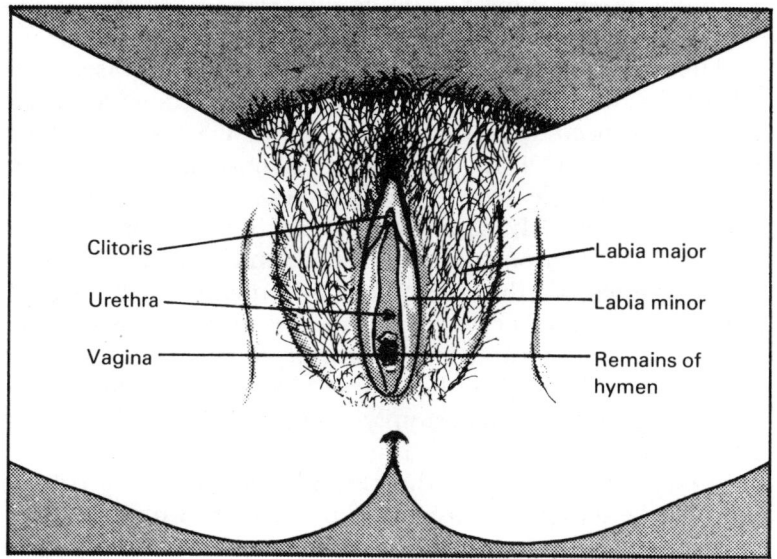

The external genitals of a woman.

orgasms when other parts of the body are stimulated, most women are best sexually aroused by stimulation of the clitoris. It's very important for a man to get to know his partner's likes and dislikes when it comes to caressing her clitoris. Because it's such a sensitive organ and because women differ so greatly as to what they find enjoyable, the attentive man will take great pains to find exactly what pleases his partner most. The best way of doing this is to get her to tell and show him exactly how she'd like him to caress her and then guide him in doing it. Not only is this highly arousing for both partners but it also lays the foundation for a good physical relationship. Many men feel that such an approach is too 'mechanical' or 'clinical' but most women strongly disagree and very much appreciate a man who takes the trouble to find out what pleases them and then sticks to it.

There isn't room here to discuss the arguments surrounding vaginal and clitoral orgasms but it has now been shown that the majority of women are able to reach an orgasm only by clitoral stimulation and that in some women when a so-called vaginal orgasm occurs, it does so because the movement of the penis in the vagina causes a rhythmical pulling on the surroundings of the clitoris or because possibly in certain coital positions direct clitoral stimulation occurs when the man's body rubs against the woman's.

This at least is the current thinking based on the research of Masters and Johnson. However, several experts would disagree, especially in the light of recent US research which suggests that at least some women have a sensitive and sexually arousable area in the front wall of the vagina called the G-spot. Indeed, many women say that their best arousal occurs when their partner's fingers or penis stimulate this area of the vagina and that the nature and quality of the orgasm such stimulation produces is totally different from that produced by clitoral stimulation. Argument will no doubt rage around this subject for years to come but many women know that this research simply proves what they have been saying for years.

Manual stimulation of the clitoris can take place before, during or even after intercourse and in some women a combination of two or even all three of these will be what they like best. Many couples find that the clitoris is best caressed (along with the rest of the woman's body, of course) *before* making love. With the vulva excited, intercourse is especially pleasurable for both partners. If the position for intercourse is carefully chosen, the man can caress his partner's clitoris with his penis inside her. This can be very exciting because it is then possible to have simultaneous orgasms, if that is what the couple wants.

I've gone into some detail about the clitoris because not only is it one of the least well understood parts of a woman's genitals (except by the woman herself, of course) but because it probably has considerable significance in infertility.

To say that an orgasm is necessary for a woman to get pregnant is clearly nonsense because millions of women never experience orgasms during intercourse yet easily become pregnant. However, in a sub-fertile couple in whom the odds against easy conception are high for whatever reason, an orgasm can probably help get the man's sperms where they're needed. It has long been known in animal husbandry that a sexually excited female's uterus actually sucks sperms into its cavity. Sperms themselves move only extremely slowly, yet they can be found within a few minutes of intercourse in the fallopian tubes. They could not have swum this distance and so were almost certainly sucked up by the negative pressures that develop in the contracting uterus at orgasm. Any woman who has orgasms knows the sensation of the womb contracting but may not realize that in between each contraction there is a phase of negative pressure. This negative pressure, together with muscular contractions induced by substances in semen called prostaglandins, probably results in the transport of sperms up the fallopian tubes far quicker than could be accounted for by the sperms' swimming alone. Sperms have been found in human fallopian tubes as soon as five minutes after insemination and sperms swim at only a tiny fraction of this speed.

So, if a woman is having difficulty getting pregnant, it pays her and her partner to so organize their sex lives as to ensure that they either climax together (which may not be desired or even easy to achieve) or for the woman to have her orgasm after her husband has ejaculated so that her womb will suck up sperms as she climaxes. I'm not suggesting that this should necessarily become a routine – there are far too many of those imposed on the sex lives of infertile couples – but an increased orgasm rate around the time of ovulation in the presence of reasonable numbers of healthy sperms in the vagina may well result in a pregnancy and save a lot of trips to doctors and hospital clinics. Also, a woman who is enjoying orgasms will almost certainly want sex more often and this will enhance her chances of getting pregnant.

Behind the clitoris is a tiny opening – that of the urethra. This is the opening of the urinary passage that runs from the bladder to the outside. It is not part of a woman's sexual apparatus. Behind this is the opening to the vagina and behind that again the anus or back passage.

The *vagina*, contrary to popular belief, isn't a hollow tube inside a woman's body. It's because it's only a potential space that it's so pleasurable for a man whatever the size of his penis. The vaginal walls are usually in contact except when something is put inside. The vagina is about three or four inches long and extends from the hymen (a sheet of skin that almost closes off the outer end in virgins) to the uterus (womb) inside the body. It runs backwards and upwards and has very elastic walls. They have to stretch to let a baby out and so have no trouble letting a penis in! The vagina is moistened by fluids produced by the cervix (mouth of the womb) and these are particularly plentiful at certain times of the month (see page 119). When a woman is sexually aroused, fluid is produced by the walls of the vagina and it is these fluids that

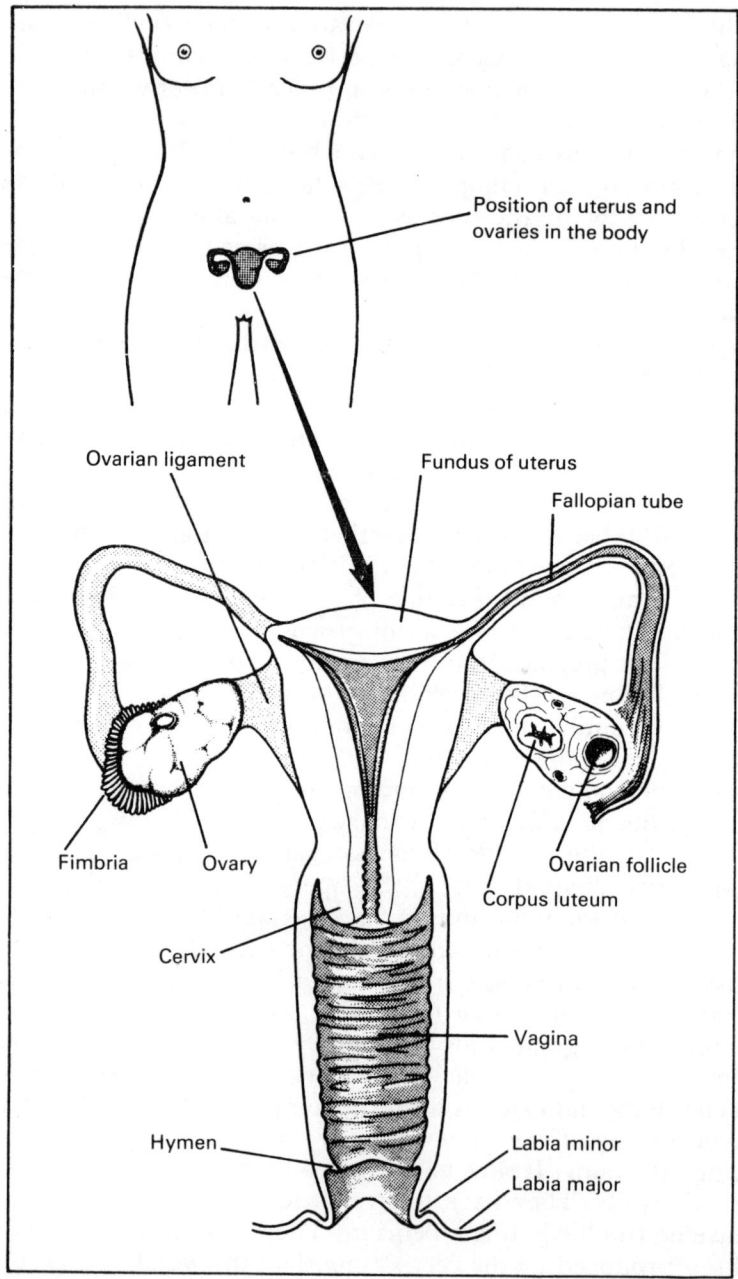

The female reproductive tract. (Ovary and fallopian tube on the right are shown in section.)

make intercourse pleasurable and painless for both partners. Many women when sexually aroused produce lots of these secretions, but, as far as is known, there is no relationship between the likelihood of conceiving and the amount of fluid produced.

Because the vagina is only a potential space, as soon as the man has taken his penis out the walls go back together again and semen and vaginal secretions can leak out. This can be a problem in couples in which the man only has a small volume of semen, because it may all leak out and so never be able to get to where it's needed. More about this on page 86.

After normal intercourse some of the semen lies in a pool at the top of the vagina near the mouth of the womb and the sperms can then swim up, possibly aided by suction, to meet an egg.

Inside the vagina, at the top end, lies the entrance to the womb (uterus). The *uterus* is a pear-shaped, muscular organ about three inches long and two inches across at its widest part (fundus). The widest part of the pear shape points down into the top of the vagina and the body of the 'pear' lies above the vagina in the pelvis. The neck or cervix of the womb (the narrowest part) lies within the vagina and it is this that can be felt with your fingers. In most women the uterus is angled slightly forwards but in about 20 per cent it is tipped backwards (retroverted). It used to be thought that women with retroverted uteri were more likely to be infertile but this is now known not to be so. Occasionally a woman with a retroverted uterus may have another reason for her infertility that is also causing her uterus to tip backwards. Endometriosis or adhesions secondary to pelvic infection can cause this but it is not the backward tilt of the uterus that causes the infertility.

The uterus has a cavity which is triangular and flat, the point of which ends in the narrow canal inside the cervix. The uterus is lined with a special type of cellular tissue called endometrium and the cervix is normally plugged up with mucus, the significance of which we shall see in later chapters. Suffice it to say that when a woman is most likely to conceive (around the time of ovulation) her cervical mucus is most encouraging to sperms, and that when this mechanism fails in some way, her partner's sperms, however plentiful, may not get past the cervical mucus barrier.

At the top of the wide end of the uterus two tubes enter. These are the *fallopian tubes* that run from the ovaries to the uterus. Each fallopian tube is about four inches long and is thinner in diameter than the lead in a pencil. They have very muscular walls, lined with hairlike projections. Both walls and projections move in such a way as to waft ova (eggs) progressively along from the ovaries to the uterus. Cells lining the tubes produce substances that alter sperms so that they can fertilize an egg – indeed, fertilization of an egg by a sperm occurs in the fallopian tubes. The open ends of the tubes are called the *fimbriated ends* and are a sophisticated collection apparatus to ensure that eggs are caught and channelled down into the fallopian tubes. There are numerous nervous, hormonal and chemical mechanisms at work in normal fallopian tube function and we still know very little of exactly what goes on. But just as the structure and physiology of the fallopian tubes is vital to the downward passage of an egg, it is also as important for the upward progress of the sperms. Subtle chemical changes take place in sperms as they travel along the tubes to meet an egg, changes which are essential if the sperm is to be in a condition to fertilize the egg it meets. This process of sperm maturation is called *capacitation*.

The *ovaries* lie below the fimbriated ends. They are paired organs lying one each side of the pelvis, about the size of walnuts, that have two functions. First, they release a ripened egg each month and, second, they produce progesterone and oestrogen – two important female hormones. The ovaries are amazing organs because when a baby girl is born she already has all her eggs (40,000-50,000) in her ovaries. After puberty the eggs begin to ripen or mature at the rate of one a month under the influence of complicated hormonal changes that occur cyclically. This happens every month (unless the woman is pregnant or breast feeding) until the end of her reproductive life, when the menopause intervenes. In practice, many eggs begin to mature each month but for some unknown reason only one actually ripens. The average woman has 400-450 cycles in a lifetime. The ripening and release of an egg each month is called *ovulation*.

A woman's body functions in a cyclical way, each cycle lasting about a month. It's important to remember that this is only an average and that there can be large variations in cycle length that are still quite normal. In a classical 'text book' cycle, the events run as follows. The first day of the cycle is taken as the first day of menstruation. This is the day when the lining of the womb, realizing that it is not going to be needed for a pregnancy, starts shedding itself in the form of clots, cells and blood. The brain (particularly the hypothalamus) influences a tiny gland that lies near it (the pituitary gland) to produce a hormone called follicle stimulating hormone (FSH) which stimulates the ovary to ripen an egg that month. Another hormone, luteinizing hormone (LH), is produced in only very small quantities early in the cycle. Suddenly, in the middle of the cycle (somewhere around the 13th day in a woman with a 28-day cycle) a surge in the level of LH starts. The egg is usually released about 30 hours after the beginning of the surge when the production of LH reaches its peak. The release of the egg usually occurs 30-36 hours after the start of the surge and is helped by the production of prostaglandins in the follicle. This exact timing of ovulation is more important for *in vitro* fertilization (see page 201) but is of considerable importance too in naturally occuring pregnancies. The release of the egg is called ovulation and it is at this stage that a woman is most likely to conceive. Some women experience abdominal discomfort at this time

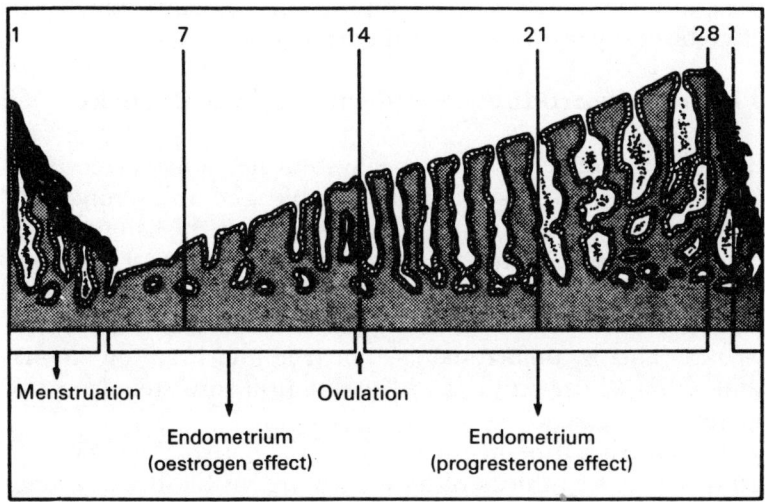

Diagram to show how the lining of the uterus builds up over a menstrual cycle – to be shed at the end of the cycle.

(mittelschmerz – the German word for middle-of-the-cycle pain).

Each month then, an egg is released from one of the ovaries and 'collected' by the fimbriated ends of the tube. It takes about three days for an egg to pass along the tube. While this is all going on, the ruptured egg sac on the ovary turns into a functioning gland called a *corpus luteum* which produces another hormone called progesterone. Progesterone together with oestrogen, acts on the lining of the uterus in such a way as to build it up, ready to receive a fertilized egg. Oestrogens produced in the first half of the cycle prime the endometrium and encourage growth. Without it, progesterone produced in the second half of the cycle cannot act properly to ripen the endometrium ready to receive the fertilized egg, If the egg isn't fertilized, the corpus luteum, which has an independent lifespan of only about fourteen days, begins to cease functioning. Progesterone and oestrogen levels fall and eventually the lining of the womb sloughs off during a menstrual period. If a fertilized egg is present, other changes occur as we shall soon see.

These then are the female reproductive organs and faults or malfunctions can occur at almost any level to cause infertility. These faults range from psychological or emotional problems which influence the brain and so alter hormone production by the pituitary gland, to purely physical problems which can often be easily overcome with medical help.

The male reproductive system and how it works

Because the male reproductive system lies outside the body people tend to think it's more simple and that things are unlikely to go wrong with it. I feel sure that this is one of the reasons why women usually blame themselves for 'their' infertility and many have told me that a man's system seems so obvious and straightforward that it couldn't possibly go wrong. This is, unfortunately, not true and it is now known that about 40 per cent of all infertility problems stem from the male.

The *penis* is a tube-like structure at the base of the abdomen. Only about two-thirds of its length are visible because one-third is buried in the body. Although it looks like one tube, it is in fact three. As you look down on the penis from on top there are two tubular masses of tissue under the skin called the *corpora cavernosa*. They're called *cavernosa* because they're

THE BASIC EQUIPMENT AND HOW IT WORKS 33

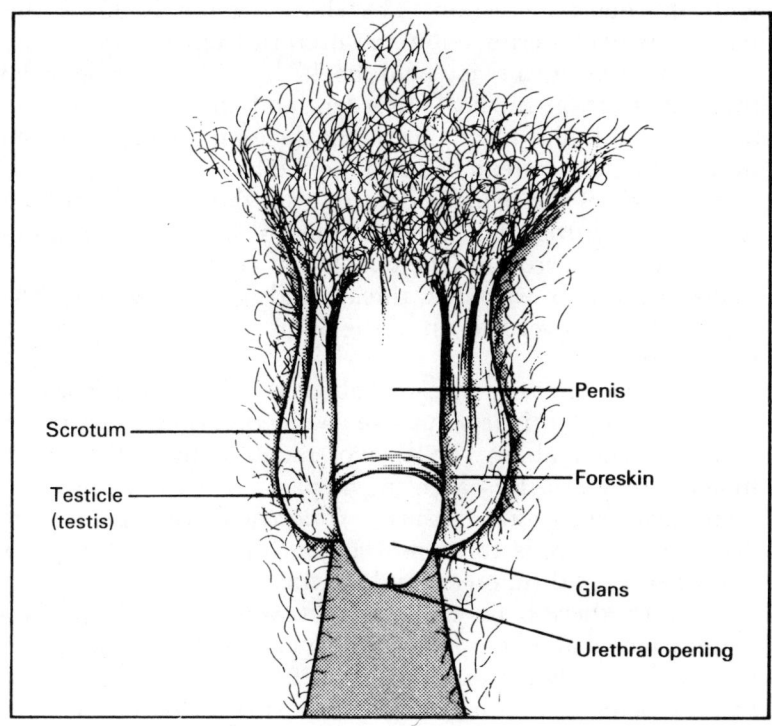

The external genitals of a man.

cavernous in structure and can swell to accommodate large volumes of blood. The third cylindrical structure in the penis lies on the under surface and is called the *corpus spongiosum*. It ends in a bulbous swelling (the glans), the sensitive tip of the penis.

The three cylindrical parts swell when a man becomes sexually aroused and an erection occurs because more blood flows into the penis than is allowed to flow out. The penis has to swell and become rigid to fulfil its sexual function – that of placing semen high up in a woman's vagina near the cervix.

The *urethra* is the tube that carries urine from the bladder to the outside, and terminates at the tip of the penis in a thin, slit-like opening. Semen comes out of this same opening, so the urethra has a dual urinary and sexual function in men but not in women. Because the urethra runs through the corpus spongiosum it is compressed and virtually shut off when the penis is erect. This is why it is difficult for a man to pass water when he has an erection. The shut-off point is above the level at which sperms enter the urethra from the vasa deferentia so that urine is 'held back' but semen is allowed through. Certain medical disorders and some drugs can so alter this muscular mechanism that the man ejaculates semen into the bladder instead of down the uretha.

The shaft of the penis is covered with darkened, loose skin which looks rather delicate and thin and this skin continues below over the scrotum (the pouch that contains the testes or 'balls') as a more wrinkled, thicker and hairier covering. The skin protrudes over the tip of the penis as a loose fold called the prepuce.

Just as women are concerned about the size of their breasts, men worry about their penis size. Women, however, are much less concerned about the size of men's penises than men imagine they are. Research in the past few years shows that men have been unnecessarily concerned with penis size because not only is there no relationship between the penis size when flaccid (unerect) and the final erect size but, even if there were, there is no evidence that women like big penises better than small ones. The vagina adapts to fit any size penis and anyway only the outer third of the vagina is really sensitive to penis size, One New York survey found in close interviews with sexually very experienced women that they did not find large penises particularly exciting. According to one expert, some women prefer their partners to have large penises while others prefer small ones because they think they are 'sweet'.

From an infertility point of view, there is no evidence that men with smaller penises are more likely to be infertile. Provided the man with a small penis can get an erection and maintain it long enough to place his semen high up his partner's vagina, he stands as great a chance of impregnating her as does the man with a large penis.

The *scrotum*, as we have seen, is a large bag of skin inside which are the sperm-producing organs, the testes. The skin of the scrotum is composed of several layers, the most important of which is muscular. These cremasteric muscles, as they are called, act as a heat-regulating mechanism which helps keep the testes at exactly the right temperature. This is important because normal sperm development can only occur if the testes are maintained at a temperature of about 2-3°C lower than that of the core of the body. Both fear and cold cause the

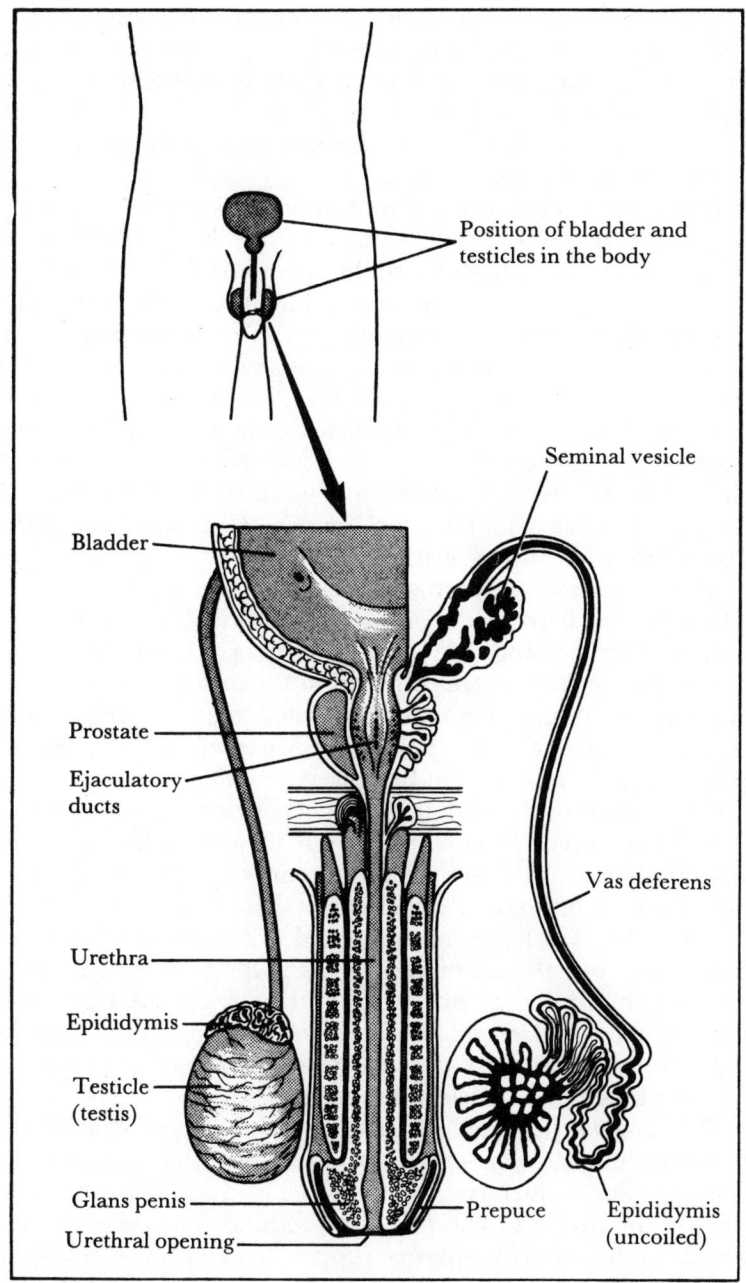

The male reproductive tract. (Testis, epididymis, vas deferens, seminal vesicle and prostate on the right are shown in section.)

cremasteric muscles to contract and so draw the testes nearer to the body. A mass of veins surrounds the artery that supplies the testis on each side, producing a counter-current heat-loss system that loses heat from the artery to the veins. In this way the testes get blood at a lower temperature than that supplied to the rest of the body.

Each *testis* is composed of several hundred little lobes, each of which contains a number of highly convoluted seminiferous tubules. These eventually straighten out and converge to form the five or seven ducts that open into the epididymis. The testis produces not only sperms but also male hormones, the latter in special cells called Leydig cells. Testosterone is responsible for a man's secondary sexual characteristics (his muscular body, beard growth, distribution of body hair, deep voice and aggression), affects his metabolism and his psychological behaviour and also stimulates the formation of various chemicals in his reproductive tract that ensure the production of healthy sperm.

The formation of sperms takes about two weeks. Sperms, when they're first produced, are not motile, (i.e. they don't move). After passing through the miles of tubules that forms the testis, the sperms are collected in the *epididymis* where they are stored. While they are here they mature further and become motile. From the epididymis the sperms enter the *vasa deferens*, a fine, muscular tube, and travel along this, up out of the scrotum into the abdominal cavity. It is the bottom end of the vas deferens that is tied off in men undergoing a vasectomy. The vas deferentia gently milk the sperms along by muscular action to their upper ends where they widen to form the *ampullae*. Most sperms are stored in the epididymis as we have seen, but the ampullae act as secondary storage sites, Beyond the ampullae are two blind bags off the vasa deferentia called the *seminal vesicles*. They are important because they produce a sugar called fructose which feeds the sperms on their long journey to fertilize an egg.

The *prostate gland*, which makes about 10 per cent of the seminal fluid (semen – the ejaculated fluid that contains the sperms), lies at the base of the bladder and surrounds the first part of the urethra. The prostate produces substances which act as a vehicle for the sperms, supply them with nutrients and buffer them against attack from acid vaginal secretions. It is because it needs to counteract acid vaginal secretions that semen is so alkaline.

Beyond the prostate is a pair of small glands called *Cowper's glands*. These add a small amount of lubricant to the seminal fluid before ejaculation takes place. Rather less than 10 per cent of the volume of any ejaculate is composed of fluid from the testes and epididymes; about 80 per cent comes from the seminal vesicles and the remaining 10 per cent from the prostate.

The whole process of maturation of a sperm from the day that it starts in the testis to the day it is ejaculated takes about three months, most of which time is spent in the epididymis while the sperm matures. Once a man becomes sexually excited his penis enlarges and the vasa deferentia increase their muscular milking action and send more sperms into their ampullae. A combination of muscular contractions of the pelvic structures produces an ejaculation of the semen and when this happens the seminal vesicles, prostate and Cowper's glands all add their secretions to the sperms which are discharged as semen via the penis. While this is happening, the internal muscle of the bladder shuts off the bladder's opening so that semen isn't forced back into the bladder instead of onwards down the penis. Sometimes this nervous mechanism goes wrong as we shall see later. Sperms form only 5 per cent of the volume of semen and a normal man ejaculates between 2 and 5 millilitres of semen after a day or two of abstinence. Men who have large volumes of semen are not necessarily more fertile than those who don't but volumes of less than 1 millilitre are sometimes associated with infertility because there isn't enough fluid to maintain contact with the cervix.

Many men who are infertile (or fear they may be) are concerned about the colour or consistency of their semen. Thick, milky semen does not indicate that it is rich in sperms and conversely, thin, watery semen doesn't mean a man is infertile. Semen varies enormously in its colour and consistency according to many factors, the main one of which is frequency of ejaculation.

Just as in the female, hormones play an important role in the sexual functioning of men. Although research is beginning to show that male hormones may be produced cyclically as in women, there is no obvious cycle in men, who produce sperms and seminal fluid all the time. There is no time of the month when a man is more or less fertile as far as we know in the light of current knowledge. Just as in women, follicle stimulating hormone (FSH) and luteinizing hormone (LH) are important but in men they are essential throughout a man's reproductive life to ensure the normal production of sperms in the testes. But just how important these hormones are, where they act exactly and the amounts needed for optimal functioning of the testes are not known. Just as in women, the control of these hormones is maintained by the brain and this means that both external and internal stimuli can affect the production of sperms. Having said this though it seems likely that male infertility of psychological and emotional origin is mostly penis-centred, rather than sperm-production-centred. This can be said with some certainty because although some psychological factors prevent a woman from ovulating in any one month (and so ruin her chances of conception), a man's sperms have been developing for months in his testes and simply need to be put in the right place to initiate a pregnancy. However, there is almost no research which has looked at the effects of emotional and psychological trauma on sperm counts three months later, so the question of temporary hormone imbalance and sperm formation must remain an open one.

The miracle that is a baby

As we shall see later, the conception of a baby is not the inevitable outcome of sexual intercourse. Western men and women are at their most fertile around the age of eighteen to twenty and after that their fertility begins to decrease. Fertility declines fairly rapidly after the age of thirty.

In a couple making love on an unrestricted basis, the average time to conception is 5·3 months. Twenty-five per cent of couples will have conceived in the first month, 63 per cent by the end of six months, 75 per cent by the end of nine months and 80 per cent by the end of a year. A further 10 per cent (bringing the total to 90 per cent) will have conceived by eighteen months.

As we have seen, the male and female reproductive systems are highly complex. Factors from the brain, hormone-producing glands and several specialized parts of the body all have to be in perfect balance for a baby to be conceived. It's no surprise therefore that something somewhere along the line may go just slightly wrong at some time and it's for this reason that a baby doesn't result from every single act of unprotected intercourse. In addition to this, intercourse may take place at a time of the month when there is not fertilizable egg present.

Nature has so ordained things that sperm are 'cheap' (easily produced in their millions throughout a man's post-pubertal life) and eggs 'expensive' (only one is produced per month over only half a woman's life span). A man can clearly impregnate many women and has historically done so in cultures in which polygamy was practised. Women and their valuable eggs are thus much more prized in biological terms and it could be for this reason that women (and some men) are so willing to see reproductive failure as the woman's 'fault'.

Let's look at how conception occurs because that will give us the basis on which to build our knowledge of infertility.

There are several basic necessities for conception. First, the man must be able to produce normal, healthy sperms in large enough numbers and be able to place them near the opening of the womb so that they can get up to an egg in the fallopian tube. Second, the woman must produce a healthy egg. Third, the egg must be in the fallopian tube so that it can be fertilized. Fourth, the sperm and the egg must be in the right place at the right time. This may not be easy because eggs live for only up to a day (and sometimes for up to only twelve hours) and sperms for a very few days, although some have been removed from the fallopian tubes as late as six days after intercourse. Fifth, the egg, once fertilized, must lodge in the wall of the uterus and start growing into a healthy baby. And sixth, there must be a healthy and functioning corpus luteum for several weeks until the developing placenta makes enough progesterone of its own to maintain a pregnancy. Assuming that all this has happened and that the uterus and the baby are both normal, after nine months the baby will be ready for the outside world.

With all these odds seemingly stacked against us it seems amazing that people have babies as easily as they do but the system works because women have a chance every month to get pregnant (unlike so many of the animal kingdom which come into season much less frequently and often only once a year) because our males produce so many sperms (after all, you only need one to do the job), and because, unlike all other animals except for other primates, we're willing and able to copulate at any time.

On ejaculation then, sperms begin to propel themselves at a

rate of about 1 to 3 millimetres per minute, depending on the environment. The muscular contractions of the uterus together with the sucking action produced during orgasm carries them into the uterine cavity. Subtle chemical changes take place in sperms as they travel through the mucus of the cervix, up to the uterus and along the tubes to meet the egg, changes which are essential if the sperm is to be in a condition to fertilize the egg it meets. This process of sperm maturation is called capacitation and includes the acrosome reaction. The acrosome is a protective cap that covers the head of the sperm. It is shed before the sperm enters the egg; but a chemical in the acrosome helps the process of penetration into the egg. When sperms have just been ejaculated their chances of fertilizing an egg are small. Eventually the egg and sperm meet in the fallopian tube, the sperm penetrates the egg and the male sex cell fuses with the female one.

Most of the body's cells are so small that they can only be seen under a microscope, yet an ovum (egg) is as large as a full stop on this page. A sperm on the other hand is 100,000 times smaller than an ovum. They both have one thing in common though – they each contain only half the genetic material that is contained by every other body cell (except other sperms and ova) of the person they've come from. It is this mixing together of the two half-sets of chromosomes that is what sexual reproduction is all about. As we have seen, 85 per cent of the time the system works perfectly within a few months of trying. Many of the people who make up the other 15 per cent can be helped to have a baby – sometimes by doing the simplest of things.

CHAPTER 2

Helping Yourselves

Although most couples who can't conceive when they want to come to the conclusion, albeit reluctantly, that there must be something wrong with either or both of them, very few, it seems, ask themselves if there's anything that *they* might be doing which makes conception less likely. In this chapter we'll look at things a couple has at least some control over and can do something about, even before going to the doctors for help. Masters and Johnson, the renowned sex researchers, found that simple advice on technique and attention to basic things such as are outlined in this chapter proved to be the answer in one in eight of the 'infertile' patients attending their clinics. So, clearly, simple things are worth trying.

Sexual technique

Most of us, whether we're trying unsuccessfully to conceive or not, imagine we're normal and that what we do sexually is what everyone else does. Unfortunately, there is still such ignorance of sexual matters that a small number of couples (probably about 5 per cent) end up at infertility clincs with no evidence of intercourse ever having taken place – the woman is still a virgin. Case histories abound in the infertility world but it is no joking matter that some young, often intelligent people persist in anal (back passage), umbilical or even urethral (urinary passage) intercourse, often to their personal discomfort, for months or years before going for help because they can't conceive. It must be said that there is only one way to become pregnant – by vaginal intercourse. A man's penis must penetrate the vagina (preferably deeply) and leave some sperms there at the time of the month when the woman is ovulating. Oral sex or intercourse with any other part of the body will never result in a pregnancy.

Although the number of women attending infertility clinics as virgins because they don't know their basic anatomy is falling, there is another group of virgins that is rising in number – those who are virgins because of impotent husbands. We shall discuss this more fully below. Other women have never allowed intercourse because of pain on penetration (or even an attempted penetration), while others have vaginismus, a reflex spasm of the muscles around the vagina that starts if anyone tries to put anything into it, but more of that later.

Let's assume then that you are one of the majority who are putting the penis in the vagina. If both of you are ever fertile you stand some chance of conceiving – so why aren't you?

TIMING

For most couples who are very active sexually, the time of the month at which they have intercourse hardly matters because they are making love so often that by pure chance alone they will be having sex at around the time of ovulation. As we have seen (Chapter 1), an egg lives about a day and sperms for about two or three days, so if you make love any time from three days before ovulation to one day after, you've got a fair chance of getting pregnant. This assumes that both sperms and ovulation are normal, of course. In most couples who make love about two or three times a week (the average as shown by several surveys), the chances are fairly high that there will be sperms in the vagina when ovulation occurs.

However, if the man is a shift-worker, works away from home a lot, if a husband's or wife's working shifts alternate so that you rarely see each other, if either of you is ill or if for any other reason you're not together very often, then you obviously reduce your chances of getting pregnant.

FREQUENCY

There is no 'normal' for the number of times you should make love each week or month – every couple is different. The normal for you is what you both find enjoyable. Many surveys have found that two to three times a week is the most common frequency of intercourse. Some couples have intercourse several times a day and others only once or twice a month. Provided both of you are satisfied, it doesn't matter how often you have intercourse – until you want to get pregnant that is. Very many couples attending infertility clinics are having intercourse as little as once or twice a month, which may be fine for their sex lives but may well not result in conception unless they happen to make love very close to the time of ovulation. If they are also slightly sub-fertile, the fertile 'window' may be as short as one or two days and the chance of one of their twice-monthly sexual encounters coinciding with this is small indeed.

Remember that even with unrestricted and unprotected intercourse, only one-quarter of couples will conceive in the first month of trying and this is on average with about twelve intercourse experiences. So, it must be said that if you're making love as infrequently as once or twice a month you are stacking up the odds against your getting pregnant.

However, the answer may not be as simple as it at first appears because for many couples a very low frequency of intercourse is all they can tolerate. In fact several people working in the infertility counselling area tell of the adverse effects on a relationship as the couple try to step up their intercourse rates. The reasons for low intercourse rates are many but the stage might come when you are both found to be anatomically and psychologically normal and will simply have to have intercourse more frequently in order to conceive. Sexual dysfunction (see below) may be the cause and indeed evidence shows that more and more men are affected by premature ejaculation and impotence as society puts the pressure on them to perform. A more likely cause even than this is the psychosexual make-up of one or both partners. A woman who, because of her upbringing, finds sex distasteful will submit to her husband's desire to have sex as infrequently as she feels she can and still keep him happy. On the other side of the coin, a shy man married to a powerful woman may be so intimidated by her that he cannot function properly sexually or puts off doing so either to protect himself or to punish his wife. Both of these are extremes of a spectrum but in between there are millions of couples who tolerate their sexual intercourse frequency because it suits them mutually to do so. What many of the 'reluctant' women have to realize is that unless they make love more frequently, they stand little chance of getting pregnant, so the choice is theirs. If you feel that you'd like to make love more often, talk first to your partner and see what can be arranged between the two of you. Very often the problem is simply a practical one and is nothing sinister at all. Some women, for example, feel at their sexiest in the morning and are tired after work in the evening. The husband may, on the contrary, not feel like sex just before going off to work because it makes him sleepy. Couples like this find they are putting off sex more and more until the conditions are perfect for both – which is rarely and not necessarily around ovulation time.

If after discussing the matter you think there are underlying problems that could benefit from specialist advice, see your doctor, who may then refer you to a psychosexual specialist. One of the reasons that infertility is still one of the great taboo subjects of the western world is that it implies that you're somehow incompetent sexually. This is one of the things that puts off men especially from seeking specialist help. Nobody wants to be thought of as a sexual cripple when the rest of the world are sexual athletes. The fact that most of the world is desperately ordinary when it comes to sex should be made known to more people. Nobody is going to censure you for your sexual appetite, or lack of it, but specialist help could make an enormous difference to your marriage and get you pregnant into the bargain.

A lot of people wonder whether they should be saving up sperms so that when they do have intercourse they'll stand the best possible chance of conceiving. There is some truth in this as sperm counts are definitely reduced if the man ejaculates every day. However, after two to three days, sperm counts are back up again to normal levels so there's no point in 'saving up' for longer than a couple of days. There are also other negative effects of the saving-up technique because if you're aiming for D-day with a husband bursting with semen, the chances are he'll ejaculate prematurely from frustration and excitement and although the increased numbers of sperms may make pregnancy more likely, they won't get to the right place and will also leave a very unsatisfied woman. Also, if you've been saving up for the target day and one of you is unwell or tired, you'll feel terribly depressed (and many women express great anger) if you don't make love at the appointed time. Men become very concerned with having to perform like a stallion during the fertile period and this can lead to considerable friction in the relationship. It's best to continue with your normal sex pattern but to abstain for a day or two prior to ovulation so that the man has a good supply of the best sperms he can produce at the time of the month when it matters most.

LOVE-MAKING POSITIONS
If you are very fertile as a couple, it really doesn't matter how you make love – the woman will get pregnant. If the odds are stacked against you in any way though it makes sense to have sexual intercourse in such a way as to ensure the best chance of conception.

When a woman becomes sexually excited, her vagina balloons out at the top and distends in such a way as to form a small depression below the neck of the womb with her lying on her back. When intercourse takes place with the woman on her back then, assuming her uterus is positioned normally, semen forms a pool in this area of the vagina and the cervix lies in the pool. As the woman's sexual tension subsides, the opening of the cervix widens and this, together with the dipping of the cervix into the pool of semen, makes it easy for the sperms to swim up into the uterus. During orgasm or immediately after, the muscular action of the uterus sucks up the sperms and this is aided by muscle contracting substances called prostaglandins which are present in the semen. Making love with a pillow under the woman's hips so as the emphasize this pooling effect increases the chance of sperms entering the uterus as does the continued presence of the man's penis after he has ejaculated. To be even more certain, the woman should remain lying down for half an hour after intercourse, with the pillow still under her hips. Ideally, she should go to sleep in this position but this may be difficult.

For a woman whose uterus is retroverted (tilted backwards), raising the hips might remove the neck of the womb from the pool of semen, so it makes sense to use the rear entry position for lovemaking. In this the woman kneels with her elbows and forearms on the bed, either with her head up or on the bed too. This allows exceptionally deep penetration by the penis and gives an excellent chance that the cervix will be bathed in semen.

Deep penetration is helpful in whichever position you use because although the highly fertile man with a high sperm count and with sperms of good motility can get a woman pregnant by placing sperms at the opening of her vagina, the less fertile man will need to place the sperms very deeply inside the vagina. Because of this if you're having difficulty in conceiving, get a good sex book that tells and shows you the best positions for deep penetration. If this is painful or impossible for any reason, see your doctor because it could be that there is an underlying painful condition that has been preventing deep penetration, and thus pregnancy, for some time.

In order to penetrate a woman deeply a man doesn't have to have an especially long penis. It's important to say something briefly about this here because many men (fertile and infertile alike) worry about penis size. Some infertile men with a short penis worry that it's this that prevents their wives from becoming pregnant. The medical facts are somewhat different. Very few men have such a short penis that they can't impregnate a woman, provided their semen is normal. On the contrary, a normally fertile man and woman can conceive if he inserts only the very tip of his penis into her vagina. Clearly penis length isn't a crucial factor.

However, a man who has very low semen volume or a very poor sperm count will need to ensure that what he does produce gets as near his partner's cervix as possible. This can be done by using intercourse positions in which the woman's legs are pulled right back onto her tummy or chest or by using rear-entry positions. To reassure yourself on this the woman can lie flat on her back and then she or her partner can feel her cervix become easily within a finger's reach as she pulls back her thighs. This effect is enhanced even more if a pillow is placed under her hips. Few men have an erect penis shorter than their middle finger and so can usually see the fallacy of blaming their penis size for their inability to make their wife pregnant.

If for some anatomical or other reason the man cannot satisfactorily place his penis deep in the vagina, artificial insemination may have to be resorted to. (See page 172.)

ORGASMS

It's not necessary to have an orgasm in order to get pregnant but in my opinion it helps in two ways if you're having trouble in conceiving. First, the uterus definitely sucks up sperms more actively during an orgasm and this must make it more likely that one sperm will reach an egg in the fallopian tubes;

second, a woman who is having lots of orgasms will desire sex more often and so increase her chances of conception. This doesn't mean that you should go all out for an orgasm at any cost on every occasion as this can be a restriction, especially on the man who feels he has to perform so as to produce an orgasm for his partner each time. There are lots of ways around this. You can masturbate after your partner has ejaculated or even while he is still inside you. You can bring yourself to a climax at the same time as your partner or he can caress your clitoris to produce the same result. Whatever methods you use, don't get wrapped up in producing an orgasm – you'll be quite concerned enough about the time of the month to get further embroiled in more technique. Relax and enjoy your love-making and you may find you conceive unexpectedly. It's very common for a supposedly infertile couple to conceive on holiday when they are relaxed, enjoying sex more and so having intercourse more often.

AFTER LOVE-MAKING
Once you've made love, the woman should stay in bed and lie with her hips on a pillow as described above. If she gets up too quickly sperms will leak out of her vagina and if her partner has produced only a small volume of semen it may all be lost, once again making pregnancy unlikely. It's best to remain lying down after intercourse for at least an hour. Some women feel like passing water immediately afterwards and get up for this reason. Try to keep lying down if you possibly can.

Many women wash or douche *before* intercourse. Simple washing of the outside of the vulval area is fine but washing or douching is definitely prejudicial to conception. Never use creams, petroleum jelly, other jellies or lubricating fluids because they all have some spermicidal effect. If lubrication is necessary, use saliva because this is natural and won't kill sperms. The ideal of course is to ensure that the woman's vagina is well lubricated by her own secretions produced during foreplay.

Sexual dysfunctions

There are two fairly common types of infertility-producing sexual dysfunctions in each sex. Women may be frigid or suffer from vaginismus and men may be impotent (unable to maintain an erection) or suffer from premature ejaculation.

With any or all of these types of sexual dysfunction, conception may be difficult or impossible yet it is extremely rare for couples attending infertility clinics to volunteer any information that might lead to a diagnosis of sexual dysfunction. Only on deeper analysis, often in the hands of a psychosexual counsellor, does the underlying problem emerge. However, the problems are all fairly obvious and can often be treated in expert hands, so it's well worth getting help. Don't let the years tick by with the woman becoming less and less fertile, get help early.

FRIGIDITY
This is an inadequate word that ought to be banned. It is a word that can mean many things to different people and even to the same people. It is used to describe a range of female sexual unresponsiveness from a complete lack of sex drive to a desire for sex less frequently than her partner demands it. Some psychoanalysts define any woman who doesn't achieve vaginally induced orgasms as frigid but this unfortunate definition rules out most women.

However, there are undoubtedly many women who find sex distasteful for a variety of reasons and because of these they put off having sex as often as possible and so stand little chance of getting pregnant. Rigid religious backgrounds form the basis for most so-called frigidity according to many surveys. If sex has been linked with sin for long enough throughout a girl's formative years, then she'll be unable to function properly in a sexual relationship. Another reason why some women function poorly sexually is that they don't relate satisfactorily to their partners. If you consider your man is a bore, a slob, too fussy, badly dressed or in other ways a 'turn off' it's very difficult to give yourself to, in your eyes, such a second best person. A woman married to a man who himself has a sexual dysfunction is often labelled as frigid simply because she is over-concerned with her partner's adequacy or lack of it. Other so-called frigid women are latent lesbians or have arrested sexual development at the teenage homosexual stage and haven't found the right man to lead them out of it; yet others are simply not interested in sex.

Having said this, although a woman with any of these problems needs help, she probably won't have difficulty in conceiving (unless intercourse is extremely infrequent) because even one act per month at the right time could result in the pregnancy she so wants. If you feel that you fall into one of the groups outlined above and if either you or your partner is unhappy about it, get professional help. After all, being married isn't only about having babies.

VAGINISMUS
This is an uncommon condition that can first present itself as infertility. Women who suffer from this condition experience involuntary tightening or spasm of the muscles around the outer third of the vagina when penetration is attempted. This contraction can be so severe that it is impossible for the woman to have intercourse and some couples go on for years without it. Whilst such a reaction can be caused by painful conditions inside the vagina, this is rarely the case as this latter group of women allow penetration and then complain that it is painful. The woman with vaginismus, however, will often not allow a doctor to insert even one finger into her vagina and shrinks away up the examination couch. No one is suggesting that vaginal examinations are pleasant but this 'running away' reaction is only seen in women with vaginismus. If the doctor forces entry into the vagina the problem can become more difficult to treat, so patience is called for.

Vaginismus shouldn't be confused with a rigid or unusually tight hymen. Should this be present it can easily be treated surgically.

Many women with vaginismus are married to impotent men. Whether the men were impotent in the first place which led to the women's condition, or whether the men became impotent because of it isn't known. Many sexual counsellors find that if one partner in a marriage suffers from a sexual dysfunction, the chances are that the other eventually will do so too. This is another reason for getting help as soon as possible. The second factor that produces vaginismus is found in the family background which shows a 'sex-is-dirty/sinful' pattern time and time again. Similarly, religious taboos can produce vaginismus. Rarely, pre-marital sexual assault or very inept teenage intercourse experiences can so linger in a woman's unconscious mind that she rejects the thought of anything entering her vagina.

Truly painful intercourse can usually be cured once a doctor has made a diagnosis – but in order to be able to do this he has to be given a chance, and that involves doing a vaginal examination. The majority of women with vaginismus though do not have a physical cause and simply need careful, patient help to realize that their vagina can accept penetration without pain or horror. Some specialists demonstrate the spasm of the vaginal muscles to the husband and the patient by getting the woman herself to feel the contractions as she inserts her own finger into her vagina. Once she realizes the problem is so simple she's usually open to treatment. A doctor can give a woman dilators to insert – first small and then large – until she is confident that her vagina will take a penis. Other doctors advise the woman to use her fingers, either well lubricated during masturbation or in the bath. Once the physical problem is resolved, the increased confidence this gives the woman improves her relationship with her partner and a cure is commonplace. The vast majority of women with vaginismus can be treated successfully, although help from an outside specialist is often necessary to give the woman the confidence to overcome her fears.

PREMATURE EJACULATION
Like vaginismus, this is a condition that, after an initial period of professional help, can be sorted out by the average, caring, loving couple. You may feel after reading this section that you can effect a cure for yourselves.

Premature ejaculation is a condition in which the man ejaculates before his penis is inside the vagina and because of this, the chances of his partner conceiving are very small indeed.

Most men who complain of this disturbing and frustrating condition tell the same story. Their early sexual attempts were hurried and often unpleasant. A young man having intercourse in his fiancée's house when her parents are at home, in the back of a car in a lovers' lane, or in public places, gets used to ejaculating quickly and then eventually finds it impossible to control himself. Rapid ejaculation, once imprinted, is difficult to eradicate, except by special techniques. These are simple and although first invented by another doctor, were modified and made popular by Masters and Johnson.

The pattern of marriage with a premature ejaculator is consistent. At first, when the newlyweds discover the problem they console each other and assure themselves that things will improve. For some, they do and they enjoy a normal married

HELPING YOURSELVES

life and the woman gets pregnant. For many others the problem remains. Slowly the wife's attitude changes. She begins to feel that her husband is concerned only with his own pleasure and doesn't care for her sexual needs. This occurs particularly if foreplay has been long and the woman is aroused and yet has no release. Eventually the woman withdraws commitment to the marriage and loses her confidence in herself as a woman. The man becomes more humiliated at his failure to satisfy his wife and the marital hostility may end in divorce or in armed, childless neutrality.

Many ways of getting over this problem have been suggested. The commonest piece of advice is for the man to think of something which 'turns him off'. Mental distractions such as counting backwards from 100 to 1, thinking of a business problem or pinching himself may work temporarily, as may anaesthetic creams applied to the penis, but these are all of little use in the long term.

Treatment is ideally carried out in a professional setting in the first instance with counselling from sexual therapists. In the UK though facilities lag a long way behind the numbers of those needing help, so many couples resort to self-help, often with considerable success. The basis of the treatment is the squeeze technique as described by Masters and Johnson. The principle involved is not one of avoiding penis caressing (as was so often taught) but exactly the opposite. Using a controlled touching technique the couple attains a freedom they never dreamed of.

Over the first few days the couple practise 'pleasuring' each other without even attempting intercourse. If the man ejaculates it does not matter but during the pleasuring sessions the genitals are not the focus of attention so their response is not of prime importance. For further details of this pleasuring procedure the reader should get a Masters and Johnson-influenced sex manual because the subject is too complex to do justice to it here.

The specific technique for treating premature ejaculation starts with the woman sitting up on the bed and leaning on a pillow with her back against the headboard. The man lies on his back facing her with his hips between her legs and with his feet flat on the bed outside hers. The woman caresses the man's penis in any way that he likes until he has an erection. As soon as he is fully erect the woman takes the penis between the thumb and first two fingers of the same hand. With the thumb placed over the frenulum (the little vertical ridge on the underside of the penis rim) and the other two fingers on the opposite side of the penis, one on each side of the ridge that seperates the glans (top) from the shaft, she squeezes hard for several seconds. This pressure makes the man lose his urge to ejaculate and he may or may not lose some of his erection. After fifteen to thirty seconds the woman renews her manipulation and caressing of the penis and brings her partner to full erection again. By repeating this procedure the penis can be maintained erect for as long as twenty minutes or more and yet the man will not ejaculate. Eventually the woman allows her partner to ejaculate but the technique is not aimed at this end. After two or three weeks of this training the couple will have complete ejaculatory control and this alone gives both partners a tremendous sense of pleasure and achievement.

Once this stage has been reached, the next involves the placing of the penis in the vagina with the woman sitting on top and facing the man. In this way with the woman not moving the man gets used to being inside her with no immediate urge to ejaculate. The woman's restraint produces control in her partner. As the days go by, the man can slowly move his penis more and more without ejaculating until after some time they can resort freely to female superior intercourse and then to other positions. The male superior position is the most difficult in which to attain ejaculatory control.

When the couple has perfected these skills, premature ejaculation will be a thing of the past but some further training in the early months is still advised by the experts in this method. They suggest that the couple practise the squeeze technique at least once a week for the first six months and that they should also do it for fifteen to twenty minutes at some time during the woman's menstrual period. It may take six to twelve months for the squeeze method to produce perfect ejaculatory control but the effort will be well worth it; the method is exciting for both partners anyway. Masters and Johnson found that when using this technique they had only a 3 per cent failure rate in the treatment of premature ejaculation.

IMPOTENCE
This is a condition where the man is unable to maintain an erection long enough to have intercourse. Most people think

that an impotent man is not virile but mistakenly they often also assume that he is infertile. Most impotent men *are* fertile. The vast majority of impotent men have no physical disease to explain their problem. Those that are physically ill may be suffering from diabetes, a debilitating disease or may be taking certain drugs (see page 107). If you are impotent it's well worth discussing the matter with your doctor because he may be able to help. However, the majority of impotence is caused by other reasons which will often need professional help if the problem is to be resolved. Most of this 'psychological' group can masturbate quite easily yet cannot have satisfactory erections in the presence of a woman.

Anxiety about intercourse, fatigue, work problems, grief and a host of other daily trials can all produce temporary impotence. Some sub-fertile men or those normal ones whose wives are undergoing investigations and treatment for infertility commonly become impotent with the pressures put upon them. Many normal men who were virile before 'intercourse to order' around ovulation , find they have problems because the spontaneity of sex has been removed. Many have told me that they feel like they are being used like a medical tool and that this turns them off, albeit unconsciously.

Most normal couples accept occasional impotence for what it is and can usually find a way around the problem between them. However, if after a few times the woman begins to make her man feel he's a failure and is letting her down, the man become anxious, fears failure even more and is rendered impotent for a long period. His early 'I don't want to know' becomes 'I can't' and that spells trouble that needs expert help.

Even in this permissive society many people embark on marriage in a state of ignorance on many sexual matters and quite naturally bring with them their cultural and environmental fears, inhibitions and shames. Strict religious backgrounds and repressive childhoods brainwash some children into believing that pleasure, especially sexual pleasure, is sinful. Such a young man often cannot accept that the pleasure he gets from his relationship with his partner is 'permissible' and his unconscious mind turns off the nervous system that controls his erection. Some men are obsessed by the size of their penis, fearing that it is too large or too small or looks peculiar. Some uncircumcised men become upset by the fact that they're not and vice versa.

But it's the fear of failure that's the biggest problem and the main cause of impotence. A thoughtless remark by an old girlfriend, a jibe by a prostitute or a hurtful comment from a wife can all trigger off impotence in a susceptible man. If you think this is silly or unreasonable, remember that a woman doesn't need to maintain an aroused state in order to fulfil her role as the receptable for sperms and so become pregnant. A man is physically incapable of intercourse if he is disinclined, uninterested or otherwise debilitated. A man cannot will an erection. Any negative feelings therefore, however deeply seated immediately reveal themselves to his partner who feels cheated or hurt and possibly even suspicious (that he's gone off her), reproachful or inquisitorial (has he got another woman that he does have erections with?). With all this so evident, the man dreads the threat to the stability of the relationship which might well be otherwise perfectly acceptable to both partners, and so becomes more impotent. This sort of impotence can be treated but it may take time, so in the meantime it's probably worth getting on with the procuring of a pregnancy.

Artificial insemination with the husband's sperms (AIH) is probably the answer unless a speedy cure for the impotence seems likely. Once the woman is pregnant time can be devoted to curing the impotence. Ideally, of course, the impotence should be treated before AIH, if only because it might be considered unsatisfactory to bring a child into the lives of a couple who are having a rough time sexually. This must be a matter for discussion with your doctor and your partner. Often, a woman given her desired goal of a baby will take the 'pressure' off her husband and so allow him, perhaps with professional help, to function normally again. The pressures of being impotent are quite bad enough without also having to worry about the baby you both want.

Heat

As we saw in Chapter 1, the testes have to be kept at 2°-3°C below body temperature in order to function. A simple thing that's worth trying is to reduce the number of situations under which the man's scrotum gets hot. The excessive use of jockstraps (athletic supports of the penis and scrotum), tight pants and jeans, saunas and hot baths are the most obvious overheating situations. However, the exceptionally large numbers of men in infertility clinics who simply have sedentary jobs make doctors suspect that far less dramatic heat changes could be responsible.

Seemingly miraculous results can be obtained simply by changing from tight underpants to loose-fitting boxer shorts and by bathing the scrotum in cool water morning and night for five minutes. Results take about three months because, as mentioned earlier, that's how long it takes a sperm to go through its whole generative cycle.

Other self-help methods

LOSING WEIGHT

This can be helpful. Fertility is known to be reduced in obese women and a man's obesity can directly affect *his* fertility in two ways. First, the heavy pad of fat hanging down from his abdomen near his testes can so insulate them that they are permanently too hot. Second, the fat may actually prevent him from having satisfactory intercourse because he can't penetrate the woman deeply enough. A reduction in weight will thus improve his sperm count if it is low and will make him healthier anyway. Weight reduction in an obese woman has also been shown to increase her chances of conception. Perhaps weight reduction also has a positive effect by making the person feel better about his or her body image and so more likely to have sex more frequently. Also slimmed 'fatties' say they have more energy for sex.

SMOKING, DRINKING, SOFT AND HARD DRUGS

These habits are known to reduce fertility so it is well worth cutting down or cutting them out if you're determined to have a baby. Medicinal preparations known to cause infertility are listed on page 95, but you should never stop taking these without prior consultation with your doctor.

STRESS

Stress and its relation to infertility is a much debated subject. In women, stress may inhibit ovulation, acting through the hypothalamic area of the brain (see page 60), and some experts claim to have proved that some women's fallopian tubes go into spasm under stress. Research on effects of stress on men is more definitive. It was first reported in Nazi concentration camps during the last war that sperm production went down under the physical and emotional stress experienced and other more recent work has shown that city dwellers are consistently less fertile (in Sweden anyway) than are country dwellers. Stress in men though seems to manifest itself mainly at the penis level and not at the testicular level. A man under stress may become impotent and for this reason be unable to fertilize his partner. Too often, the twentieth-century bogey of stress is used to explain phenomena for which we haven't found all the answers and infertility may well be another of these.

THE SPLIT-EJACULATE TECHNIQUE
If a man's ejaculate is collected in two containers it is found that there are significant differences between the semen in each container. Several researchers have found that the first few spurts of ejaculate contain more sperms of greater motility and viability than do later parts of the ejaculate. Why this should be so is not entirely certain but it's possible that fluids added to the later ejaculate (from the seminal vesicles) may depress sperm activity and survival. One large study of 500 men attending a subfertility clinic found that the sperm count in nearly nine out of ten of them was higher in the first part of the ejaculate and this sort of result has been repeated elsewhere. This work led the researchers to use the first part of the ejaculate in artificial insemination (see page 175) and so to produce pregnancies in a greater proportion of couples than when using the whole ejaculate.

Many couples can't or won't use artificial insemination and so can't benefit from this recent piece of research. However, one of the world's leading experts in infertility has suggested that the method can be modified to allow near-normal intercourse. He instructs his male patients to withdraw their penis immediately after the first spurt of semen and to let the rest go anywhere but inside the woman's vagina. He only recommends this withdrawal technique for use around the time of ovulation because it would be unnecessary and unpleasant for the couple to practise it as the norm. This method rapidly resulted in pregnancy in many women who had been childless for years and is well worth trying for a few months if you're having trouble in conceiving.

* * *

None of the self-help methods outlined in this chapter will be of any use if the man has no sperms, if the woman is not ovulating or if her tubes are totally blocked. However, many couples do not have these problems so these simple things are worth a try. If you are both under thirty and have not been trying for more than six months already, you could use all the suggestions in this chapter that are applicable to your situation for up to a total of a year before starting on the medical approach. If after this you are still unsuccessful, the chances are that you'll need medical help. Chapters 3 and 4 look at what can go wrong and what can be done and Chapter 5 looks at how the problems can be sorted out.

CHAPTER 3

Female Infertility and its Treatment

Although many people think of infertility as being the woman's 'fault' most of the time, this is not so. Male and female factors contribute about equally to infertility problems. Having said this though, female causes are a lot more responsive to currently available treatment than are male ones and this has led both the medical profession and the public to believe that time spent on the investigation and treatment of female infertility is more worth while. This is in fact true.

Female infertility is usually investigated and treated by gynaecologists although increasingly the gynaecologist forms part of a much larger team which investigates and treats the couple together. However, as we will see in Chapter 5, the majority of couples are represented only by the woman at infertility clinics, so understandably the majority of the medical effort is focused on the woman, at least in the early stages.

Because women have monthly cycles (which often have to be charted and regularized before treatment can begin) any medical action, either for treatment or investigation, revolves around these monthly time-spans. Because of this, the investigation and treatment of female infertility can be very long drawn out because each cycle can be used for only a limited number of investigation or treatment procedures. If, in addition, one waits for a few months to see if the last treatment has had any effect before knowing where one stands, a year can easily go by and that seems an age for someone trying to conceive.

Unlike the reproductive system in a man, a woman's is very distinct from her urinary system. By and large the important parts are all inside her body which means that more intrusions are necessary if she is to be investigated and treated successfully. But when you're going through all the tests and treatments it's encouraging to remember that you have a better than 50 per cent chance of being helped. A woman also has something of a psychological advantage when it comes to the investigation and treatment of her infertility because she is already very aware of her monthly hormone cycles and will usually have had vaginal examinations or even other procedures when seeking family planning advice.

By and large it's fair to say that women fare better than men in the treatment of their infertility because research into contraception has provided a body of knowledge which can be applied to the problems of low fertility. It's ironic that the desire of most women *not* to have babies has helped the minority who can't.

A woman may be infertile for one of three main reasons and in about 35 per cent there are two or more of these operating in any one woman. First, something mechanical may be blocking her cervix, uterus or fallopian tubes and this obviously prevents sperm and egg from meeting. Second, her glandular (endocrine) system may be at fault, thus producing problems with ovulation., Third, she may have structural abnormalities of her reproductive organs. Survey results vary when it comes to deciding which of these factors is the most prevalent cause but ovulatory disturbances are probably most common, followed by blocked fallopian tubes. In about 12 per cent of infertile women, no cause of any kind is found.

Ovulation problems

Most women ovulate every month, except under times of stress or illness, or when they are pregnant or breast feeding on an 'on-demand' basis, and the fine balance of their hormones produces the desired result of a fertilizable egg each month. Some women ovulate very irregularly and some not at all. The first cycles immediately after the menarche (onset of monthly periods) and those just before the menopause are usually anovulatory (that is, there is bleeding but with no ovulation preceding it). In fact many early-teenage girls go on for as long as four to five years having anovulatory periods. Normal women have anovulatory cycles once in every twelve or fifteen cycles; in some women they seem to be an almost constant occurrence.

Most women who don't ovulate either have irregular and scanty periods, or very heavy periods or even none at all (amenorrhoea). Normal women don't necessarily ovulate optimally *every* month and it is thought that this explains why some normal, healthy women don't conceive at the first opportunity. Some eggs are also probably of poorer quality than others but no one knows why.

One of the commonest causes of amenorrhoea is the post-Pill syndrome. If the contraceptive Pill has been used to suppress the pituitary and hypothalamus glands for a long time, ovulation may not return for months or, rarely, years. This occurs most commonly in women whose periods were irregular before they went on the Pill and in those who started their periods late. But having said all this, the Pill is not considered to reduce fertility rates to any significant extent (see also page 61).

There are three ways in which a doctor can tell if a woman is not ovulating properly. First, her menstrual history (see above) will be abnormal; second, her basal temperature (see page 114) will be monophasic and not biphasic; and third, the blood levels of the hormone progesterone will be low throughout the cycle (instead of rising during the second half of the cycle). It is usually fairly easy to decide whether a woman is ovulating or not although one can never be absolutely sure of course, except by actually seeing the process happen. All other evidence for ovulation is presumptive. The absence of periods though is pretty convincing evidence that a woman is not ovulating and there are many causes of this.

The hypothalamus is a sensitive centre in the brain that controls the action of the pituitary gland, which in turn is the master of the body's endocrine glands. Anything that affects the hypothalamus can therefore affect ovulation. Weight change in either direction can produce amenorrhoea. Anorexia nervosa, a condition in which a girl stops eating, becomes extremely thin and ceases to have periods, is an uncommon cause of infertility because it occurs mostly in

FEMALE INFERTILITY AND ITS TREATMENT

teenage girls and this is not in general an age group that is trying to get pregnant. Any serious weight gain can also cause anovulation. Loss of the excess weight results in the return of periods and of fertility. Oral contraceptives cause a complete loss of periods and cessation of ovulation.

The bleeding that occurs on withdrawal of the contraceptive pill each month is a chemically-induced 'period' and isn't in any sense a natural, body hormone-induced one. We have just seen how the hypothalamus can be shut down for long periods after discontinuing the Pill and this can be a real problem for young women today, many of whom have been on the Pill all their fertile lives. One expert has called this 'planned infertility' but to be fair, post-Pill anovulation probably occurs in only about 2 per cent of women who were on the Pill and most of these respond to the fertility drug clomiphene (see page 62). Some tranquillizers too can cause anovulation and the cessation of periods. Lastly, of the factors that act on the hypothalamus, psychological disturbances undoubtedly produce a loss of periods.

Some severe mental illnesses (such as depression) can produce anovulation but, on a more day-to-day level any girl knows that around examination times, times of stress, changes of time zones (for example, in air stewardesses), and under a host of other emotional conditions her periods may not appear as usual. For more details of the the influence of the emotions on infertility (psychogenic infertility) see page 141. It's interesting that up to 30 per cent of women have an increase in the number of their anovulatory cycles as a direct effect of the stress of being infertile. Some women start off with normal ovulatory cycles but become anovulatory as the months of investigation and treatment progress.

The hormones of the body may also be at fault and so cause a loss of ovulation. A tumour of the pituitary gland, an under- or over-active thyroid gland, cystic ovaries and conditions that lead to a poor build-up of endometrium each month can all cause amenorrhoea.

All of this complex hormonally-based collection of conditions has to be carefully sorted out by the doctor, but this task has been made a lot easier now that there are sophisticated hormone-measuring methods available. The assessment and treatment of ovulation disorders depends on measuring blood levels of the hormones FSH, LH and prolactin, and the outlook for women with ovulation disorders is very good. About

70 per cent of infertile women have normal FSH, LH and prolactin values and 15 per cent have normal FSH and LH values with only raised prolactin levels. Three-quarters of this raised prolactin group leak milk from their breasts and a tiny percentage are found to have a tumour of the pituitary gland. Only about 1 or 2 per cent of women with amenorrhoea of six months or more duration have a tumour of the pituitary gland, though it will always be looked for because some of these glands enlarge during drug treatment to induce ovulation and others enlarge during a subsequent pregnancy.

WHAT CAN BE DONE?
First of all, let it be said that a significant number of women with infrequent or completely absent periods of less than one year's duration recover spontaneously and conceive while the investigations are going on. This also occurs with women suffering from the post-Pill syndrome and presumably happens because of the reassurance they get once they start to be cared for by the medical team. Some teams give a placebo (a safe, inactive tablet) to boost this reassurance effect and claim ovulation rates of 40 per cent and pregnancy rates of 20 per cent.

However, most women who are not ovulating are going to need treatment with active drugs. Before these 'fertility' drugs are administered, the doctors will have made absolutely sure that the cause of anovulation in fact arises in the ovaries. Other causes will be corrected first, if present. The first treatment of choice is clomiphene citrate (Clomid), unless the blood levels of prolactin alone are raised in which case a specific prolactin-lowering drug called bromocriptine is used. Clomiphene citrate is an anti-oestrogen which stimulates FSH production by the hypothalamus. It is usually started on day 5 of the cycle and is continued for five days. In women in whom bleeding cannot be predicted, a period is sometimes induced by giving norethisterone twice daily for five days. This ensures that therapy isn't started unnecessarily during a period of spontaneous ovarian activity. In most women who haven't had periods for a year or more though, the chances of spontaneous ovarian function are small and therapy is started without delay. Ovulation usually occurs between four and ten days after the last dose of clomiphene is taken. A woman will know if she's ovulating by keeping her daily temperature chart (see page 114 for details).

About 80 per cent of women ovulate when given clomiphene and pregnancy rates of 40 per cent are claimed in several studies. This low pregnancy rate is thought to be due to the slight anti-oestrogen effect that clomiphene has on the cervical mucus. This can be corrected by giving small doses of oestrogens a few days before ovulation is due. This drug is not one that causes the multiple births for which fertility drugs are so notorious. In well-controlled dosage the multiple birth rate is only 6 per cent and most of these are twins. Clomiphene is usually given to a woman only after it has been ascertained that her husband is normal and that her tubes are open. If in the presence of ovulation the woman still doesn't conceive, further investigations will have to be done to find out why.

There are two main groups of women who don't respond to clomiphene. The first include a small proportion of those suffering from cystic disease of the ovaries (see page 78) and the second have a gonadotrophin deficiency at hypothalamic or pituitary levels.

The next group of drugs used to stimulate ovulation are the two gonadotrophic hormones. There are two main types and these are used only if clomiphene has had no effect. The first, HCG (human chorionic gonadotrophin), is obtained from the urine of pregnant women and the second, HMG (human menopausal gonadotrophin), comes from the urine of post-menopausal women and is marketed under the name Pergonal. It is a white powder which, when disolved in saline, has to be given by injection. Pituitary gonadotrophins (extracts of pituitary glands) are used in many countries but are not on sale in the UK. Gonadotrophins are the most potent ovulation stimulators because they bypass the pituitary and hypothalamus and act directly on the ovaries. Even ovaries that have lain dormant for decades can be stimulated to ovulate within ten days of starting treatment with these drugs. There are problems though. Gonadotrophins are expensive and in very short supply. The treatment is time-consuming, needs careful monitoring at expert centres and can be hazardous unless the dose is strictly controlled. For these reasons, gonadotrophin therapy is usually reserved for those women who fail to respond to clomiphene or bromocriptine therapy, who have normal, functioning ovaries and who are very strongly motivated. Specialists can obtain gonadotrophins for their patients.

The main problem with gonadotrophins is that the

difference between the minimum effective dose and the maximum that will not cause too great a stimulation of the ovaries is only 33 per cent. The minimum effective dose varies from woman to woman and has to be worked out before starting the course of treatment. From this base level the dose in increased every five days until serum oestrogen levels begin to rise. Once oestrogen levels exceed a certain critical level the gonadotrophin is discontinued and another type of gonadotrophin is given in the full ovulating dose forty-eight hours later. The couple is advised to have intercourse during the following twelve-hour period. With this procedure (which varies from clinic to clinic depending upon their particular experience) 90 per cent of women ovulate and 60 per cent get pregnant.

HMG (Pergonal) is the drug that caused all the furore over multiple births after its use in the treatment of infertility, and it certainly has produced quadruplets and quintuplets. These dramatic multiple births are very much less common today because infertility experts have now perfected the dose-regulating methods; even so about 20 per cent of all HMG births are multiple (usually twins).

Bromocriptine is a drug that specifically suppresses the production of prolactin by the pituitary. Prolactin is the hormone normally increased during lactation (breast feeding). When prolactin is increased in the body, FSH is decreased and this produces amenorrhoea. About one in seven of all women with amenorrhoea have raised prolactin levels and suppression of these produces a rapid return of ovulation. Gastric side effects are not uncommon and can be avoided by taking the drug with meals. Ovulation rates of 95 per cent are common and pregnancy results in about 75 per cent. The drug is discontinued as soon as a positive pregnancy test is obtained.

It must be stressed that apart from clomiphene, all these drugs are very potent and can only be obtained in big infertility centres where careful monitoring and blood hormone estimations can be done. Many women go to an infertility clinic and ask straight away if they can have a 'fertility drug'. The answer to this is 'not until we know if an inability to ovulate is your problem'. There is no point in giving these expensive drugs to someone who is ovulating perfectly well but has blocked tubes.

There is, unfortunately, no magic cure-all 'fertility drug' and there never will be because there are so many possible causes of infertility in a woman and the treatment of each is so different.

Fallopian tube problems

Tubal abnormalities account for about 25 per cent of all causes of female infertility. It is ironically one of the easiest conditions to diagnose yet about the most difficult to cure. Unfortunately, the number of women who are infertile because of blocked tubes is rising as venereal infection (the commonest cause of blocked tubes) increases in incidence. These statistics are also boosted by the rising number of pregnancy terminations (procured abortions) and the premature (often immediately after a birth or an abortion) performance of sterilization procedures which damage the fallopian tubes – a decision that is often all too soon regretted, if it has not been carefully thought out in advance.

The fallopian tubes are extremely complex organs. The way in which eggs are 'captured', the way they transport the egg and change sperms to make them capable of fertilizing the egg, and the whole mechanism of fertilization are only poorly understood. Research is under way to try to elucidate the roles of hormones, prostaglandins and secretions produced by the tubes, but we are a long way off understanding exactly how these delicate structures function.

One thing we do know though is that infection can so seriously change them that the fine channel down which the egg must travel to meet a sperm can be completely obliterated and so render the woman sterile. The division of abdominal adhesions (sometimes under laparosocpy) caused by a previous infection (for example, a burst appendix) can alter tubal function in a way which makes conception more likely.

Sexual intercourse with many partners is a part of everyday life among some people today. World statistics show that whenever sexual promiscuity increases, a proportionate increase in sexually transmitted infection occurs. This is particularly true of gonorrhoea and chlamydia which are now the fastest growing infectious diseases in the world. About 10 per cent of women who contract gonorrhoea suffer from an inflammation of their fallopian tubes as a result and whenever this occurs there is an increased risk of subsequent infertility. In Britain the most gonorrhoea-prone are women in the eighteen to nineteen age group and the numbers of affected women have risen dramatically. One Swedish study found that about 20 per cent of women who had gonorrhoeal infection of their tubes were permanently infertile due to tubal obstruction, so it is a subject to be taken very seriously. Such infertility was most common in those women who had had several infections with gonorrhoea.

However, not all salpingitis (inflamation of the tubes) is gonococcal; other organisms can also be responsible. Syphilis is less common, less destructive to the tubes and, if caught early, can be treated. Pelvic inflammatory disease is a broad term used to describe the infection of the reproductive tract (including the tubes) from the many and varied sources. The insertion of an intra-uterine contraceptive device (IUD) can cause long-term sub-clinical infections that go unnoticed by the woman and her doctor. This smouldering infection can produce tubal changes and is another reason why tubal blockage is on the increase as more women come off the Pill and have a coil (IUD) inserted. Abortions carried out even in the best hospitals can (though rarely) cause pelvic infections and certainly any women undergoing do-it-yourself or back-street abortions run extremely high risks of subsequent pelvic infection and then infertility. However, it's only reasonable to bear in mind that the risks of becoming infertile as a result of an abortion in a hospital are small. It has been calculated that it's twice as safe to have such an abortion (before 12 weeks of pregnancy) than it is to go through with the pregnancy – at least from an infertility point of view. The tubes can also be affected after other abdominal infections such as a burst appendix. One Danish study looked at eighty women who had had appendicectomy operations as children and examined their fertility status. They found that those women who had been operated on for perforated appendicitis had an increased level of infertility compared with women of the same age who had not. They suggested that it might be advisable in the light of their research to ensure that young girls have their appendix out whenever there is the slightest indication that anything is wrong. However, this view is still open to debate.

Any pelvic inflammatory disease (such as burst appendix) can produce bands of tissue which link one organ inside the abdomen to the next. These thick, fibrous bands are called adhesions and can substantially alter the functioning of the fallopian tubes or even shut them off altogether. So, after pelvic infection, a combination of scarring and adhesion formation may damage the tubes and render the woman infertile. One sort of infection, however, doesn't cause scarring and adhesions yet renders women infertile – this is an infection with T-mycoplasma (see below). The infection is usually symptomless but seems to affect a woman's ability to carry a fetus and can cause miscarriages. Two Swedish doctors have done most of the research on this organism. They found T-mycoplasma in the semen of some infertile men and in the cervical mucus of some infertile women. T-mycoplasma can be killed by an antibiotic called doxycycline and when this drug was given to a group of infertile women, 29 per cent of them became pregnant. Research has also shown that T-mycoplasma organisms bind to sperms and reduce their motility. Tuberculosis is now a rare cause of pelvic infection in the West but is still common elsewhere in the world.

WHAT CAN BE DONE?
Here is an example of prevention being better than cure. Girls should be made aware of the dangers of promiscuous sexual relationships because it is they, and not their men who end up suffering the most. Gonorrhoea in men produces symptoms fairly early and only rarely produces permanent damage. A substantial proportion of women with gonorrhoea, though, have no symptoms and can thus pass the disease on to a man who will then infect someone else. It is this pool of unwittingly infectious women that is so worrying. The greater use of the Pill and the IUD have further increased the likelihood of transferring gonorrhoea, or indeed any venereal infection, as a sheath definitely provides some protection against the disease. The wider use of condoms would undoubtedly reduce the numbers of women who suffer from infected tubes but this is a trend that is unlikely to occur (although the sheath is still the most widely used form of contraception in the West). Efficient contact tracing is also essential if the source of the gonorrhoea a woman has spread to other men and their partners is to be discovered and treated. The early detection of gonorrhoeal infection in the absence of symptoms as part of routine medical check-ups can't be relied upon to be successful because the chances of discovering the infection in its early phases are small. In one study only one case of gonorrhoea was detected among 625 women attending a clinic for other reasons. Unfortunately, too few women realize that even if an infection has been treated successfully, once the tubes are

affected the chances of subsequent infertility are still high.

Once tubal damage is done, however, surgery at the very best centres can offer some hope. The degree of success likely to be achieved depends on the severity of the tubal damage. As we will see on page 133, a hysterosalphingogram itself may open the tubes. However where adhesions surround the tubes, division of the adhesions (salpingolysis) is essential. About half of all women undergoing this operation (which can sometimes be carried out under direct vision down a laparascope thus avoiding an abdominal operation) will get pregnant. When the tubes are completely blocked by previous infection, microsurgery is needed to create a new opening of the tube into the uterus. Alternatively, the diseased section can be cut out and the two ends of good tube joined up again. These procedures are extremely delicate, can only be carried out in a handful of centres in the UK and have very low success rates (5-20 per cent). These low success rates come about because, although the plumbing may be restored to near normality, the normal functioning of the tubes does not necessarily return so they may not conduct eggs and sperms properly or may not provide the right environment for fertilization.

If the damage to the tubes was done by tubal ligation (as a sterilization procedure), rejoining the tubes results in pregnancies in 50 per cent of cases. However, heat applied to the tubes (a common way of sterilizing women, especially in conjunction with laparoscopy) causes so much tissue damage that the chances of reconstituting the tubes are very small indeed.

The outlook for the future of women who have irreparably blocked tubes lies not with improved microsurgical techniques, which will always be extremely time-consuming and expensive, but with *in vitro* or 'Test-tube babies' (see page 201).

Endometriosis

This is a condition in which endometrial tissue, which is normally only found lining the uterus, appears in other places in the abdominal cavity and the pelvic organs. The disease occurs most frequently in women aged between thirty and forty, though it can first appear in the twenties. It is commoner in women who put off having children until their late twenties or early thirties and this makes it an increasingly important cause of infertility. Endometriosis is clearly associated with infertility – about 40 per cent of all women with this condition are infertile.

No one knows why endometriosis occurs but it is thought that normal endometrial tissue comes out of the fimbriated ends of the fallopian tubes, possibly during menstruation, and that the cells implant themselves in the tubes, on the peritoneal lining, on the ovaries or even on the bowel or bladder. Unfortunately, these particles of endometrium behave just as if they were still in the uterus and undergo cyclical changes, including bleeding during menstruation. Obviously, normal menstrual blood flow can leave the uterus but patches of endometrium elsewhere produce a menstrual flow which can't escape and so causes local inflammation and eventually the formation of scar tissue. In really bad cases, bands of fibrous tissue (adhesions) can cause deformations of the uterus, tubes or ovaries. Endometriosis causes infertility not only through the mechanical effects of the patches which may block the tubes but also because it seems to produce a hormonal upset that results in poor cervical mucus and a failure of ovulation in about 50 per cent of cases.

The signs and symptoms of endometriosis are fairly clear-cut. About one-third of all women with the condition have no symptoms but the rest have a combination of painful intercourse, painful periods and heavy periods. If the periods are painful, the pain is often described as coming on a few days before the period actually starts. The pain is dull and persistent and may go through to the back or the back passage. The diagnosis is made from the woman's story, a careful pelvic examination and, most useful of all, a laparoscopy. With a laparoscope the plaques can be clearly seen and any cysts on the ovary (so-called chocolate cysts because they become filled with dark red blood) can clearly be visualized.

Ultrasound is now being increasingly used by gynaecologists and infertility specialists not only to diagnose the presence of ovarian cysts, fibroids which have degenerated and ectopic pregnancies but also ovulation. Repeated ultrasound pictures give very accurate measurements of the size of the Graafian follicles in the ovary and are now used increasingly to pinpoint ovulation both in test-tube baby pregnancies (see page 201) and in predicting ovulation in normal cycles and in women who are to have AID (see page 176).

The best treatment for endometriosis is, ironically, pregnancy but since nearly half of all women with the condition cannot get pregnant, this is not a helpful answer. Pregnancy produces a cure by suppressing the cyclical stimulation of the endrometrial plaques and possibly by enlarging the cervical canal, so allowing menstrual products to flow out easily and not be refluxed back up into the peritoneal cavity.

WHAT CAN BE DONE?
The infertile woman with endometriosis can have two types of treatment: medical – with drugs, or surgical. The first of the drug treatments involves going on the Pill for a year continuously, so suppressing ovulation and menstruation. This treatment cures the less serious cases of endometriosis but there are problems because after a while many women have breakthrough bleeding on the Pill and need to receive higher and higher doses in order to suppress their periods completely. This may be unpleasant because of the increasing levels of oestrogenic side effects as the dosage is stepped up. Recent research suggests that the risks to older women on large doses of the Pill are unacceptably high, so it is unlikely that your doctor will be as keen to use this course of treatment as he would have been only a few years ago.

Male-type hormones are now used successfully – danazol (Danol) with its anti-gonadotrophic action being the most popular. These drugs cause an artificial menopause which reduces ovarian function and so enables the patches of endometriosis to heal. There are some side effects, notably weight gain, acne, a decrease in breast size and sometimes some growth of new body hair. These symptoms disapppear when the drug is stopped.

In really severe cases in which scarring is very bad, drugs have little or no effect and endometrial plaques may have to be operated upon. At the operation adhesions can be removed, the uterus resuspended (to prevent the formation of further adhesions), plaques cauterized and sometimes drug therapy is combined witht the surgery. About half of all women undergoing surgery for endometriosis subsequently get pregnant – the outcome depending upon the severity of the disease in the first place, the woman's age and the duration of the infertility before surgery.

Unfortunately, endometriosis cannot ever be said to be 'cured' by any of these methods; they simply stop further deterioration. Some women have few symptoms after successful treatment but others may have to have a hysterectomy in an attempt finally to cure the problem.

Infections of the urinary and genital systems

There is now increasing evidence that genito-urinary infections are a major factor underlying infertility. Of course, it has been known for centuries that venereal diseases such as gonorrhoea and syphilis cause infertility by inflicting damage on the fallopian tubes and we have already seen how this occurs and how it is treated.

This section though deals with infections that don't do anything quite so obvious, yet which appear to impair fertility.

There seem to be three ways in which infections of the genito-urinary tract can produce ill effects on reproductive physiology. First, they can have deleterious effects on sperms; second, they can affect gland functioning; and third, they can induce immunological responses in both partners. Often, more than one of these mechanisms is at work.

Let us look first at sperm function. Sperms can't be considered to be mature until they've been ejaculated and further development still takes place in the vagina and even as 'far away' as the fallopian tubes. Because of this, it's essential that the environment in the vagina, uterus and tubes is just right, so that sperms stand the best possible chance of success. There are many reports of organisms causing poor sperm function. In one study, 180 out of 190 infertile male partners had prostatic fluid which contained organisms. Eighty-nine per cent of these men also had Trichomonas vaginalis organisms present. Their positive cultures were correlated with decreased sperm motility, a reduction in sperm life and increased sperm clumping. Other studies have looked at the effects of bacteria on sperms when the bacteria are added to normal cervical mucus and have repeatedly found that several common genito-urinary bacteria cause decreased sperm motility and that one, E. coli, causes sperm clumping.

As we saw above, T-mycoplasma, an organism half-way in size between a virus and a bacterium, has been linked with infertility for years. In a study of 678 infertile males, one researcher found that this organism was the cause of increased ejaculatory volumes, decreased sperm counts, increased abnormal sperm forms and decreased motility. Other workers have found that women with T-mycoplasma infection not only have a higher incidence of infertility but also of ectopic pregnancy and spontaneous abortion. It has also been found that in women, this T-mycoplasma infection is usually not clinically obvious either to doctors or to the women themselves.

Common vaginal infections such as moniliasis (thrush) and Trichomonas vaginalis both cause decreased sperm motility and moniliasis also makes sperms clump.

For some reason or other, genito-urinary infections in women are very common. It is known that the common vaginal and urinary infections are more prevalent in those women who wear nylon pants, tights and similar garments. Perhaps there are other environmental factors involved of which we are as yet unaware. But whatever the reason, it seems certain that when a woman opens her bowels, the area around her vaginal opening becomes contaminated with bacteria. Contamination also occurs if the woman has a true urinary infection, which can be remarkably common, even in quite normal healthy women.

The recurrence of genito-urinary infections might be caused by hormonal changes. It is well known that the urine of women who are on the Pill is more favourable for bacterial growth and this gross, clinically-induced hormonal change is only a more blatant extension of the hormonal changes that go on every month in a woman not taking the Pill.

Treatment of genito-urinary infections in either partner can be notoriously difficult. If a woman (or indeed her partner) is carrying an identifiable organism, treatment with specific anti-bacterial agents might cure the infertility. As we saw above, this can sometimes be the case with T-mycoplasma after it is treated with doxycycline. Unfortunately, reports of the successful treatment of infertility caused by genito-urinary infection are hard to interpret for several reasons. The woman might have conceived anyway, even in the presence of the infection; too often there is poor follow-up to see what really happened; many of these infections recur; there are too many different treatment schedules to be able adequately to compare the values of each; there have as yet been too few well-controlled trials of therapy; and lastly, many clinics don't go to enough trouble to find out whether the infection is actually causing the infertility or not.

Most experts agree that even if only one of the partners is infected with an organism, the other should be treated too because the transmission of organisms at intercourse is so common. Unfortunately, one of the commonly used drugs for urinary infections, nitrofurantoin (Furadantin) can actually depress sperm formation in its own right but there are many alternatives available. Duration of treatment is a vexed problem, but experts in this field agree that it makes sense to go on treating the infection until the sperm parameters return to normal.

A lot more research is needed in this area but it could well be that a substantial proportion of women who at the moment are labelled as infertile 'cause unknown', could be suffering from a sub-clinical infection. It's certainly worth trying a full course of doxycycline because pregnancy occasionally occurs as a result of this simple treatment when all else seems to have failed.

Cervical factors

Since the cervix is the gateway through which sperms have to pass in order to get to the egg, any disorder of this important area can render a woman infertile. It has been estimated that between 10 and 30 per cent of infertile women have a cervical factor causing their infertility. Sperms may be completely barred from passing through, or simply held up long enough to render them incapable of reaching the egg by one of several conditions: longstanding infection of the cervix (cervicitis): cervical stenosis (narrowing): thick, impassable mucus; or what has been called a 'cervical hostility factor'.

In the last-mentioned case, these women produce mucus which is inhospitable to sperms and this hostility may be specific to their partner. The mucus is of good quality but repeatedly kills sperms as judged by post-coital tests. This is especially likely to occur if there is very little semen as the enzymes in the sperm heads are needed to get the sperms through the mucus, and too little of the enzymes will fail to break the barrier. If the semen volume is normal though, it suggests that there is something in the mucus which is killing off the sperms. This 'something' may be antibodies that the woman has produced in response to her husband's sperms (see below) or there may be other, as yet unidentified, factors in the mucus itself.

In a post-coital test (PCT) two important aspects are checked: the number of sperms and how many are actively progressing through the mucus. Simple motility is no good if the sperms are swimming in circles or beating away without progressing.

However, a PCT is only valid and useful in the presence of normal mucus, so often one finds either that the PCT is bad because the mucus was poor or that the test was done on the wrong day (too early or too late in relation to ovulation). For practical details of the PCT see page 129.

So if one post-coital test is negative then it is more practical to proceed to a sperm invasion test (SIT) or penetration test. This test, although more complex for the doctor, is as simple for the patient as the PCT. It is fact a combination of a seminal fluid aetysis test and the ability of the sperms to pass through mucus (penetration test). It also has the advantage that in the event of no penetration or poor motility of the sperms, a second stage (cross-matched sperm penetration test) can be carried out. Here, normal sperms (from a donor) are checked against the wife's mucus and donor mucus is checked against the husband's sperms.

In the first part of the test a seminal fluid sample is checked carefully (see page 125), then a small known amount of semen is put into a glass chamber in which is placed a fine glass tube containing the wife's mucus. Using a microscope, the penetration of the mucus by the sperms can be watched. Normally, sperms move freely and rapidly up the tube through the mucus. If, however, the mucus is hostile, then the sperms die after penetrating a short way. If antibodies are present sperm clumping takes place without penetration. If an abnormal result is obtained then the second part of the test (a cross-match test) confirms whether it is a sperm or mucus problem. The penetration test can also be used to test the effect of treatment either on mucus or sperms; for example, treatment with oestrogen to thin the mucus or with hormones to improve sperm numbers or motility.

But all this talk of cervical 'hostility' may be too simple because the latest research suggests that it may well be more a matter of spermatic 'suicide'. Recent research shows that sperm antibodies are present in about 2 per cent of fertile and 14 per cent of infertile men. A study in Holland suggested that sperm antibodies in men *are* important (many doctors have questioned their importance) and clearly showed that over a ten-year follow-up, untreated men had increasing antibody levels which resulted in a decreasing likelihood of subsequent fertility. As we have just seen, sperms get trapped in so-called 'hostile' mucus. This led to studies being done in which fertile donor sperms were tested against the woman's cervical mucus. But these and other tests suggest that the mucus is mostly normal and that it's the sperms that kill themselves off because they are pre-sensitized with antibodies. But this mechanism only seems to come into play if the man has sperm antibodies in his semen and not in his blood serum. This could explain why it is that a vasectomy is often successfully reversed in the presence of serum antibodies to sperms. A recent report in *Science* by Professor Nancy Alexander led to widespread concern about the safety of vasectomies. This research demonstrated that monkeys with anti-sperm antibodies following vasectomy who were fed on a high-cholesterol diet developed more extensive atherosclerosis than dummy-operated animals. She blamed this on serum antibodies which, she thought, became deposited on artery linings. There is no evidence that vasectomy or anti-sperm antibodies do this in man although several studies are under way to examine the possibility.

WHAT CAN BE DONE?
Cervical narrowing is rare. Probably only about 10 per cent of women with a cervical abnormality leading to infertility have this. No one knows for certain why cervical narrowing produces infertility but it could be because of the smaller area of mucus-producing cells. Some women become pregnant after very gentle dilatation (stretching) of the cervical canal by a specialist.

About half of the 'cervical' group of infertile women have abnormal mucus. About half of these have poor quality mucus that is too sticky, while the other half have very little mucus. Oestrogen therapy can produce good results in some of these women.

If a post-coital test (see page 129) shows that the cervical mucus is normal yet sperm penetration is poor, the use of a cervical cap containing the husband's sperms produces pregnancies in about half the number of women treated. Because sperms normally don't live in the vagina for more than about half an hour it makes sense to give them a longer time to get into the cervix by placing them very close to it in a cap for several hours.

So in summary, all infertile couples should have a properly

performed post-coital test. If abnormal mucus is found, oestrogen therapy will help nearly 50 per cent and about 90 per cent of these will get pregnant. If the defect is secondary to poor quality sperms or to immobilized sperms, the cervical cap should be used. About 50 per cent of these women will get pregnant.

Alkaline douches are said to promote fertility if the cervical mucus is too acid. To obtain the maximum effect the douche should be used immediately before making love. Long-term infections of the cervix can be cured by freezing (cryosurgy), by cauterizing the area or by the use of antibiotics, and mucus quality can be improved (as we have just seen) by using oestrogen around ovulation time.

So clearly there are several reasons why a woman's cervix may be a barrier to her husband's sperms. In addition, she might well have formed antibodies to his sperms, making them clump together so that they don't swim up the cervix. The whole question of sperm antibodies is still not clear especially as anti-sperm antibodies are found in the serum of perfectly fertile women. Much more work needs to be done, but certain rays of light are being shed on the matter.

Antibodies develop in a woman as a result of her body's reaction to her husband's sperms and it has been shown that prostitutes, who come into contact with many men's sperms are more likely to develop antibodies than are other women. In relation to sperms, antibodies cause two main problems. First, they may agglutinate them (clump them together) so that they can't swim and, second, they may immobilize or even kill them.

Both men and women can form antibodies to sperms. In one study, of 400 infertile couples, 18 per cent of the women had sperm antibodies in their blood. When a woman has sperm antibodies (which she develops for some unknown reason against the 'foreign' protein of her husband's sperms) there are several ways around the problem.

The first of these is for the couple to use a condom for at least a year. This is not a very good method but it is thought that because sperms no longer come into contact with the woman's reproductive tract, the sperm antibody level probably falls away. Subsequent intercourse results in pregnancies in about 50 per cent of these women.

The second method involves the washing of her husband's sperms, on the assumption that any antibodies in his semen can be carefully washed away. The washed sperms are then inseminated into the woman at or very close to the time of ovulation. The insemination is either direct into the uterine cavity or into the cervical canal.

The third method involves giving immunosuppressive (antibody-suppressing) drugs to either the man or the woman. A steroid (methylprednisolone) is given in very high dosage for seven days to either sex. In women receiving the drug there was no disturbance of ovulation as judged by basal temperature charts in one survey. This survey found that the suppression of antibody formation produced no ill effects in the women treated and resulted in pregnancies in one in seven of them.

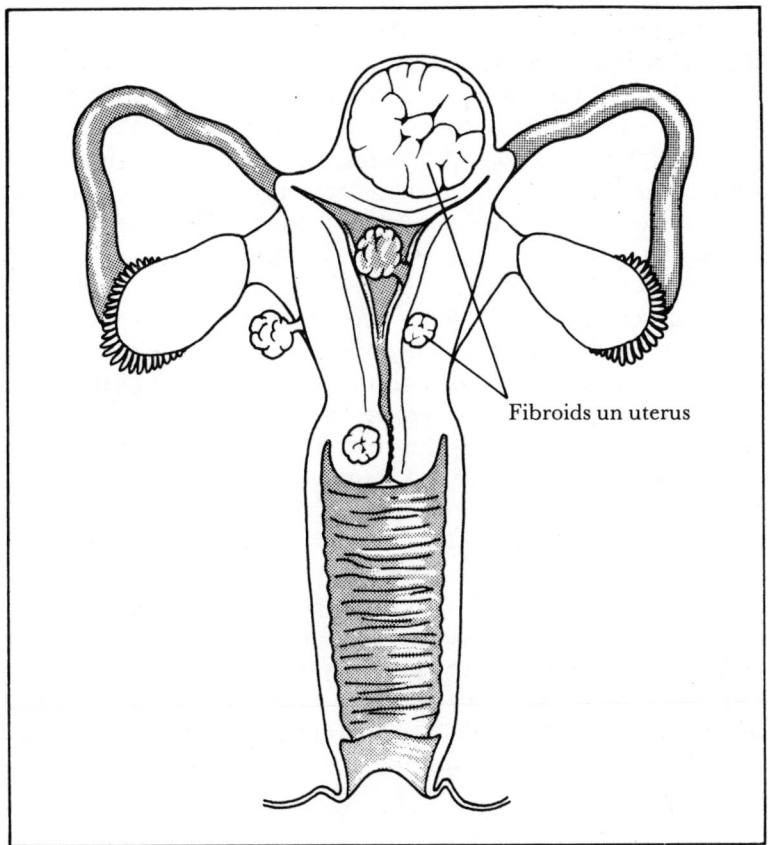

Fibroids in various parts of the uterus. Not all these sites would necessarily be affected in any one woman.

Abnormalities of the uterus

Although abnormally shaped uteri can cause miscarriages it is rare for them to cause infertility. Uterine fibroids are about the only cause of infertility brought about by abnormalities of the uterus and these are a rare cause of infertility under the age of thirty. In some women fibroids actually obstruct the opening of the fallopian tubes, but in the vast majority the tubes are open and the mechanism by which fibroids produce infertility is obscure. Pregnancy can occur after the removal of fibroids – the success rate is about 50 per cent.

Other causes

STEIN-LEVENTHAL SYNDROME (Polycystic ovaries)
This is a fairly common condition in which the ovaries are tough and fibrous and covered with many cysts. It causes irregular or absent ovulation. There may be more than one cause for the condition and it presents in many different ways. Obesity and hairiness (in a male distribution) and irregular and unpredictable periods may be features. Treatment is with clomiphene on its own or with gonadotrophic hormones, and surgery is only necessary if these methods fail. Some women with the condition suddenly recover, become normal again and start ovulating. Any form of operation on the ovaries can change them back to normal and so re-start ovulation. The most usual operative procedure though involves removing a wedge of tissue from each ovary. This surgery is performed only on women who have not responded to ovulation-inducing drugs.

TURNER'S SYNDROME
This a rare congenital condition in which the ovaries are absent because the woman has only one-half of her sex chromosome complement. This gives her an XO chromosome pattern instead of XX. These women have the outward appearance of a female but never menstruate or develop sexual characteristics. Nothing can be done to alleviate this condition.

X-RAYS
Repeated X-rays to the pelvic area may affect conception but probably do more harm to the future fetus than to the poten-

tial mother's chances of conception. Radiographers and other women working in X-ray departments should wear protective garments when they are anywhere near X-ray sources in use and should carry a monitoring badge to check how much exposure they're getting.

MENSTRUAL BACK-FLOW INTO THE FALLOPIAN TUBES

A Norwegian gynaecologist noted that some women have very slack support for their uteri and that the ovaries and tubes of these women hang limply, causing congestion in the veins and poor muscular function in their tubes. During a menstrual period, he operated on twenty-three women who were infertile and in whom no cause could be found. He discovered that they all had menstrual blood refluxing back along the tubes, so he pulled up the tubes and stitched them to the abdominal wall. Twenty of the women became pregnant.

GENERAL DISEASES

Acute infectious illness can temporarily reduce a woman's fertility but has no permanent effect. More serious diseases such as TB or diabetes probably have no effect on normally fertile women but might just tip a marginally sub-fertile one over the brink into infertility.

It is usually disease of the endocrine glands that causes infertility mainly by interfering with ovulation (as we saw on page 60). Severe malnutrition, severe depression, anorexia and gross obesity can also suppress ovulation.

VITAMIN B12 DEFICIENCY

It was noticed that women who develop pernicious anaemia in later life had suffered from infertility when they were younger. This led to the proposal that some women might be infertile because of a sub-clinical vitamin B_{12} deficiency. Whilst it should not be considered a treatment of first choice, it makes sense to give this injection to any woman in whom no cause for infertility can be found. It can do no damage and does occasionally produce a pregnancy.

STRESS

Whether stress has any relation to female infertility is not known. For years experts suggested that the fallopian tubes went into spasm under emotional stress but research now shows that this is not the case. If stress affects women's fertility at all it is most likely to do so via the higher centres of the brain turning off the hormones which stimulate ovulation. Even research into this is very confused, some reports clearly showing that ovulation is delayed or absent in the presence of stress and others showing exactly the opposite. More research is needed. Recent work has found that women under stress have raised levels of prolactin, which could be a cause of infertility.

So, as with male infertility there are many causes. The difference with female infertility is that a lot more can be done. Investigative techniques and treatment methods are improving all the time, which means that the 12 per cent of women who today end up infertile for no known reason will stand a better chance in the future. This is an area of medicine where things move quickly. Changes in the last five years have revolutionized the outlook for the infertile woman and there are signs that the next five will be just as eventful.

CHAPTER 4

Male Infertility and its Treatment

Until only a few years ago it was generally assumed that if a couple was infertile it was the women who was 'at fault'. Today we know differently. In about 40 per cent of couples attending infertility clinics it is the man who has the underlying cause of the problem. Until the last decade, male infertility fell into the domain of urologists, simply because as specialists in genito-urinary troubles they were used to dealing with the male sex organs and could be said to be most familiar with them in health and disease. This state of affairs was somewhat unsatisfactory though, because whilst the urinary and reproductive organs seem to be very closely linked anatomically (or even to be the same organs in certain cases), in reality the two systems are more distinct than at first appears to be the case and so need separate consideration and study. The flaccid, 'urinary' penis, for example, is a very different structure from the erect reproductive organ so essential for fertilization.

Recently though, especially in the US, the study of male reproduction has been growing and there are now specialists in this field of medicine known as andrologists.

Very briefly, there are four things that can go wrong with a man's reproductive system: he can fail to produce sperms; the sperms he produces may not be healthy; there may be a blockage that prevents normally produced sperms getting to the penis; and there may be a problem that prevents him ejaculating the sperms into his partner's vagina.

The following are the major causes of male infertility.

Varicocele

A varicocele is a varicose vein around the top of the testis, usually the left (see illustration, page 109). It can also affect the right testis. About 30 per cent of all cases of male infertility are thought to be caused by this simple and treatable problem. Ten per cent of normal, fertile men are found to have varicoceles though, so clearly it is not a condition which *necessarily* produces infertility. This is just one of the many unsolved mysteries surrounding varicoceles, as we shall see.

Just why a varicose vein around the top of the testis should cause infertility isn't understood but there are several theories. As long ago as 1956 one expert suggested that because of the increased blood flow through these varicose veins, the temperature of the testes was raised and that it was this that depressed the production of sperms. This has never been proven to be the answer. Further studies showed that blood from the left side of the scrotum mixes with that in the right in men with a varicocele. Similar studies with radio-opaque dyes injected into the veins leading from the adrenal glands and the kidneys show that in men with a varicocele, blood refluxes abnormally from these organs, possibly carrying toxic metabolic substances from the adrenal gland and kidney to the testes. No one has yet discovered what these substances are but they arrive at the varicocele from the left adrenal and kidney veins and then spread to the right testicular veins. This helps explain why it is that a condition only seeming to affect the left testis should produce infertility.

We don't know why the varicose veins develop in the first place but it is possibly a combination of two factors. First, a man's upright posture may lead to increased gravitational forces on the valves in the veins, so leading to a gradual distention and eventually to a failure of the valves. This is how varicose veins in the legs are thought to arise. Second, it might be caused by straining at stool for year after year as a result of the very low roughage (dietary fibre) diet we eat in the western world. Many surveys have shown that varicose veins generally are very much less common in countries where the people do not strain to pass their motions. Research has also found that on straining at stool, the pressure inside the veins at the tops of the legs goes up enormously and it is postulated that these bouts of high pressure damage the valves in the veins and eventually cause varicose (enlarged, twisted and distorted) veins.

The diagnosis of a varicocele is not always easy because sometimes a very small varicosity of the veins can cause a serious depression of sperm production. During examination, you'll be asked to stand upright in a good light and then to cough or strain hard while the doctor feels the scrotum.

But varicoceles, whilst being the subject of considerable study, still present the medical profession with dilemmas. Why should many men with a varicocele have perfectly normal semen? Why are some men with even quite large varicoceles fertile? What are the toxic substances that reflux down the veins from the kidneys and adrenal glands? Why do some men not respond to surgery even though their varicoceles look exactly the same as those who do respond? Only more research will find answers to these questions.

WHAT CAN BE DONE?
Varicoceles are one of the most rewarding conditions to treat in the field of male infertility. A simple operation under general anaesthetic, usually involving only a very short stay in hospital, produces improved sperm counts and motility in 80 per cent of all cases. At the operation the left spermatic vein is tied off and this leads to such an improvement in sperm production that about 50 per cent of the partners of these men become pregnant within a year of the operation. The results seem to be particularly encouraging if the sperm count before the operation was below 20 million per millitre.

Testicular failure

Nearly one in seven infertile men have some malfunction of the testis which shows itself as poor, or even absent, sperm production.

A condition called Klinefelter's syndrome (characterized by small testes, no sperms, high blood FSH levels, an extra X chromosome and feminized features) is surprisingly common.

Mumps causes testicular inflammation quite often if it is contracted after puberty (rarely before) but in about 70 per cent of affected men the inflammation affects only one side. If there is testicular swelling at the time of the mumps, there is about 50 per cent chance that the affected testis will eventually become small and produce few sperms. If this atrophy of the testis affects both sides, some degree of infertility will result. If the inflammation of the testis doesn't go on to produce atrophy later, then there'll be no permanent drop in sperm production but normal levels may not return in that testis for a year or so.

Trauma and injury to the testes occur both accidentally and during surgery. A twisting (torsion) of the testis must be quickly corrected in order to preserve the sperm-producing potential of that testis. As this is such a painful condition the chances are that the sufferer will seek medical help very quickly anyway. Some experts feel that if one testis has twisted spontaneously the other one should be fixed at a minor operation so that it can't twist and so endanger future fertility. Any severe trauma to the testes can cause permanent damage and needs medical attention quickly.

Surgical damage to a testis during, for example, a hernia operation, is not uncommon.

Endocrine problems

'Glandular' or hormonal problems are thought to account for less than 10 per cent of all cases of male infertility. Some of these are caused by low levels of pituitary sex hormones and can be treated with human chorionic gonadotrophhin or mare's serum gonadotrophin with approximately a 30 per cent success rate.

Men don't seem to have a cyclical release of gonadotrophins as do women but studies of the breakdown products of male hormones in the urine can sometimes be helpful in elucidating the cause of or treatment needed for certain endocrine imbalances.

Rarely, the thyroid gland is underactive and this causes lowered sperm production. However, most authorities feel that the once fashionable diagnosis of 'thyroid deficiency' is now rarely acceptable as a cause of infertility.

Sexual problems

We will consider the main factors arising from difficulties with intercourse in Chapter 5. In one series of patients attending infertility clinics, as many as 5 per cent of otherwise normal couples were thought to be infertile simply because of poor sexual technique or frank sexual problems.

As explained already, there are *disease* conditions such as diabetes, neurological disease, endocrine disorders and post-operative states (especially after sympathectomy, major operations for rectal cancer and prostatectomy) that cause organic impotence. Many drugs (see page 107) can do so too. All these conditions will be ruled out before the doctor considers looking for psychosexually-based causes of impotence.

The frequency and timing of intercourse can be crucial in a couple who are not very fertile – this is discussed on page 42. Too infrequent intercourse or masturbation can lead to the production of poor quality semen and so to infertility in susceptible couples.

Obstruction to the vasa deferentia or other sperm ducts

The commonest place for the ductal system of a man to be obstructed is at the epididymis. The causes of this are usually congenital or secondary to TB or gonorrhoea, both of which can produce inflammation and subsequent blockage of the epididymal tubules. This usually results in the production of no sperms at all in the ejaculate and can occasionally be corrected by an operation. Any such operation will always be preceded by a testicular biopsy to ensure that the testis is in fact producing sperms.

Infections of the male reproductive system can be very difficult to diagnose (except for the obvious venereal diseases that produce pain and a penile discharge) and can be extremely resistant to treatment. Venereal disease has now attained epidemic proportions throughout the western world but men are more fortunate than women with regard to gonorrhoea and infertility because the signs of infection are more quickly noticed and can be treated before the organisms produce permanent damage. However, as we have just seen, the ducts of the epididymis or vas deferens *can* be blocked by gonorrhoeal infection. T-mycoplasma infection is a recognized hazard of intercourse. For more details see page 71.

The vasa deferentia can be blocked or may never develop in some men. An increasing number of males with obstruction to their vasa deferentia have the 'obstruction' created at their own request. Vasectomy operations are now extremely commonly performed and a proportion of men eventually decide they want to reverse the procedure. Contrary to popular belief, vasectomy can be reversed but only in about 50 per cent of couples does a pregnancy subsequently occur. This is often not because the tubes weren't put together properly but because about 60 per cent of men develop sperm antibodies which seem to keep them permanently infertile even after the 'plumbing' has been restored. The answer to this 'second thought' infertility problem is for a clinic to deep-freeze some of the man's semen before he undergoes a vasectomy operation.

Semen volume

Infertility can occur with either too high or too low a semen volume. A very low volume (less than one millilitre) even if the quality of the semen is otherwise good, can lead to infertility either because there is too little of it to reach the cervix or if, because of the low volume, there are too few sperm enzymes to break down cervical mucus. Men with very high semen volumes (over five millilitres) often have poor quality sperms. When the semen volume is high the first portion of the split ejaculate (see page 56 for details) contains most sperms of good quality and can be used for artificial insemination.

WHAT CAN BE DONE?
Semen volume can occasionally be increased by the administration of gonadotrophins in high doses but probably the best method of treatment in men with low volumes of otherwise normal semen is to use the semen to inseminate the woman artificially. After all, what there is of it is good and can produce a pregnancy.

Men with a high volume of semen can use the withdrawal method (withdrawing half-way through the ejaculation) of intercourse around the woman's most fertile time. Alternatively the man can produce a split-ejaculate specimen and this can then be artificially given to his partner. (See page 174 for details of AIH.)

Ejaculation disturbances

Ejaculation can be faulty in several ways. First, and most commonly, sperms may reflux up into the bladder instead of out down the penis. This is called retrograde ejaculation. Second, there may be no ejaculation and third, there may be premature ejaculation outside the vagina. The last of these conditions is discussed on page 50.

Retrograde ejaculation is the commonest of the foregoing dysfunctions (except for premature ejaculation, which is really a sexual dysfunction) and usually comes about as a result of surgery on the prostate gland or as a result of taking anti-hypertensive or certain tranquillizing drugs. It can, however, arise spontaneously for no apparent reason. Retrograde ejaculation may also be the first sign of early diabetes and, unfortunately, does not improve once the diabetes is treated.

Under normal circumstances, the muscles around the base of the bladder are kept contracted as the ejaculate reaches the back part of the urethra just below the bladder. In men who ejaculate retrogradely this contraction is faulty and although they get a sensation of ejaculation and are relieved by it just like other men, they do not ejaculate anything from the penis – the semen refluxes back up into the bladder.

WHAT CAN BE DONE?
The condition can sometimes be cured by reducing the drug dosage the man is taking, or by changing to another drug to achieve the same effect, but often treatment will involve obtaining sperms to inseminate the man's partner artificially. Sperms can be retrieved from the man's urine and used to inseminate his partner. The man takes bicarbonate of soda on the day before he goes to the doctor to make the urine alkaline. The doctor inserts a catheter into the man's bladder and washes it out with a special solution. The man is then asked to masturbate and the fluid from the bladder is let out complete with the sperms that are now floating in it. This fluid is spun down in a centrifuge and the sperms used to inseminate the man's partner artificially.

Undescended testes

While a baby boy is in his mother's womb, his testes move down from inside the abdomen into the scrotum. If a boy is born early the testes may still be up in the abdomen, but will normally come down within a few days. Many boys have testes which cannot easily be felt because they are what is known as 'retractile' – that is they shoot back up from the scrotum into the pouch above the scrotum. A doctor can gently push these testes down, though they may pop back up again.

The reason that doctors worry whether a boy's testes are 'down' in the scrotum is that there is now good evidence that if they are not down by the age of five years, irreversibile damage starts to take place from this age. If a testis remains outside the scrotum until puberty, it will never produce sperms. This occurs because the temperature within the abdomen is 2-3°C higher than the optimal temperature for sperm production and is usually sufficiently high to prevent sperm formation.

The longer a testis stays inside the abdomen, the more its structure is altered, until by the age of thirty or so it even stops producing sex hormones as the active hormone-producing cells are replaced by fibrous tissue.

Another reason why doctors worry about undescended testes is that they become cancerous in a very large proportion of cases. It is thought that cancer of the testis is forty-five times more common in undescended testes than in descended ones.

WHAT CAN BE DONE?
Treatment is usually started soon after the age of five years. Hormone therapy can sometimes bring the testes down. If this treatment is unsuccessful a surgeon can pull the testis down and tether it with a small stitch to the bottom of the scrotum. Sometimes a combination of hormonal and surgical treatment is employed.

Sperm agglutination

Sometimes, and for no apparent reason, semen samples from infertile men are seen under the microscope to contain sperms clinging (clumping) together. This is known as spern agglutination and affects fertility because the clumped sperms cannot move and so fail to get through the cervix. This is an example of the body's antibody system producing infertility.

The subject of immunity and infertility is a vexed one and experts are currently trying to sort it all out. Suffice it to say that it is possible for a woman to produce antibodies (such as she would produce against an infection, for example) to her husband's sperms. It is also possible for a man to produce antibodies against his own sperms. When this latter situation occurs it is usually after a vasectomy, trauma or infection, all of which may induce an antibody reaction. Fifty to sixty per cent of men in their first post-operative year after vasectomy have sperm antibodies, produced as a reaction to the reabsorbed sperms that can no longer be ejaculated, but there are now signs that the condition can be treated if necessary in some men and anyway the level of sperm antibodies falls naturally over a long period.

It has been found that between 14 and 30 per cent of men attending infertility clinics have sperm antibodies and some workers in this field think that if all other factors look normal and the woman still hasn't conceived after a year of trying, then sperm antibodies should be looked for.

There are probably about thirty antigenic substances in human serum. Some are unique to sperms and others are found in human serum, milk, saliva, gastric juices, urine, vaginal secretions and cervical mucus. Antibodies to sperms are usually measured in blood serum, so the discomfort in diagnosis is very small as the only procedure involved is the taking of a blood sample. Just why some men develop antibodies to their own sperm is not known. For some reason the sperm cell components become recognized by the body as 'not-self' or 'foreign' and antibodies are produced. The interesting thing is that not only do the sperm antibodies cause clumping in the affected men themselves but they also cause clumping of the sperms of normal men.

WHAT CAN BE DONE?
Until recently very little could be done but research in the US has now made strides forward with four new techniques. The first of these involves washing the man's sperms. The man produces a masturbated specimen of semen which is then assessed for sperm count and motility. The semen is diluted and spun down in a centrifuge. This washing is repeated and at each washing more and more of the antibodies are washed away. The final washed sperms are then artificially inseminated into the woman.

The second method uses immunosuppressive drugs. A high dose of a steroid drug is given for seven days. Steroids are known to suppress the formation of antibodies if given in large enough doses. Striking reductions in sperm antibodies are found in some cases, with pregnancy occurring in the partner of 35 per cent of those men treated.

The third technique involves giving hormones that damp down sperm production for three months in the hope that if no sperms are being produced there will be none to which the man can form antibodies and that on discontinuing the suppressive androgens there will be a rebound of normal sperm production. This method seems to work for some men.

The last technique is based on the knowledge that semen contains natural anti-clumping substances, one of which is known to be vitamin C. The management of these patients involves giving them 250 milligrams of vitamin C by mouth three times a day. This has resulted in normal, non-clumping semen in many cases.

Necrospermia

The production of semen which contains only dead sperms is uncommon and is at present untreatable. The affected men are usually normal in every other way and have high sperm counts with good looking, normal sperms, except that they are all dead. This is a completely untreatable cause of infertility at the moment.

High sperm density

A very few infertile men have extremely high sperm counts (600-700 million per millilitre). High counts are often associated with poor sperm motility, thus causing infertility.

High seminal viscosity

Very rarely the semen may be so thick that motility of the sperms is unusually restricted. An alkaline douching method has been devised to overcome this rare problem.

Genito-urinary infections

Although infection is generally thought of as playing a much larger part in female infertility than in the male disease counterparts, infection is nevertheless becoming increasingly recognized as an important precipitating factor in male infertility, mainly because of its ability to produce antibodies to sperms.

At a gross level, obstruction to the duct system (vasa deferentia) can occur just as an infection can cause obstruction to female ducts (fallopian tubes). Duct obstruction is much less common in the male than the female.

The second type of change that can occur after infection is in the sex glands (prostatic and other sex-gland function changes temporarily after infections affecting them).

Thirdly, sperms themselves may be affected adversely, mainly in such a way as to induce antibody formation which makes them clump together and so renders them unable to swim normally.

In addition to all of these, there is the ever-present danger that any genital infection in a man can be transmitted sexually to his partner who might then suffer from the effects of the infection herself.

The commonest organisms to cause obstruction in the male ducts are M. tuberculosis, gonococci and colon bacteria but others (Chlamydia trachomatis, for example) seem to affect younger men especially.

Inflammation of the prostate (prostatitis) can affect male fertility. The man with acute prostatitis is easy to spot. He has a fever, chills and some difficulty in urinating. Chronic prostatic infection though is more difficult to recognize and the diagnosis may be made only after culture of the urine and/or the semen. Just how infections of the prostate cause altered fertility isn't known but it probably changes the nutrient environment that the sperms need in such a way as to reduce semen quality critically.

The role of infection in infertile men with sperm antibodies has been well described by many researchers. In one survey of 109 infertile men with genital infection and/or obstruction, 50 were found to have infection alone and 59 to have infection and/or obstruction plus sperm antibodies. It is also interesting that as genito-urinary infections are treated, sperm clumping disappears, sperm counts rise and the numbers of abnormal sperms fall.

An interesting linking factor between infection and infertility could be the trace element zinc. Zinc is present in foods such as oysters, herrings, pork, bran, cow's milk, peas and carrots in especially large amounts and is present in smaller amounts in dozens of other foods. Whilst there is an enormous amount of medical literature on the effects of zinc and its lack in the body, the medical profession, in the UK at least, is still loath to take the subject of zinc very seriously. In the field of reproductive physiology, however, there are facts which cannot be ignored. Zinc is found in the prostate in a higher concentration than anywhere else in the body and in prostatic infections the level falls to one-tenth of normal. Zinc is known to be essential for the production of active sperms and for their normal motility. The reason for the high level of zinc in vaginal secretions is as yet unknown but may well be something to do with the further maturation of sperms that takes place within the female reproductive system.

That zinc is essential for the activity of sperms was studied in a Yugoslavian survey which found zinc levels of 20 milligrams per cent in normal, active semen: 14 milligrams per cent in semen with decreased sperm motility; and 8 milligrams per cent in that without active sperms. At one centre in the US certain patients have been successfully cured of their infertility, it is claimed, simply by eating a diet rich in zinc-containing foods. It is thought by this group of researchers that cadmium (a common industrial pollutant) reduces body levels of zinc and could possibly be a factor in infertility. Much more work needs to be done on the role of both infections and zinc (and the link between them) before we can be sure just how important they are in infertility.

Drug allergies

Acute allergies to drugs (including penicillin) can cause a temporary shut-down of sperm production.

Ageing

This is not a major cause of male infertility. Men become slowly less fertile over the age of forty and by the age of eighty, three-quarters of all men are impotent or infertile. By and large though, the men coming to an infertility clinic for help are very much younger and ageing is not a problem.

Stress

It is generally agreed that stress, anxiety and emotional tension can all affect sperm production. This is probably brought about because the higher centres of the brain affect the hypothalamus which in turn controls the sex hormone production of the pituitary gland. Psychogenic factors also affect potency and the ability of a man to deliver normal sperms to the cervix.

The effects of stress on infertility have as yet not been sufficiently researched though and much more needs to be done.

Nutrition

Studies in this area have been poor and are difficult to interpret. We assume that adequate nutrition is essential for sperm formation but it is not known at what level of malnutrition sperm production ceases. Vitamin A deficiency can cause reversible damage to sperm-producing cells and vitamin B is known to be essential for adequate pituitary gland function. Vitamin C plays a vital role in preventing sperms from clumping together and vitamin E has been shown to be essential for rats' sexual functioning. There is no evidence that taking vitamin E produces any positive effect on sperm production in man.

Obesity is known to depress the sperm count, so slimming is a reasonable thing to do for the man whose count is low.

Radiation

Of the body's cells, the testes are especially sensitive to radiation. Irradiation renders sperms incapable of fertilizing an egg but the effects are usually temporary, recovering over several years. Because X-rays not only cause a suppression of sperm production but might also cause mutations in the sperms' chromosomes which could produce abnormal babies later, every man having an X-ray of any region of the body near the testes should wear a lead protector. Very small doses of X-rays, for example in the dentist's chair or from the occasional chest X-ray, using good, modern equipment, almost certainly present no hazard at all to the testes.

Heat

The seminiferous tubules of the testes are very sensitive to heat. This heat can be produced externally (such as in a furnace room, a hot bath or sauna) or internally (for example by a fever) or with undescended testes. The temperature of the scrotum is maintained at 2-3°C lower than that of the rest of the body as we saw on page 34. If the seminiferous tubules become overheated, sperm formation is arrested but returns to normal about three months after the removal of the heat source. This was demonstrated very effectively in one study which showed an 86 per cent drop in sperm count in normal males who wore insulated underpants for ten weeks, with a rapid return to normal levels once the underwear was discarded.

The way to avoid external heat is to avoid taking hot baths, saunas or Turkish baths, using close-fitting underpants and jock straps, sitting for prolonged periods (especially driving), and any other conditions under which the scrotum becomes overheated. The problem with treating overheating is that you have to wait three months to see if the remedy has had any effect!

Internal heat (a fever) can occur for one of many reasons, the commonest being everyday infectious illnesses. Even after a fever with influenza, a man's sperm count can be reduced. This fall reaches a maximum around three to four weeks after the fever and in every case returns to normal by three months. Because of this, if your doctor finds an isolated poor semen specimen, he may well ask you about recent feverish illnesses. Viral diseases such as infectious mononucleosis (glandular fever) or hepatitis are particularly known to reduce sperm production temporarily.

Other diseases

MYOTONIC MUSCULAR DYSTROPHY
This condition can cause infertility. About 80 per cent of afflicted men have atrophy of their testes.

CYSTIC FIBROSIS
This is a condition affecting one in 1,000 men. It causes infertility because it results in an absence of the vasa deferentia. Surgical correction can be offered in highly specialized centres.

LONG-TERM KIDNEY FAILURE
This can produce impotence, loss of libido, small testes and breast formation, and the persistently high urea levels in the blood of these people depresses testosterone levels. Both men and women seem to be less fertile after renal transplantation but conception is by no means impossible.

SEVERE OR CHRONIC ILLNESS

Such illness can affect a man so that he doesn't want to have sexual relations with his partner. This is not a true cause of infertility as such because the man is strictly speaking fertile, but it can be a reason for a woman not conceiving when she would like to. All except the most severely ill (either mentally or physically) can masturbate and the semen from this can be used for artificial insemination. However, severely ill people would do well seriously to question the sense of trying too hard for a baby. Doctors will try to help them in coming to a decision.

Drugs

Drugs can render a man infertile in two ways. First, they may affect his drive for and his ability to have intercourse; and second, they may depress sperm formation.

In the first group come alcohol, narcotics, tranquillizers, antidepressants (especially monoamine oxidase inhibitors) and some antihypertensive drugs (guanethidine and methyldopa, especially).

Drugs affecting sperm production include methotrexate, sex hormones (male and female), nitrofurantoin (Furadantin, used for urinary infections), amoebicides and anti-malarial drugs, busulphan (Myleran), arsenicals, colchicine and medroxyprogesterone (Depo-Provera).

If you are in any doubt about the drugs you are taking ask your doctor.

Blood groups

There seems to be a relationship between blood groups and infertility. Even though Groups 'O' and 'A' are the commonest in western populations, there is a significantly higher incidence of infertile men in these groups. Group 'A' especially seem to have larger numbers of men with no sperms or very low sperm counts and this has led experts to wonder whether infertility could be genetically determined (as are blood groups).

The treatment of male infertility

The treatment of male infertility poses some of the most

difficult problems in modern medicine. A few conditions can easily be treated as we have just seen but most of the others are much more difficult. Part of the problem has been knowing at what level of the sperm count to take action. Thirty years ago it was thought that any man with a sperm count of much less than 60 million per millilitre was unlikely to father a child, whereas today the figure that is generally accepted is 20 million and some experts feel this is still too high. Because of this it is now widely believed that provided there are *any* active sperms present it is probably worth completing the female examinations and investigations in the knowledge that pregnancies have occurred in women whose male partners have had very poor semen indeed.

In general it would be fair to say that until recently the stated aim of most specialists was simply to try to raise the sperm count, assuming no clear-cut cause was found (and no cause at all, let alone a treatable one, is found in 5-10 per cent of the men who are deemed to be 'at fault' in an infertile partnership).

For decades thyroid extract was given in the hopes of raising sperm counts but in spite of various studies which seemed to prove its value it has now been shown to be of no use unless there is a proven thyroid deficiency, which is uncommon. One survey found that 9·4 per cent of the men attending a particular infertility clinic were suffering from an extremely mild thyroid deficiency, yet on comparison with normal, fertile men this percentage proved not to be high.

Oestrogen has been tried in short, discontinuous treatment courses but again it was found to be of little value and caused problems of feminization, eventual depression of sperm production and loss of libido.

The testosterone rebound method of treatment enjoyed its heyday in the fifties. In this form of therapy the man was given the male hormone testosterone on the understanding that when the drug was withdrawn, his natural gonadotrophins would be released in large compensatory amounts and so would produce lots of sperms. However, although it is quite easy to show that intramuscular testosterone depresses sperm production (in fact it could be used as a male contraceptive if the side-effects weren't so unacceptable), it is much more difficult to show a sustained rise in sperm counts in these men after its withdrawal. There is also a danger that permanent sperm suppression may occur.

More recently newer hormones used to treat infertility in women have been tested in men. Clomiphene citrate (Clomid) acts on the hypothalamus of both sexes to stimulate an increased production of the hormone FSH. As FSH is known to be important in stimulating sperm formation it was supposed that this would be a valuable drug, but it has turned out not to be so. It is far less effective at stimulating sperm production in men than in provoking ovulation in women. Unfortunately, Clomid also has the disadvantage of producing sterility if the dose is too high, so this treatment involves very careful dosage and monitoring. However, there is yet no definite proof that Clomid is useless, so the case must remain open until more research is done.

The hormones chorionic gonadotrphin (HCG) from embryos and human menopausal gonadotrophin (HMG; Pergonal) from the urine of post-menopausal women have also been tried, but with very inconclusive results. All this suggests that it is not simply a shortage of FSH that reduces sperm production: there must be other, as yet unidentified, stimulator substances. However, a few pregnancies have been recorded using HCG, so perhaps the method simply needs more research and a greater refinement of the initial diagnosis to be more widely effective.

* * *

So it is clear that male infertility therapy is still pretty much in the Dark Ages, apart from the simple treatments outlined under each heading above. In many animal species and especially in those whose husbandry has commercial importance, the scientific literature is bursting with data. In man, however, much more work needs to be done as so little of the animal work can be applied to him. Apart from treating many cases of varicocele, most cases of poor pituitary function and simple things such as overheated testes or over-drugged patients, we aren't doing very well on the male infertility front. This has mainly come about because the study of infertility and its treatment is understandably linked with the study of fertility control (contraception) and the burden of responsibility for contraception has always been carried by women. Ironically, this relative lack of research has backfired on men but things will change for the better over the next decade as male contraception becomes more possible and acceptable.

CHAPTER 5

Sorting Out the Causes

To most infertile couples who end up seeking medical help the worst part of the whole thing is suddenly finding themselves being treated as 'patients', often for the first time in their lives. Previously they'd considered themselves to be fit, healthy and normal (as indeed many infertile couples are) and then at a stroke they join the throng attending hospitals week after week. Most couples though start off with their family doctor. Over three-quarters of all couples with an infertility problem go to their family doctors within two years of starting to try for a baby and half go in the first year, according to a UK survey carried out by the National Association for the Childless.

The general practitioner is usually the first port of call and seeking his advice is probably the biggest step the infertile couple takes. After all, once you've committed yourself to going to the medical establishment with your problem it's difficult to back out without seeming defeatist, ungrateful or discourteous. Many women in particular put off the first visit because they fear having to have a vaginal examination and both partners are loath to have their sex lives probed in case they are found to be lacking in some way. In addition to these factors, many couples fear that by 'medicalizing' the problem they'll end up with a hard, factual answer to their infertility problem which might be difficult to accept. As long as you're still trying, there's always hope but the day the doctors tell you you can't have a baby, that's the end of it. With this attitude operating both unconsciously and consciously it's often easier to put off going to the doctor and so avoid a medical verdict for as long as possible. This same psychological mechanism is sometimes seen in those who fear they have cancer.

In more than two-thirds of couples it is the woman who starts the medical ball rolling. In only about a quarter of couples do the man and woman go together. Clearly, consulting the general practitioner is seen as woman's work. This comes about for several reasons. First, the woman is usually the more concerned of the two about having children. Even with the modern trends in society women still assume the major role in caring for children and so are in for a far bigger change in life-style than their partners. Second, women are much more used to going to the medical profession about reproductive matters and therefore feel easier about it than do their husbands. But most important of all, most people assume that the woman is 'at fault' and that it is she who'll need the treatment. Most couples with whom I have discussed the matter feel that the female reproductive systems is much more complex than the man's so that there's simply much more to go wrong. Or they believe that women have obvious signs and symptoms in gynaecological disorders, whereas the male reproductive system rarely seems to go wrong. The majority of couples don't realize that the onus of responsibility for their infertility is just as likely to be laid at the man's feet as at the woman's. If they did, they'd be more likely to go as a couple to sort the problem out.

Many couples feel it's a waste of time going to their family doctors because they've read or heard that they can do so little to help. This can put them off getting medical help and means that most couples use their general practitioner simply as a means of getting access to a specialist at an infertility clinic. The family doctor can indeed offer relatively little aid to the infertile couple. He can advise on the timing of intercourse; start the woman off on a temperature chart; advise on sexual positions and give other low-key advice. For some couples this is all that is needed and research has shown that 40 per cent of women become pregnant after the first consultation – even before any treatment or investigations have begun.

According to one survey, half of all those attending their general practitioners for help with infertility were offered no advice at all. This clearly indicates that family doctors don't see themselves as being able to offer much to the average infertile couple – a fact which was borne out by the finding that most general practitioners refer couples to a specialist fairly quickly. Eighty-five per cent in this survey were referred to a specialist clinic within twelve months of first seeing their family doctor and almost 75 per cent had gone to such a clinic within six months. Most people are passed on to a specialist centre either on the first or the second visit to their family doctor. Although a large proportion of couples put off getting advice for months or even years, there is no doubt that getting help sooner rather than later really pays off. A large survey in Israel found that the average time before the start of treatment in 258 women who eventually became pregnant was 2·8 years compared with 4·3 years in the 254 women who did not become pregnant. They concluded that any couple who fear they might be infertile should certainly seek help within three years of realizing their problem. To this I would add that if you are over thirty you should go for help after a year of trying to get pregnant.

Just as it is women who go first to the family doctor with an infertility problem, so also they form 75 per cent of those referred first to a specialist clinic. In only 10 per cent of cases are men the first to go and only one in nine couples go together to the clinic on the first visit. This probably doesn't matter too much in the long term because so long as the couple is eventually investigated by a specialist, it doesn't matter whether it is the woman or the man who initiates the contact at the clinic. The doctors know that eventually both partners will probably have to be investigated and that if the man refuses to attend there's little they can do.

Unfortunately, many men don't realize that they might be subjecting their wives to unnecessary tests and hospital visits simply because they will not go for a sperm test. And here's the irony – it's men who are loath to be investigated for infertility yet it is they who could with the greatest ease provide the information that could render many of the tests on their partners unnecessary. Apart from those who have religious scruples about masturbation (to produce a specimen of semen for analysis) – and there are even ways around that, as we shall see – there can be no reason for any loving husband (who presumably wants a baby, or his partner wouldn't have taken the step of becoming involved in the medical merry-go-round) to put off the simple matter of a semen analysis.

Going to a specialist clinic is undoubtedly a serious step to take, the day you start on the investigation process is a red letter day and many couples tell me that this is what they fear most about getting help. They fear the nature of the investigations – often unnecessarily as it transpires – and also fear, quite rightly in my opinion, that once you're on the merry-go-round it's very difficult to get off. As investigation and treatment can go on for months or even years, this fear is not without a basis in fact. One survey in the UK found that over 50 per cent of infertile couples take a year to get a diagnosis from the day they first see a specialist, and that at two years only 75 per cent are diagnosed. Having said this, though, research has shown that most couples undergo their tests willingly and once into the medical system, are determined to see things through until a pregnancy results or the doctors announce a dead end. Women have many more tests than men, as we will see, – in fact only about 10 per cent of men have any tests other than a semen analysis.

Let's look now at what happens when you go to an infertility clinic. Obviously each is managed somewhat differently and reflects the interests and abilities of those running it but the following gives a fairly middle-of-the-road picture. There are three main areas to be considered: (1) questions you'll be asked; (2) examinations that will be performed; and (3) special tests and investigations you may have to undergo.

Questions you'll be asked

One thing is certain and that is you'll be asked lots of questions. The other certainty is that *you'll* want to ask questions too. Be sure that you make a list of all the things you want to know and when the doctor has finished with all his questions, ask him those on your list. He won't think this is silly or rude – in fact by answering your queries he can get across things he wants you to know in the way you most want to know them. After all, he can't give a half-hour standard lecture to each couple – he hasn't the time and lots of it probably wouldn't be of interest to you anyway. Make sure you leave the first consultation with answers to all your questions – there's no point in going home upset about things when simple reassurance could have sorted them out.

Many clinics see the partners separately after an initial joint interview. This is helpful and shouldn't be seen as a plot to split you up. Often, one member of the pair is reluctant to discuss sensitive things in public in front of his or her spouse, but will happily do so alone with a doctor. The doctor will be able to find out all kinds of sensitive information about frequency of intercourse; problems with intercourse; previous venereal disease (about which the spouse might be ignorant); and previous children (also perhaps unknown to the other partner). After all, if the woman has had a pregnancy (or even an abortion) before the couple were married, this can rule out a lot of unnecessary time, expense and worry and the man can be concentrated on. Similarly, the man may have got a girl pregnant before he was married, or even during an extra-marital affair and he'd understandably be loath to reveal this to the doctor in front of his wife. Doctors are bound by the strictest ethical rules not to divulge this kind of information to the other partner and, even if they weren't, they'd scarcely be doing the job they are if they were interested in doing anything to harm couples or break them up. On the contrary, the vast majority of doctors working in this field of medicine are extremely sensitive to the delicate nature of the subject they're dealing with and won't ever knowingly do anything to jeopardize your relationship with your spouse.

The formal questioning will include details of your age and your religion. Age is important. A twenty-year-old girl is far more likely to conceive than a forty-year-old woman, simply because fertility falls off over the age of thirty. Similarly, a man is likely to be more fertile when he is younger. Whilst on the subject of age, some women fear trying too hard for a baby when they are over the age of thirty because they fear the child will be born abnormal. Until after the age of thirty-five there is no significant rise in the odds of producing an abnormal child and anyway after this age most women's fertility is falling off fairly quickly – perhaps this is one of Nature's protective mechanisms.

With the increasing availability of amniocentesis to diagnose some abnormalities before birth, even women over thirty-five need have no fears about producing abnormal babies. Religion is important too because orthodox Jews, Roman Catholics and Muslims to mention but three, have strict rules on subjects such as masturbation (to produce semen specimens) and artificial insemination. Another problem can be the orthodox Jewish woman who ovulates before the seven days of prescribed abstinence after the end of her period. This can be overcome though because the doctor can delay ovulation with drugs. Knowing the religious position helps the doctor to prepare himself for any difficulties he may have in selecting the best treatment and tests for each couple, and prevents unnecessary embarrassment for the couple when at some stage they feel they have to stand by their religious convictions.

The next question tries to discover whether there has been a reasonable chance of conception occurring. The doctor will ask the extent of the period of unprotected intercourse. Some couples panic if after two or three months the woman hasn't conceived. This is unnecessary as we saw in Chapter 1 because it takes 5·3 months on average to conceive if you're having unrestricted intercourse and are using no contraceptives. Infertility of less than one year's duration probably isn't significant, especially if intercourse is infrequent. If the woman is in her later reproductive years it may be sensible to get started on investigations and treatment after trying for less than a year but otherwise it probably creates unnecessary trouble as the woman would probably have become pregnant anyway.

The next questions will try to find out if you as a couple are really keen to have children. Many doctors will spend quite a long time discussing the marriage in general. Having a baby to mend a marriage often doesn't work and may even produce exactly the opposite result. The investigation and treatment of infertility must be a team effort and the doctors need both partners to be wholeheartedly behind them. Social factors may be taken into account but don't worry that the doctor will reject you just because for example you're on the council house waiting list or because the odds are stacked against you socially. Assuming that you can give a reasonable home to the child you plan to have, you'll have no problem, and doctors at clinics don't ask all the searching questions that are asked by social workers working for adoption agencies. You'll both be asked if you have any other children. This may seem strange in an infertility clinic but many people have one child quite normally and easily and then can't have another. This is called secondary infertility.

Because it is known that stress surrounding your life-style and job, and excessive smoking, drinking or drug taking, can reduce your chances of conceiving, the doctor will ask you about these things too.

Questions especially for women

The doctor will want to know your age, what you do for a living, how long you've been married, whether you've been married before and whether you've had any previous children. He'll ask you if you've ever had any serious illnesses or any abdominal operations. There is some evidence that a previous burst appendix that has been operated on is associated with a higher incidence of infertility, for example. He'll ask how old you were when your periods started, the length and regularity of your cycle and how long you usually bleed for. If your cycles are irregular he'll ask you what the range is (shortest and longest) and how many you've had in the last year. He'll ask you if you've ever stopped having periods for no apparent reason and if you get any bleeding between periods or after intercourse. Painful periods are asked about, as is painful intercourse. Details of previous pregnancies if any, are of particular value. The doctor will especially want to know about infections or bleeding after the birth and how long it took for normal periods to return. Previous contraception is an important facet of infertility today so questions will be fairly detailed about this. You'll be asked whether you've been on the Pill and, if so, which one and for how long; whether you've ever had an IUD and, if so, which type and for how long and whether you ever had any bleeding or an infection with it.

Next will probably come some questions about your sex life. These are important because often quite simple advice can be offered which will effect a cure for the problem with no further investigation or treatment. Even women who'll happily discuss their personal lives over the garden fence have difficulty in discussing their sex lives with doctors they know well, but seem to be less reticent when they're in a strange clinic. It's important to tell the doctor as honestly as possible what he wants to know and not what you think he'd like to hear. If there are things you'd rather not say in front of your partner, get out of the question somehow and discuss the matter when you're alone with the doctor.

'How often do you have intercourse?' is the next question. This is a terribly important one and must be answered honestly. There is no norm for the number of times a week or a month that people make love, though the average is about twice or three times a week. Studies show that intercourse rates are actually falling in the population as a whole but for the highly fertile this probably has no effect on fertility. For the border-line couples though it could just be the last straw. It is not uncommon for a couple going to an infertility clinic to say that they are having intercourse as little as once a month or less and this can be very illuminating to the doctor. The chances of getting pregnant if you are having intercourse this infrequently are very small indeed. Certainly, one hears of girls getting pregnant after one sex act but this is very rare and presumes that her egg was just in the right place at the right time or that she ovulated because of extreme sexual arousal. Such a chance happening can't be relied upon if you really want a baby. Even the answer to such a seemingly simple question is difficult to interpret because people's ideas of how often they make love bear little relation to reality. Some doctors think they can learn a lot about the couple's sex life by asking the partners separately how often they make love. For example a man who, because of a sexual dysfunction of some kind can't satisfy his wife, usually overestimates the number of times they are having intercourse. A big American study of over 4,000 men found that in every group studied, men wanted intercourse at least three times a week, with five to seven times taking second place. Other studies have repeatedly shown that actual intercourse rates are about half this, so clearly men are having intercourse much less frequently than they would ideally like. A book such as this is no place to discuss the subject in great detail, but surveys of women also show that they'd like to have intercourse more than they do.

There's nothing magical about the number of times you have intercourse in a month – only *when* you do. After all, three sessions around the time of ovulation will be more likely to result in a pregnancy than regular intercourse throughout the rest of the month. The frequency of intercourse question is a very delicate one though because many couples are quite happy with lovemaking once or twice a month and either one or both partners would be unwilling or indeed unable to step up this intercourse rate without damaging their sexual and personal relationship. For many couples 'more' doesn't necessarily mean 'better'. The exception to this is those who can't get pregnant simply because they don't make love at the right time of the month.

'Do you enjoy intercourse and do you have orgasms?' might well be the next question. The value of this question is not only to try to discover any underlying reason there may be for infrequent (and therefore unlikely to hit the pregnancy jackpot) intercourse but also to see if the woman is at ease with intercourse. A lot of women even today find intercourse distasteful or even physically unpleasant and a helping hand with either of these areas can so improve a marriage that intercourse becomes more frequent, giving that much more chance of a pregnancy. Having an orgasm isn't a necessary part of getting pregnant, as we saw in Chapter 2, but it may help because of the sucking action of the uterus during orgasm. If you don't have orgasms during intercourse and your partner won't or can't caress you to bring you to a climax, you can masturbate after intercourse to increase your chances of conception. At the other end of the scale, the woman who enjoys intercourse a great deal and has orgasms easily may exhaust her husband's poorly fertile sperms by too frequently engaging him in intercourse and this too can result in infertility because the sperm quality doesn't get a chance to recover.

'Do you get out of bed after intercourse?' is a very pertinent question because many women get up and wash after sex. This is remarkably commonplace and in the sub-fertile or in those whose partners ejaculate only a small volume of semen, this ritual washing may kill any remote chance there might have been of becoming pregnant. There is nothing dirty about semen and no reason at all to wash immediately after intercourse. Ideally, you shouldn't get out of bed for at least half an hour after sex so as to give the sperms a chance to start swimming up into the womb.

'What position do you use?' can be a useful question because many couples don't adopt a position in which the husband's semen can be placed high up in the vagina. If you're having trouble in conceiving you have to give yourself the best chance possible and this means ensuring that the mouth of the womb is bathed in semen each time you have sex. A woman lying down with her legs nearly closed allows such a poor penetration of the penis that most of the semen leaks out before the sperms can do their job. Most sperms will have become exhausted and be dead by the time they have swum the length of the vagina to reach the cervix and even then they're only half-way on their journey to the egg.

Last on the list of sex questions will be some about what douches or lubricants you use. Some women, fanatical about vaginal cleanliness, douche their vagina before intercourse, so altering the natural environment that sperms don't stand a chance. Most lubricating jellies are spermicidal. If you need to use anything, use saliva as this is warm, natural and doesn't kill sperms.

Finally, the doctor will ask about your emotional life. Many women become very agitated when they don't get pregnant readily and this, combined with stress at work or at home, can reduce their chances of conception further. The emotional factors in infertility are so important that a whole chapter is allocated to them (see page 141).

Questions especially for men

After asking the man's age the doctor will seek details of his current marriage and any previous marriages. As with the woman, he'll ask about childhood illnesses. In men he'll ask especially about undescended testes in childhood; swelling of the testes with mumps; at what age he matured sexually; details of venereal infections, if any; his present general health; his sexual performance (including premature ejaculation or poor erection) and level of desire for sex; and he'll also try to find out if he has any psychological or emotional problems.

Once these basic medical questions have been answered, the matter of the husband's job will be raised. Because sperms are so sensitive to tiny changes in environment, it's important to know, for example, whether the man has been exposed to excessive heat. We saw in Chapter 1 that the scrotum is arranged in such a way as to keep the testes at about 2-3°C lower than the rest of the body but some men do jobs in which their testes become overheated. Sedentary workers (clerks, lorry drivers, taxi and bus drivers and airline pilots, for example) all sit for long periods with heat building up around the crutch. This is made worse if the man wears tightfitting underpants, and this is why the doctor will ask the apparently unlikely question about underwear.

Exposure to lead, iron, zinc or copper and to radiation or toxic fumes can all affect fertility in men and these will be asked about in the man's history-taking session. Men who are obese or who take very little exercise can also be infertile (as we saw on page 55). Excessive smoking and alcohol consumption both reduce total sperm counts or motility so the doctor will also ask about these too.

Some drugs are known to reduce fertility. Many psychoactive drugs (phenothiazines, mono-amine oxidase inhibitors and other tranquillizers and antidepressants) can influence sperm formation. Various hormonal agents influence the hypothalamus and nitrofurantoin (a drug used to treat urinary infections) can produce low sperm counts in some cases. Thiazide diuretics (water tablets), spironolactone (Aldactone), methyldopa (Aldomet), propranolol (Inderal), hydrallazine (Apresoline), clofibrate (Atromid-S), lithium, addictive drugs, and various tranquillizers can cause a diminished sex drive and even render some men impotent.

Lastly, the man is asked about any emotional stress that might be affecting his sex life and thus reducing his desire to have sex as frequently as the couple would like. It is not at all uncommon today for men in the infertility age group (twenties and thirties) to be so stretched at work that they arrive home too tired for intercourse. This can mean that for the few days in the month when the woman is fertile, her partner may be off sex and so another month goes by with no chance of getting pregnant.

With work stresses, redundancy fears and unemployment so commonplace some men function very poorly sexually as a reflection of these life problems. Impotence or an unwillingness to have sex at all for long periods will naturally contribute to the infertility problem.

To round off the interview, the doctor will probably discuss subjects such as the wife's work and the influence that this is having, if any. Clearly, conflicting working hours makes intercourse difficult or less likely and two tired people doubles the chance that either will be 'not in the mood'. Very frequently one or other partner asks whether the wife should give up her job so that she can 'relax' and get pregnant. This may or may not be desirable. If staying at home means having little to do but fret over neighbours' and friends' babies and her own inability to conceive, then the woman is probably better off working – though, if possible, this should not be in too stressful a situation. Should the couple and the doctor agree that the combined stress at home and work is too great, then it may be advisable to stop work and allow ovulation a better chance to occur, if indeed that is thought to be the problem.

Once all the questions have been asked and answered, it's time for the physical examination of each of you.

The physical examination

THE MAN

A general physical examination is usually carried out, including urine analysis and the measurement of the blood-pressure but special care is taken to examine the reproductive organs. The testes will be felt to see if they are of normal size. Some doctors use a kind of wooden rosary to place around each testis to measure its size. In certain conditions, the testes are small and their size is often associated with infertility (see page 83). If the man has not been circumcised, the doctor will pull back the foreskin to see if the opening is in its normal place at the end of the penis. This also gives him a chance to see if the foreskin could be giving any trouble with intercourse. If the foreskin is not retractile, sperms can collect inside it and be withdrawn along with the penis, so making pregnancy very unlikely.

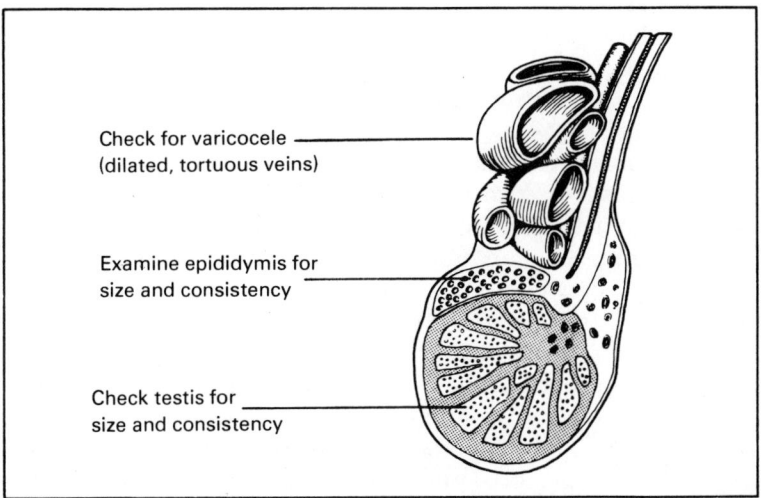

Diagram to show what a doctor looks for when examining a man's external genitals. In this case a varicocle is present.

Many doctors ask the man to stand in a good light and to bear down or cough so that they can see or feel if a varicocele (see page 82) is present. Obvious varicoceles will clearly need treatment but even small, clinically undetectable ones can cause infertility, so in some centres they use thermography (used to detect early cancer of the breast) to screen for the small temperature rise caused by a varicocele. Some clinics do rectal examinations to assess the size of the prostate gland but this is not always done in young men.

Most often, the physical examination of the male reveals nothing at all.

THE WOMAN

The physical examination of the woman is more lengthy than that of the man for two reasons. First, there's more for a doctor to assess and second, it's the woman who's going to be the one to bear the baby and this has to be borne in mind from day one.

The woman's blood-pressure will be taken and her urine analysed. She'll be weighed and examined generally. Most doctors take the opportunity to feel her breasts for lumps – not that this has anything to do with infertility but simply because breast cancer is so common and is best caught early. The doctor may also try to see if any milk can be expressed from the nipples because if milk is present it leads him straight to one particular cause of infertility (see page 61). But the majority of the examination involves the female reproductive system.

Once you've committed yourself to investigation for infertility, you're going to have to get used to internal examinations. Many women attending infertility clinics have never had a vaginal examination before and many tell me that it is the thing they worry about most before their first visit to the hospital.

There's nothing particularly pleasant about having a vaginal examination but there's nothing to be feared either. An unpleasant part for many women is the coldness of the lubricating jelly the doctor uses. Most women think of their vagina as very personal and private and find it difficult to relax while a doctor feels inside and inserts instruments. Hard though it may be to believe, it's something that you soon get used to as your investigations and treatment get under way and many infertile women have told me that after a while they get so used to internal examinations that they think no more of them than having a blood sample taken. If you find it difficult to relax, look the doctor in the face, press your bottom into the bed, open your legs as wide as possible and breathe deeply all the time.

Any gynaecological examination begins with the doctor first

inspecting and feeling your tummy. Once this is complete he'll ask you to lie on your back or side (usually the left) while he examines your vulva (external vaginal area). He'll look at the outside first, separating the lips (labia) with his fingers. At this stage, he'll be able to see any abnormal hair distribution, clitoral enlargement, varicose veins of the vulva, swellings, sores, discharges or inflammation before going on to feel for any abnormalities. Quite a few women (about 5 per cent) attending infertility clinics haven't consummated their marriage and still have an intact hymen. If the woman is still a virgin, the doctor will discuss this with her.

Although a manual examination of the vagina reveals a lot of information quickly and painlessly, the doctor will often first want to see inside of the vagina and the cervix so that a smear test can be done to rule out cervical cancer and also to assess the hormonal state of the cervix and vagina. At the same time he may take a smear to be sent for testing for gonorrhoea. This look inside is easily done by the doctor inserting a special instrument into the vagina. A speculum, as it is called, is sterilized and warmed, sometimes lubricated, and then gently inserted in its closed position into the vagina. Once inside, it is opened so that the blades push the deepest parts of the vaginal walls aside and allow a view of these and the cervix at the end of the vagina. In this position the doctor can take a smear of the cervix to test for cancer or infection and he can also look for other abnormalities. If you have had intercourse in the last twelve to eighteen hours the doctor may, if he sees a plug of mucus in the cervix, remove it for examination under the microscope to see if there are any sperms in it. This can save time later. For more details of the post-coital test, see page 129.

These preliminaries having been completed, the doctor removes the speculum and puts on a rubber or plastic glove. Next he inserts his forefinger into the vaginal opening a little way and feels the labia between finger and thumb to detect any swelling of the Bartholin's glands that lie each side of the vagina in the fat of the labia. The finger is then passed higher up in the vagina. Some doctors find they a get a more accurate impression of what is going on if they use two fingers but if this is uncomfortable for the woman he can still feel most abnormalities using one only. Once his fingers are inside the vagina, he places his hand on the woman's lower tummy just above the pubic hair and by pushing down into the

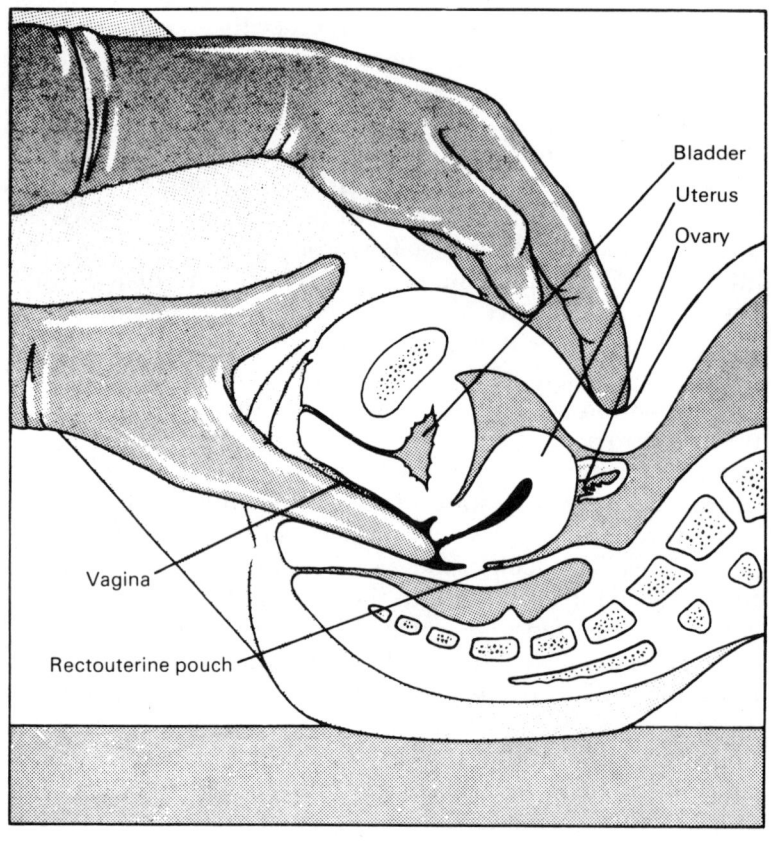

Diagram to show a bimanual pelvic examination – the common 'internal' or vaginal examination.

abdomen with one hand and up from within the vagina with the two fingers of his other hand he can feel the uterus (womb) between his two hands. This enables him to judge its size, position and consistency and to feel for swellings or lumps.

Once he has felt the uterus he moves his finger to each side to feel for the tubes and ovaries. Any cysts or other swellings can often be felt quite readily like this. By doing this he can easily feel any gross abnormalities of the internal organs that might be causing infertility and this can lead him to select the right tests to go on to next.

All this sounds complicated but a good doctor who is skilled in vaginal examinations can tell a lot about a woman's reproductive organs within a minute or so. If you get any

SORTING OUT THE CAUSES

actual pain when the doctor is examining you, tell him because it might be caused by a condition called endometriosis which frequently causes infertility and which can be treated.

Tests and investigations

Once the history and clinical examinations have been completed, the doctor will decide which tests should be carried out and when. The ideal plan is to investigate both of the partners in parallel because in that way you save time and investigations on the part of one partner. If the husband refuses to go to the clinic though, he can still send some semen along for analysis and the wife can have a post-coital test done – so all is not lost.

If you've ever talked to infertile couples about the tests they've had you could be forgiven for thinking that they are extremely numerous, complicated and unpleasant but this is really not so. Not all the tests have to be carried out in any one couple and certain results preclude certain other tests. The burden of the tests falls on the woman because so much can be learned from a simple analysis of a man's semen that other tests are rarely necessary for him.

The tests can be simply divided into three stages. The first-stage tests confirm that ovulation is in fact occurring; confirm that sperms and cervical mucus can live with each other; and look in some detail at the man's sperms. The second stage includes all the tests that tell if the woman's fallopian tubes are open or blocked. Stage three involves more detailed tests which are used to assess the endocrine (hormone) system in the limited number of cases that aren't sorted out by stages one and two.

CONFIRMATION OF OVULATION
There are five methods that doctors commonly use to try to decide whether a woman is ovulating. There is only one way to be *sure* that a woman is ovulating and that is to see it happening (which can now be done using a laproscope), but these tests provide good presumptive evidence in the absence of actually being able to see the event.

1. Basal body temperature recordings
2. Cervical mucus changes

3. Endometrial biopsy
4. Blood progesterone estimation
5. Urinary pregnanediol estimation

1. *Basal body temperature recording* Just about the simplest test in the infertility work-up is the daily recording of your body temperature. You simply take your temperature by mouth every day on waking. A normal woman who is ovulating will notice that around the middle of her cycle her temperature will rise by about 0·5–1°C and will stay raised for the rest of her cycle until her period starts. This type of chart was first described in 1904 and although lots of research has been done into the subject we still don't know why this temperature rise occurs. It is generally accepted that it comes about as a result of the increased circulating levels of progesterone in the blood. If a pregnancy occurs, the basal body temperature does not fall back to its lower level because as the progesterone levels remain elevated, so does the temperature. This can be a useful sign that you are pregnant.

A question that is commonly asked is why the temperature has to be taken in the morning. The main reasons are that it always has been and that it reflects the 'basal' or resting temperature of the body. As any woman who has done the daily temperature regime will know, it is of most use in telling her and her husband when it is best to have sex so that she is most likely to conceive.

Because of the way that most people's domestic lives are organized it is impractical to make love in the mornings, especially if it has to be on certain prescribed days and this led a South African researcher to ask whether the temperature could be taken in the evening – thus allowing the couple to make love and not have to get up immediately afterwards. He asked all infertile patients to record their morning and evening temperatures on the same graph. He found that although the evening temperatures were always slightly higher, they mirrored the morning temperatures exactly and the evening was much favoured by his patients. Obviously a woman has to be careful not to take her temperature after food or drink, alcohol or after a bath, but most people find that it is not difficult to take it at about 6.00 p.m.

There are two main reasons for recording the basal body temperature. First, it shows if the woman is ovulating and second, it helps chart the phases of the reproductive cycle.

SORTING OUT THE CAUSES

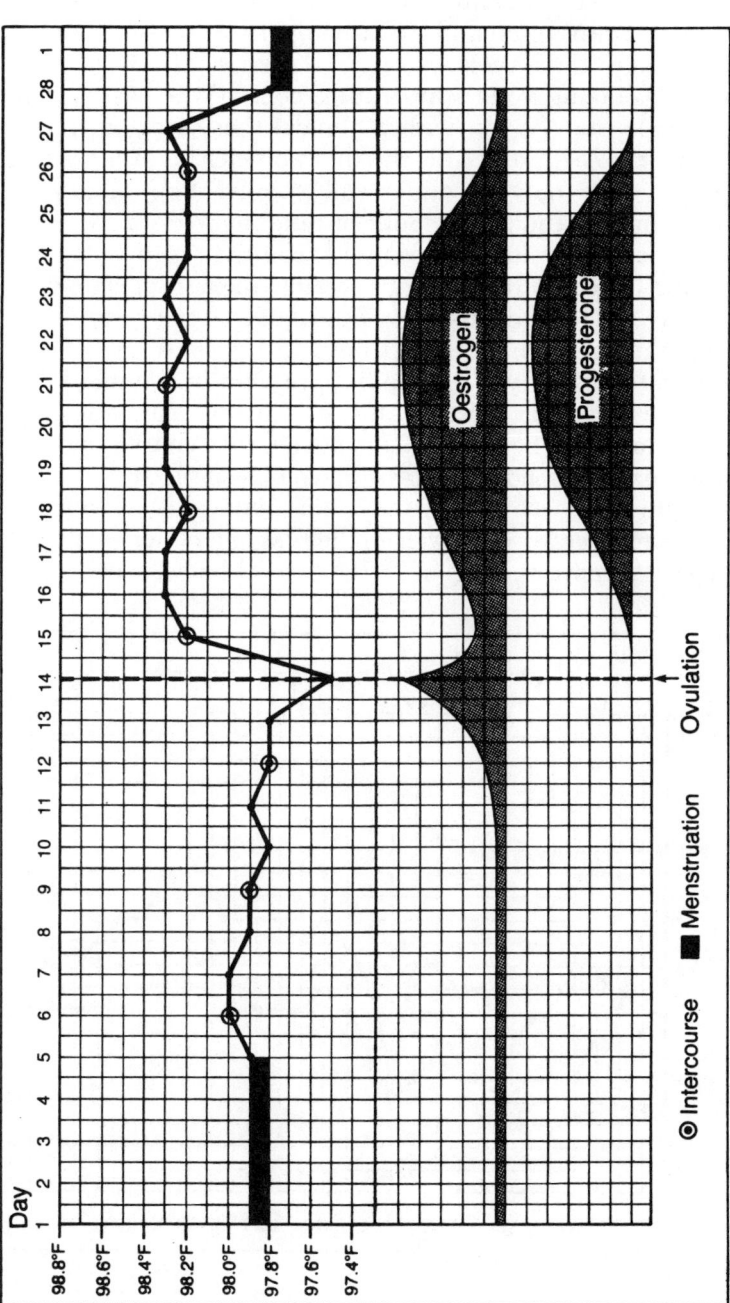

Diagram to show how the hormones oestrogen and progesterone alter during a menstrual cycle. The temperature changes are also shown.

This can be very helpful indeed later on, as we shall see, because certain tests and treatments have to be done at specific stages of the cycle.

Actually taking your temperature couldn't be easier. The clinic might supply you with a clinical thermometer or you can buy one. All you need is the thermometer and the special graph or grid that the clinic will supply. You take your temperature for the full amount of time marked on the thermometer or in the instructions and read the result to 0·1°C, recording the result on the graph against the appropriate day. If you are ill, have drunk lots of alcohol or have been doing anything unusual, mark these things on the chart against the appropriate day. If you normally have pain in the middle of your cycle, note that down against its day too. Note also with a cross or a circle the days when you have intercourse, and use another mark to denote the days on which you bleed.

As you will see from the chart opposite, a normal woman's temperature is lower in the first half of her cycle and it fluctuates more then than in the second half. At ovulation

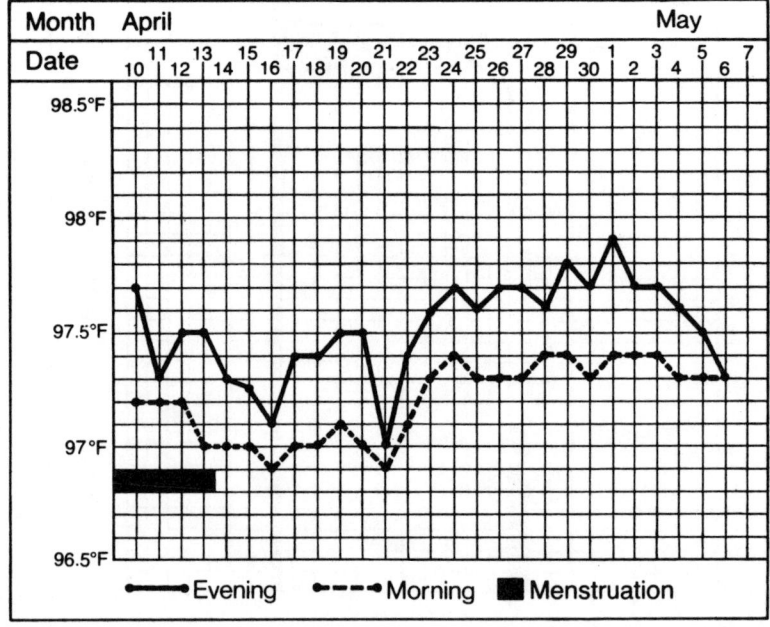

A plot of morning and evening temperatures to show how parallel they are. (From the work of Dr G. W. Rosemann.)

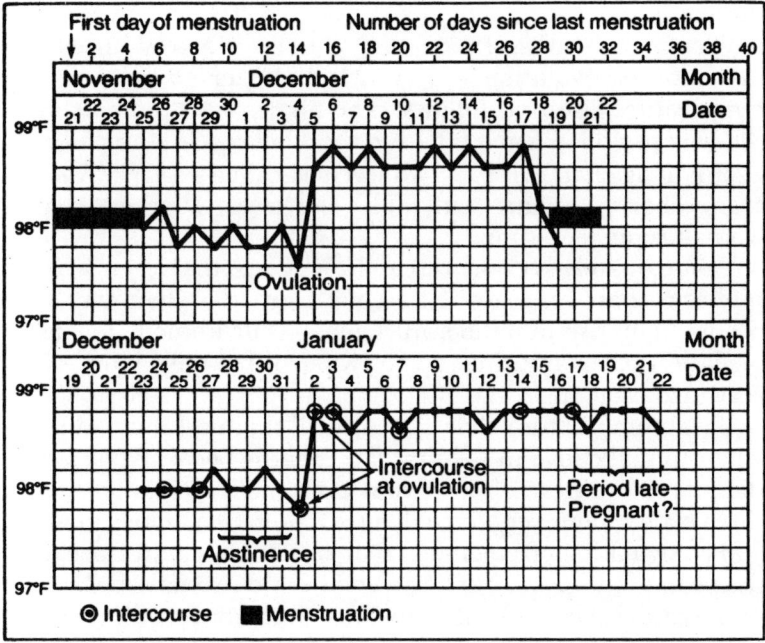

Two typical temperature charts as used in the investigation of infertility. The upper one shows the typical bi-phasic pattern of normal ovulation and the lower shows a bi-phasic pattern marked with intercourse and a persistently raised temperature when it should have fallen – a sign of pregnancy.

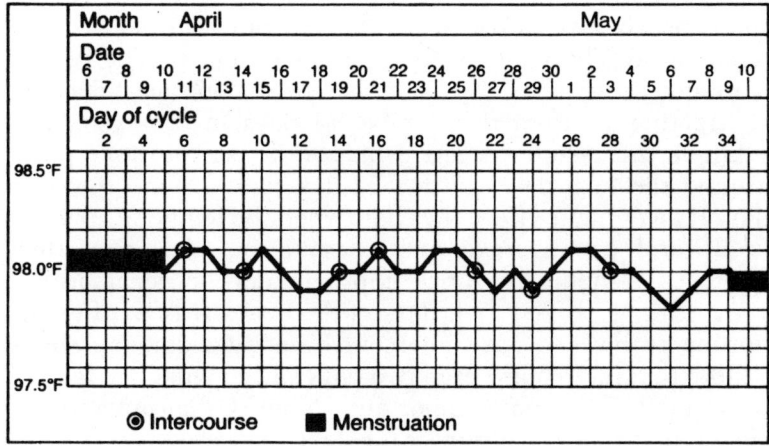

A monophasic temperature chart – probably a sign that ovulation is not occurring.

there is a dip of several tenths of a degree, followed by a rise of four or more tenths of a degree. The dip is a very unreliable indicator of ovulation – it is much better to rely on the temperature rise that follows. The higher level remains until the next period, when it falls and the whole cycle starts all over again. This chart with its two levels is called *biphasic*. A *monophasic* chart (a chart with only one level) suggests that a woman is not ovulating.

Unfortunately, recent research suggests that even a good biphasic chart may not tell a couple exactly when ovulation occurs. The rise in temperature may occur immediately after ovulation or at any time up to two or three days later – it is very inconsistent.

Basal temperature charts are not all that useful in planning when to make love in the first few months because you won't then have a pattern of what your cycle looks like. After two or three cycles, however, you will have a pretty good idea of when you're ovulating. Remember that ovulation doesn't occur at the peak of the graph but between one and two days before the temperature peak. So it's obvious that until you've settled down to charting your temperature for several cycles you can only guess when ovulation occurred because the temperature rise which you're looking for comes two days later. Even if you make love on the day of the temperature rise you may not get pregnant because the egg has a life of only two days at most and it may already be past being fertilizable. If a woman has biphasic charts on three successive months it is safe to say that she is nearly always ovulating and she can stop plotting her temperature chart unless she is on clomiphene. The couple work out the average date on which ovulation takes place by subtracting 14 from the number of days in the cycle. For example, in a 26-day cycle ovulation is likely to take place around the 12th day and in a 32-day cycle around the 18th day. If a couple see from the chart when the temperature rises occur and can average out to, say, the 15th day, then intercourse should be timed approximately to occur on the 11th, 13th, 15th and 17th days of the cycle. It is terribly off-putting to have to have intercourse on the right day and I believe that intercourse even two days earlier will often lead to pregnancy. The most important thing is that intercourse should take place on alternate nights in mid-cycle.

The way to get pregnant using a chart then is to have sex on alternate days in mid-cycle. Missing out a night gives the man's sperms time to come back up to full strength again. Obviously you won't be making love only on these alternate nights of the month: the rest of the time you'll behave exactly as you usually would.

This all sounds very cosy so far but it often turns out to be far from cosy in practice, especially if you've been trying for a baby for a long time. It's very easy for the lives of infertile couples to be dominated by their charts. Several couples I know revolve their entire social lives around the chart so that they are never out or entertaining around the crucial period. This can easily become extremely wearing and the man begins to feel like a stallion at stud. The 'best' night of the month often falls on a day when the man is late home from work, is tired, or simply doesn't feel like sex. This makes the woman begrudge the month's effort at temperature-taking and puts her another month away from her baby. The husband may feel as if he's just being used and friction can arise in the marriage.

If all this seems a bit much you can learn to tell when you're ovulating by another method – the cervical mucus method.

2. *Cervical mucus method* This method is primarily used around the world as a contraceptive technique. Millions of women use it to determine easily when they are fertile and so when to avoid intercourse. You can use it to tell when you're most fertile so that you stand the best chance of conceiving and it will also help tell the doctors if you're ovulating. This isn't the same as the 'safe-period' which is a calendar calculation based on probabilities and so can be inaccurate.

Under the influence of FSH (follicle stimulating hormone) an egg begins to mature in the ovary. At the same time the cells lining the cervix secrete mucus as blood oestrogen levels rise. Cervical mucus is produced at a rate of 20-60 milligrams per day throughout the cycle except at ovulation when the production rate is ten times greater.

Mucus is mostly water and only about 1 per cent is inorganic salt. Other substances in cervical mucus include sugar, protein and certain enzymes. The most important constituent of mucus though from our point of view here is a sticky substance that turns to jelly in the presence of water. Mucus serves many purposes. The vagina is usually kept acid and hostile to sperms and the mucus changes this acid environment to a more favourable alkaline one; it provides

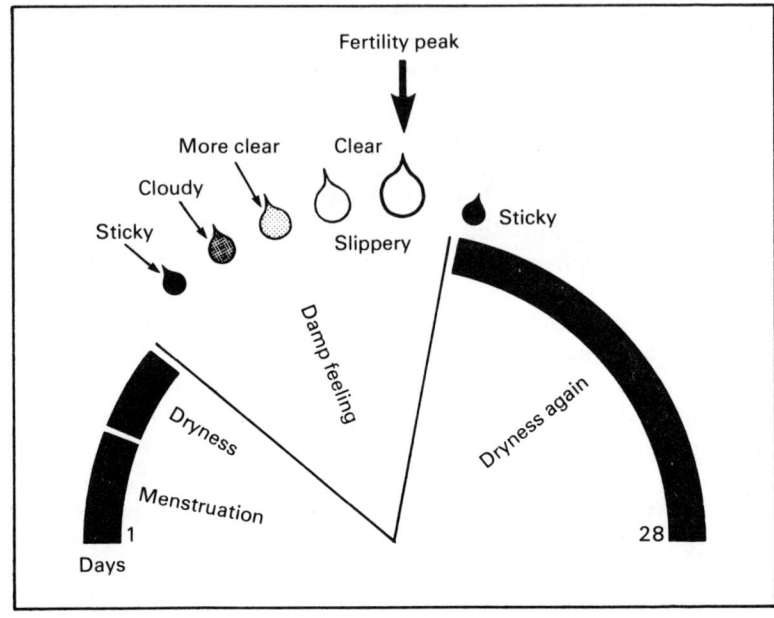

A schematic diagram of how cervical mucus changes in nature throughout a woman's menstrual cycle.

sperms with nutrient substances that keep them alive; and it attracts sperms and changes them in ways which enable them to get to and penetrate the ovum.

The quantity and quality of mucus changes throughout the month on a predictable timetable in any one woman. Unfortunately, as many young women have been on the Pill all their reproductive lives, they are totally unaware of their normal mucus patterns each month. This doesn't matter though because the patterns can quickly and easily be learned. Each time mucus production begins in a cycle it is usually thick, opaque, white or yellow, scant and sticky. You'll notice a slight stickiness in your vagina and vulva at this time and this first-stage mucus doesn't usually make your vulva feel 'wet' – as does fertile mucus.

As ovulation approaches the mucus becomes cloudy and then clear, more fluid, transparent and elastic. Just before ovulation the mucus is thin, slippery and stretchy. It has the consistency of the raw white of an egg and is discharged in 'threads'. There is a definite vaginal sensation of slipperiness and wetness at this stage. On occasions you may notice that your mucus is tinged with blood, giving it a pink or brown colour. The last of the slippery mucus days is the peak day but you can't know it's the last until the day after. Once this slippery mucus has gone there may be no mucus at all or it may become sticky and cloudy again. The uterus is now virtually closed to sperms as hormones change the cervical cells in the second half of the cycle.

Sticky mucus has a blocking effect on sperms whilst slippery mucus lets them through. Fluid, clear, stretchy and slippery mucus is the most fertile. The best thing to do then is to make love on alternate days when your mucus has *any* of these characteristics. If it could be described by any of the adjectives fluid, clear, stretchy or slippery, have intercourse if you want to because you're most likely to be ovulating then even if you don't experience *all* the characteristics of fertile mucus.

This may sound very complex and difficult to get the hang of but isn't in fact. Many millions of very ordinary women who know nothing of medicine or physiology have mastered this technique of ovulation timing very quickly and with the minimum of fuss. It takes a bit of practice to get used to the feelings of wetness or slipperiness though and here's what you can do to recognize the discharge.

Contract the muscles around your vagina. As you relax them you'll notice a difference in the feeling of the outer vaginal area around the small inner lips. If there is no mucus, the feeling is one of dryness. When there is stickiness, the inner lips stick together and separate in a sticky way and when there is slippery mucus, the lips slip past each other easily. If you've never really used your vaginal muscles before you might have difficulty in contracting them as I've described. Here's a method of getting used to the feeling of contracting them. Wait until you want to pass water but not until you're desperate, then go to the lavatory and allow a small amount of urine out. Immediately try to stop passing water and continue doing this, stopping and starting until you have perfect control. This exercise can then be repeated to produce a tightening inside the vagina at almost any time. You can practice contracting and relaxing the muscles sitting down at home, in a bus or waiting in a queue at the supermarket. After a while you'll become very expert at doing it and will be able to contract and relax your pelvic mucus at will. This will not only help you in the interpretation of the nature of your cervical muscles but may also improve your sex life because men get enormous pleasure from a woman who can contract these muscles at will. If after a period of practice you want to see the effect it'll have on your partner's penis, put one or two fingers inside your vagina and contract your muscles. You'll feel the tightening on your fingers as you alternately contract and relax your muscles. Obviously a nice thing to do is to involve your partner in this training. He'll like both the training and the results and can use either his fingers or his penis, whichever you like more.

After a while you'll be so expert that you'll be able to tell after a couple of contractions exactly what stage you're at in the month. As soon as your vulva starts to feel slippery, you're fertile. For the first few months you may find it helpful to mark your mucus conditions on a temperature chart or in your diary. Write down 'dry', 'damp', 'slippery' etc. against each day until you find it comes as second nature to you. If at first you find the vaginal contraction method a bit difficult to get used to, put one finger into your vagina an inch or two and feel what it's like. Sometimes mucus when fertile is so thin and watery that you'll think your pants are slightly damp – in fact it can produce a stiffness when it dries, especially in rayon underwear.

As well as altering cervical mucus, hormone levels affect many other areas of the body. This means that in any one woman there may be signs of fertility (ovulation) that are reliable for her and may help the doctor to decide if she's ovulating. Some of these signs are: (1) pimples on the face or back; (2) varicose veins that 'play up'; (3) swelling of the vulva; (4) a distinct vaginal odour; (5) a dull feeling in the legs; (6) a sense of pressure in the vulva ; (7) more dreams than usual; (8) an increased sex drive; (9) an increased appetite; (10) sleeplessness; (11) impaired memory; and (12) fullness or tension in the breasts.

Clearly, not every woman will get all of these symptoms but if after a few cycles of observation you know what to look for you'll soon know your fertile days without resorting to temperature charts and can thus make the whole process of 'trying' for a baby a lot less contrived. The cervical mucus method has the added bonus that after you've conceived, you will have perfected a natural, reliable form of contraception, which you'll be able to use. In this case, as soon as you feel at all slippery use a contraceptive.

SORTING OUT THE CAUSES 123

3. *Endometrial biopsy* In this test a sample of the lining of the womb (the endometrium) is taken and examined under a microscope. It can be done at any time from when you think you've ovulated until the day your period starts. The type of tissue seen in the pathology laboratory tells the doctor whether ovulation has in fact occurred.

An endometrial biopsy essentially involves the same techniques as does a D and C (dilatation and curettage) and can be performed without a general anaesthetic and as an outpatient. Some doctors use local anaesthetic around the cervix to numb it and most give some painkilling tablets beforehand. With the patient lying flat on her back and with her legs up in stirrups the doctor gently stretches the cervix with increasingly large metal dilators until it is wide enough to take a tiny scraper (curette). He then scrapes this instrument gently around the inside of the womb and removes some tissue. An alternative method involves using a thin (about the thickness of a piece of spaghetti) plastic catheter (Vabra catheter) to suck out the

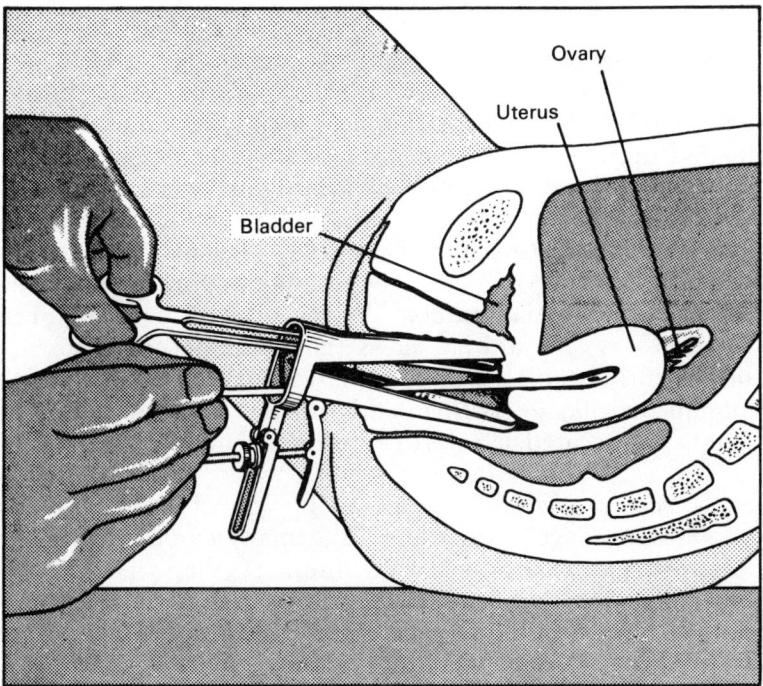

How an endometrial biopsy is performed.

uterine lining for examination. This is a much narrower tube than the curette's blade and so is not nearly so uncomfortable. Most women, especially if they have not had children, find the stretching of the cervix very unpleasant, which is why some kind of painkiller, tranquillizer or local anaesthetic is advisable. Many women have told me that if gynaecologists had experienced the procedure themselves, they would probably find another way around it. Some gynaecologists have now done so and rely much more on blood progesterone levels or they use the Vabra catheter. However, the endometrial biopsy still has a place in showing the doctor the quality of ovulation and how ready the endometrium is for implantation. In some clinics the procedure is always carried out under a general anaesthetic. Ironically, this investigation sometimes results in a pregnancy though no one really knows why. For this reason some experts advise that no other investigations are performed for three months following a dilatation and curettage in order to give the woman a chance to conceive before proceeding further.

4. *Blood progesterone levels* About eight or ten days after ovulation, the serum progesterone level is at its peak. In the fourteen days before ovulation, this level is very low but rises tenfold until its peak at six days before the onset of the next period. If you have already been investigated at another clinic, you may have to have more blood taken for another progesterone estimation because different laboratories produce different values and the results can only be compared within any one laboratory. A single blood sample taken between days 21 and 23 shows that progesterone levels are significantly decreased in infertile women who have a corpus luteum deficiency. As this deficiency is a cause of infertility that can be treated, it's worth knowing about.

5. *Urinary pregnanediol estimation* If your clinic cannot do progesterone level estimations (and many can't because the laboratory method is very complex) then its urinary breakdown product, pregnanediol, can be measured. Two consecutive samples are usually tested to ensure maximum accuracy.

So after some very straightforward (from your point of view) tests and only one that is at all unpleasant (the endometrial

SORTING OUT THE CAUSES

biopsy) you should know with some certainty whether you're ovulating or not. If you are, then it becomes important to know whether your partner's sperms are at fault. The next stage of the tests involves looking at sperms and their behaviour in your cervical mucus.

SPERM AND CERVICAL MUCUS TESTS

Semen analysis (sperm count) This test is one of the easiest to be carried out in the investigation of the infertile couple, partly because it is so simple for the man and partly because a negative result can so easily save the woman having unnecessary, time-consuming and expensive tests carried out.

Although the collection of a sample of sperms is simple, it has to be done with care so that the results aren't spoiled. The man is asked to produce a sample of sperms by masturbation. If you have religious qualms about this you may well be able to get a dispensation from your Church (the Catholic Church will certainly do this) or you can use coitus interruptus and withdraw just before you ejaculate and catch it in a jar. Most people find this unpleasant and would rather masturbate to produce the specimen. Some couples don't like the idea of the man going off to the lavatory with his jar and so do it together. There's no reason why you shouldn't have some pleasure out of the procedure!

When collecting the semen in a clean, wide-necked jar (the clinic will give you one), ensure that there is no water or detergent residue in it and be sure to collect all the semen you ejaculate. If you lose the first spurt or two you'll have lost the part that is richest in sperms, which will affect the overall result. Once it's in the jar, don't refrigerate it or leave it in the air on the window sill. Keep it at body temperature (tuck it inside your clothing next to your body) and get it as quickly as possible to the clinic. It should ideally be there within three hours.

Don't use a standard condom (sheath) to collect the semen because most have a spermicide built in, which will negate the results. Your doctor at the clinic will advise a special, non-spermicidal sheath if this is the only way that you can manage to produce a specimen of semen. If all of these methods are unacceptable to you, there is an alternative – the post-coital test (see below).

Some men wonder if they should save up their sperms to improve the quality so that the test shows them in the best light. There is some truth in this and it's probably sensible to abstain from sex or masturbation for about two to four days before collecting the specimen. No good clinic will make a definite statement about fertility after examining only one specimen and three or even four analyses carried out at intervals may be necessary to provide an accurate result.

Here are the things that the laboratory will be looking for when they examine the semen.

Volume The normal range is 2 to 6 millilitres (about a teaspoonful) and depends to some extent on when you last ejaculated. Some researchers think that too large a volume is associated with infertility problems but this is still being debated. Certainly too low a volume can be troublesome because if a man is ejaculating only 1 millilitre, there may simply be too little semen to reach the cervix as most of it will leak out of the vagina.

Sperm count The range of sperm concentration in normal men is enormous and varies from count to count in any one man by as much as 20 per cent. Anything from 20-300 million sperms per millilitre is thought to be normal. Sperm concentrations vary greatly even within one individual and this is why several repeat estimations have to be done. If the test is normal on one day, you may simply have caught a 'good' day even if on average your sperm count is usually low. Unless you happen to hit your partner's fertile period while you have a 'high' count therefore, the chances are you won't get her pregnant. It should also be remembered that any illness with a fever can damage sperm production. This depression usually shows up at about two to three weeks after the fever and can last for up to three months. Certain drugs also produce this effect (see pages 95, 107).

There is considerable debate among specialists as to what the lowest normal count is. By general consensus it is now accepted that the term 'oligospermic' (too few sperms) should be applied only to men who have fewer than 20 million sperms per millilitre. However, pregnancies occur quite frequently in women whose husbands have counts lower than this: after all you only need one sperm to do the job. Many experts feel that so long as there are any live sperms at all, there must still be a chance of conception but that under about 20 million, the chance must be small so that other ways (such as artificial insemination) are worth considering. It's also interesting to note that over the 20 million mark, the chances of a pregnancy do not increase, the higher the sperm count. One survey found that of 1,000 fertile and 1,000 infertile couples studied, 84 per cent of the infertile marriage husbands had sperm counts over 20 million and that many men with sperm counts of only 5 million were fertile.

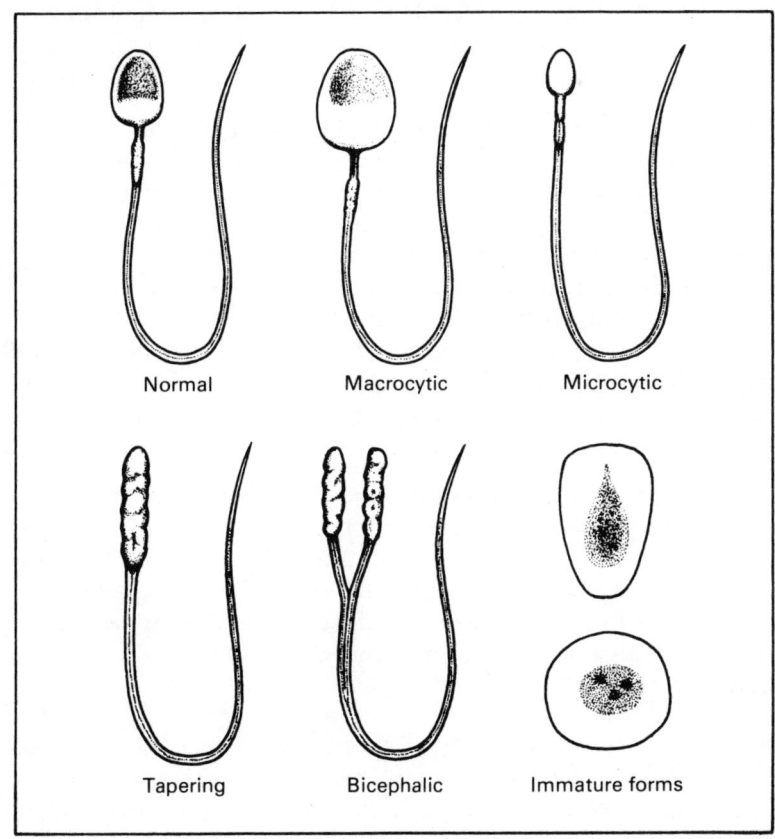

Some sperm types.

Motility Sperms are motile (that is, they move spontaneously under their own power by thrashing their tails) on ejaculation. The estimation of sperm motility is difficult and there is often a poor correlation from one clinic to another which is a shame because sperm motility is now thought to be the single most important parameter in sperm quality. Two things are looked for. First, the percentage of sperms that are motile (the normal is about 40-50 per cent within three hours of ejaculation); and second, how actively motile they are. An arbitrary scale of nought to four has been agreed upon and if sperms seem to move normally to the experienced eye then a grade of two is given. Anything under grade two is considered to be poor. It has been suggested that excellent motility will increase the chance of a pregnancy even if the sperm count is low. The study of 1,000 fertile and 1,000 infertile men showed that the infertile group had on average 40 per cent motile sperms whilst the fertile group had 58 per cent motile sperms.

Morphology Sperm cells differ in their appearance under the microscope: in fact there are about sixty different forms. In a normal, fertile man about 60 per cent of the sperms will look normal. If there are many sperms that are abnormal in form, the chances of infertility are higher because poor morphology renders the sperms poorly motile and very few of them will get to the cervix or up into the womb. All normal men have about 10 per cent of abnormal sperms. Liver diseases, infections and even allergies can cause changes in the head structure of sperms but these usually disappear within two or three weeks after the causative disease has been cured.

Liquefaction When semen is ejaculated, it is a liquid. It coagulates almost at once and then liquefies again, as its natural enzymes get to work, in about 15-20 minutes. If the semen doesn't become liquid in the normal way it may reduce sperm motility. Even after liquefaction some men's semen is still very sticky; this too can impede sperm motility and so reduce fertility.

Seminal fructose If there are no sperms to be seen, the seminal fluid will be tested for the sugar fructose. This is produced by the seminal vesicles (see page 36). If there is fructose but no sperms then there may be a blockage in the vas deferens below the level of the seminal vesicles. If there is neither fructose nor sperms, then the seminal vesicles may be completely absent. Should this be suspected, a special X-ray of the vasa deferentia can be done to find the exact blockage point or any other structural abnormality.

If your first semen analysis is normal, you will not need to have another done, but if it is abnormal, a good clinic will do at least another two or three tests to see exactly what is happening.

Once the doctors have found that the man's sperms are normal and that the woman is ovulating regularly, the next question to ask is why the two won't work together. This can be tested for in two ways: tests carried out on the couple and tests done in a laboratory.

As we saw on page 119, cervical mucus changes markedly in character and amount throughout a woman's cycle. At ovulation it is formed of 98 per cent water and is slippery, thin, clear and highly 'fertile'. Sperms can most easily swim in this thin mucus and although sperms can penetrate from the ninth day of the cycle the penetration of mucus reaches a peak at ovulation. Two days after ovulation, sperms have a more difficult job in getting through the mucus barrier.

THE POST-COITAL TEST

Once you get to this stage you may be feeling for the first time that you're a guinea pig in a laboratory. Many people can come to terms with temperature charting and making love at about the right time of the month but for the post-coital test to be successful you'll have to make love within a very few hours (6 to 18) before you go to the doctor. This usually means on the morning of the test (one or two days prior to ovulation).

Strictly speaking it isn't a 'test' at all because all you have to do is make love, lie in bed for about half an hour afterwards so as to give the sperms the best possible chance of getting into the cervix, and then get up as usual (no bathing, douching or vaginal washing is allowed) and go to the clinic.

A tiny amount of cervical mucus is sucked out (painlessly — nothing is put into the womb) and examination under the microscope tells the doctor about the quality of the mucus and the level of sperm activity. The test should only ever be done if ovulatory (thin, watery) mucus is present, and it's probably best to abstain from sex for three days beforehand. If the mucus looks good yet the sperms are clumped together, there may be an infection in the cervix or there may be an immunological reaction causing the clumping (see page 88). Rarely, there may be no sperms to be seen at all. If there has previously been a normal semen analysis, this latter finding proves that the couple has a sexual technique problem that needs sorting out. When you remember that on average about 200-500 million sperms are deposited around the cervix during intercourse between a normal couple, the chances of there being no sperms in the cervix at all after normal intercourse are very remote.

The post-coital test doesn't necessarily replace seminal analysis – it's a backup to it, except in couples whose religion or other scruples preclude any other technique for studying sperms. If on a post-coital test there are no motile spermatozoa at all, then obviously a semen analysis must be carried out, as it must if the spermatozoa are moving round in circles or are agglutinated. The so-called *fractional post-coital test* is a new procedure in which a tiny tube is pushed into the cervix by a doctor after intercourse. The doctor then attaches a syringe to the end and sucks a little cervical mucus into the fine tube. A three-centimetre length of tube is then cut into half-centimetre lengths and the sperm content of each is measured. In normal women, the number of motile sperms is the same at the outside of the cervix and at the point where it enters the inside of the womb. In some infertile couples there is a marked fall-off in both number and motility of sperms the further up the cervical canal the tube goes. A couple could therefore have a normal post-coital test yet still remain infertile because the man's sperms are being inactivated on their journey through the cervix. The fractional test usually provides the answers in such couples.

Other laboratory tests include placing mucus from the cervix and sperms side by side on a microscope slide and watching the speed of sperm penetration of the mucus.

All these tests have their place but it must be remembered that if they are negative (showing that nothing is wrong) it doesn't necessarily mean you are infertile. A positive result, however, especially if repeated, shows that something is going wrong higher up in the woman's reproductive system. After all, if the sperms are normal, the woman is ovulating and you are making love in a way that produces a normal post-coital test, then something else must be preventing a pregnancy from occurring.

TESTS TO ASSESS THE UTERUS AND FALLOPIAN TUBES
So far, none of the tests for infertility that we have discussed have been time-consuming or particularly unpleasant, or have involved a stay in hospital. The next step – assessing the uterus and the tubes – is more complex because there is a large number of tests that can be performed. The difficulty that doctors face is that of knowing how many to do to be as sure as possible of the facts before telling a woman she can't have a

baby. After all, these specialists realize only too well the impact of such a statement on the couple concerned and so will want to be very sure before they commit themselves. However, being sure often means many tests for the woman, a few of which are unpleasant and all of which involve trips to hospitals, time off work and away from home, worry in advance and anxiety about the results. Let's look then at the most commonly performed tests.

Tubal insufflation (Rubin test) This is the oldest of the tests and was first described by Dr Rubin in 1920. The essence of the test is as follows. Just before ovulation is thought to be due, the woman goes to the clinic as an outpatient. She is positioned with her legs in stirrups and an instrument with a nozzle is inserted into the cervical canal. Carbon dioxide gas is blown down this tube under pressure, and the pressure carefully observed. The gas escapes from the ends of the fallopian tubes if they are open. The doctor listens with a stethoscope over the lower part of the tummy to hear if the gas is escaping and then asks the woman to sit up. As she does so the gas rises to the top of her abdominal cavity (under the diaphragm) and causes pain to be felt in the shoulder. This in itself is diagnostic that the tubes are not blocked because if they were, the gas couldn't have got there. The gas is absorbed harmlessly by the body and leaves no after effects. The problem is that the Rubin test is uncomfortable for the woman and does not produce reliable results. It's very difficult to tell whether a tube is really blocked or is simply in spasm; you never know whether one or both tubes have let the gas through; and it can produce both false negative and false positive results.

In its favour, it is easy and quick to perform; the discomfort is not too great; and it can even sometimes clear small blockages in the tubes. Because of these advantages it has not been entirely abandoned but most experts would rather rely on other methods. The best known of them and the most widely available is the hysterosalpingogram.

Hysterosalpingography (HSG) This is an X-ray procedure which gives a lot of information about the inside of the uterus and the tubes. It is carried out in an X-ray department but is done as an outpatient procedure.

Many women find this test very unpleasant, so doctors give a tranquillizer and painkiller to be taken before the patient attends for the test. About 35 per cent of infertile women have blocked tubes though, so it's worth going through with it if you really want to get to the root of your problem. The test is normally done in the first half of the cycle so that the chances of an egg being there and getting a dose of X-rays is small.

Once on the X-ray table you may be given a local anaesthetic injection around the cervix to reduce the pain as

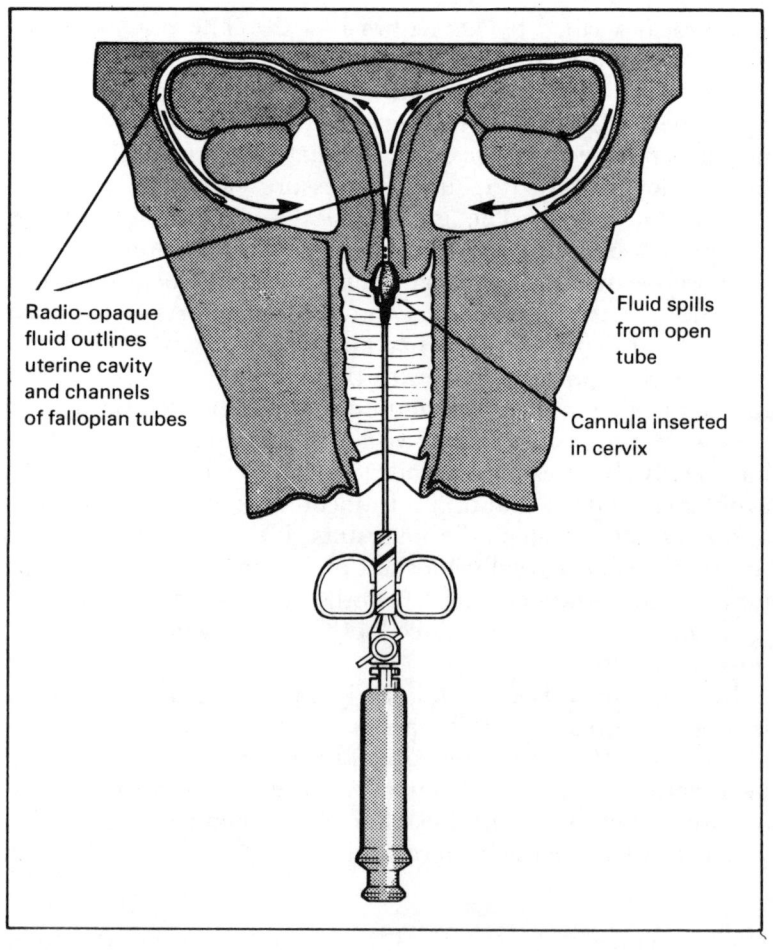

Diagram to show how a hysterosalpingogram is done.

the special nozzle is inserted into the cervical canal. It's this stretching that is painful and if it is too much you should tell the doctor. With the nozzle in the cervical canal, a radio-opaque substance is injected into the uterus and X-rays are taken as it passes up the tubes and out into the abdominal cavity. You may experience painful cramps like severe period pains when the substance is injected but if you tell the doctor he can allow the cramps to subside before proceeding further.

If the radio-opaque substance can't travel along a tube (the whole process is usually also shown on a TV screen) the doctor will wait for a while in case the tube is in spasm. If the spasm goes and the tube is then clear, all is well. Even with this fairly sophisticated test, about 40 per cent of the results show no abnormality at all when in reality there is one, and because of this and the false positives that can occur, some experts in this field are loath to accept HSG results alone as final. One study, for example, found that 'HSG was completely inaccurate in 19 per cent' (of women).

A recent German study found that the results of laparoscopy (see below) and HSG concurred in 76 per cent of the women they examined and that in the remaining 24 per cent of the so-called 'normal' findings on HSG had to be reconsidered after laparoscopy and vice versa. HSG therefore hasn't been overtaken by laparoscopy – the two should be used as complementary to each other.

As with tubal insufflation, some women seem to have their tubes cleared by this procedure and conceive after the test. Why this should happen is not known but whether the fluid under pressure actually breaks down small blockages and debris or whether the tiny dose of X-rays stimulates the ovaries, the result is an unexpected but welcome pregnancy in a small percentage of women. Some doctors think that the stretching of the cervix may be what enables a pregnancy to occur because some women get pregnant after having an endometrial biopsy and in this test nothing is done to their tubes. Whatever the reason, some doctors will suggest that you keep on trying to conceive for a clear three months after either of these tests before embarking on anything else, simply because they may be curative in themselves, whatever the test result. This is just the kind of advice which makes infertility testing such a long-term undertaking. The difficulty with all infertility testing is that of balancing the couple's mutual desire to find an answer tomorrow with the doctor's reluctance to unnecessary tests on a woman who might well become pregnant as a result of the last test. There is no rigid timetable for infertility tests but a clinic may condense the test programme if the woman is over thirty-five as each year lost makes everyone's task more difficult.

If these two tests reveal no abnormality or if they are difficult to interpret, the next group of investigations – those which allow a direct look at the reproductive organs – is carried out. There are at present three ways in which a woman's reproductive organs can be directly visualized. *Hysteroscopy* allows the doctor to see inside the uterus, and *culdoscopy* enables him to see the tubes, ovaries and uterus inside the abdomen as does *laparoscopy*.

Hysteroscopy In this technique, a fine telescope is inserted into the uterus through the cervical canal. Looking inside the uterus is technically very difficult because of the problems of getting enough light; because the cervix is so tight that the telescope has to be very small in diameter; and because it's very hard to distend the uterus so that the walls are parted sufficiently to allow their inspection. With the development of fibre-optic instruments which allow a powerful cold light source to illuminate even the darkest holes, hysteroscopy has now become a reality even though it is still something of a research tool.

The instrument is inserted into the uterus via the cervix either under a general or local anaesthetic. Because stretching the cervix is so painful, many doctors prefer general anaesthesia. The cervix is stretched, the telescope inserted and the uterine cavity filled with fluid or carbon dioxide gas. The doctor can then see the whole of the lining of the uterus, the openings of the tubes and any abnormalities in its shape and structure. This method often gives far more accurate results than does a hysterosalpingogram (HSG) because with an HSG, small filling defects with the radio-opaque substance often make the test difficult to interpret and small areas of trouble can escape detection altogether. Hysteroscopy followed by laparoscopy is probably more valuable than a hysterosalpingogram and is now replacing it in some centres.

Laparoscopy This is a procedure which has only been generally available for about fifteen years but has caught on in a big way because it enables the specialist to learn and treat so much. It

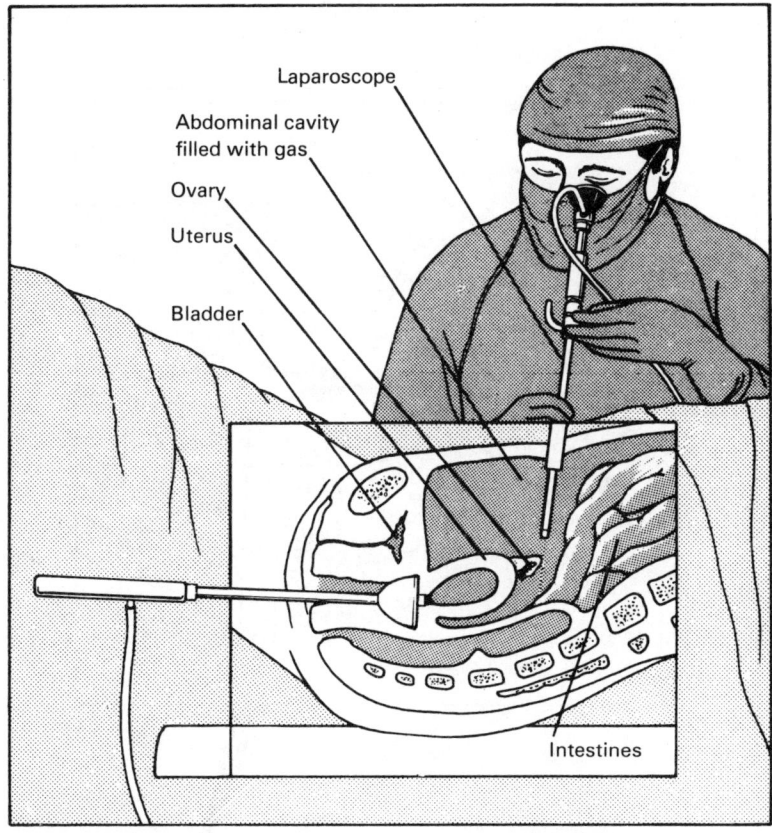

Laparoscopy.

is a slightly more major procedure than the others but it yields excellent results in women in whom no cause for their infertility can otherwise be found. One survey found that 60 per cent of the women studied had pelvic disease that could be related to their difficulty in conceiving. Of these, one-third were found to have pelvic endometriosis, most of which was minimal and undetected even by very careful medical history-taking. A further 20 per cent had pelvic conditions which would otherwise have been missed. Laparoscopy, because of the excellent all-round view that it affords, also allows the surgeon to examine the ovaries in some detail and even to perform minor surgical procedures while he is looking down the telescope. Many experts feel that in the absence of any other positive test results a woman who is persistently infertile

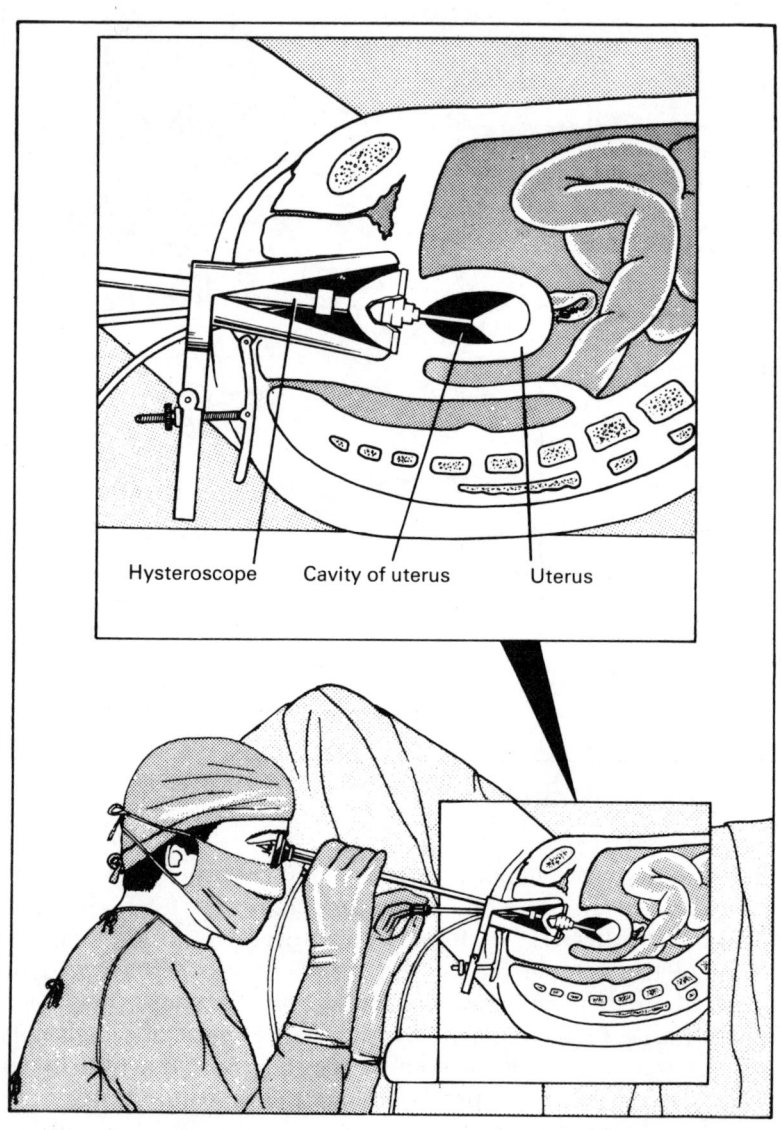

Hysteroscopy.

should have a laparoscopy performed, so often does it provide answers to the problem.

The procedure is almost always carried out under general anaesthesia but can be done under a local anaesthetic. The only preparation necessary is an enema. After first introducing carbon dioxide gas into the abdominal cavity via a needle inserted at the umbilicus, a one-centimetre-long incision is made at the navel (so that the scar will be invisible later) and a long, thin instrument called a laparoscope is introduced into the abdominal cavity. The carbon dioxide gas separates the organs, to allow a good view once the telescope is inserted. The surgeon then does a systematic review of all the pelvic organs. He can assess ovarian function, can see ovulation if it happens to be occurring at that time, can check for patches of endometriosis, can look for scarring or adhesions from past abdominal operations, and can look closely at the open ends of the tubes to see if they're functioning properly.

The surgeon introduces a dye through the cervix and via the laparoscope watches the fimbriated ends of the tubes to see if it comes out as it should if the tubes are not blocked.

Once the procedure is over, there may be a little shoulder-tip pain but there is usually no other discomfort. You'll be allowed home the same or the next day.

Laparoscopy isn't only a diagnostic tool; it can also save you from having to have major surgery later. One survey found that in 61 per cent of a series of patients in whom laparoscopy was done purely on clinical grounds, the procedure prevented the necessity for major surgery which would have had to have been done before the invention of the laparoscope. Laparoscopy is now a very safe procedure and fewer than 4 in 100 women suffer from any complications at all, whereas the discomfort and potential hazards of major surgery to arrive at the same facts are far greater. By means of tiny scissors, hooks and caterpillar forceps inserted down the tube which carries the telescope, the surgeon can often divide troublesome adhesions and with another instrument can take biopsies of organs for study under the microscope.

Culdoscopy, a way of looking into the pelvic cavity by inserting a telescope through the top end of the vagina, is now almost never used in the UK and so will not be discussed here.

OTHER TESTS

Occasionally, if the problem is difficult to sort out, the clinic may have to resort to other tests. Very briefly these are:

Vaginal cytology In this test the cells of the vagina are studied by an expert to assess the stage of the menstrual cycle. This is a difficult and time-consuming procedure for the technical staff and is wide open to misinterpretation and error caused by factors beyond the control of the doctor and his back-up staff. Vaginal cytology is therefore not widely used in infertility studies.

Vaginal cytology is very valuable in searching for trichomonas and candida as well as, of course, being valuable to exclude *pre*-malignant conditions. Even when trichomonas and candida cannot be seen on the slide the cytologist can tell the clinician whether there is an infection or not and this points to the need for further testing.

Blood tests These are performed on both the male and the female and include the measurements of follicle stimulating hormone (FSH), prolactin, luteinizing hormone (LH) and testosterone levels. Many of these tests can only be done in very large centres which have the necessary laboratory back-up. They can often provide an answer in very difficult cases but are too expensive for routine use. You'll probably have several blood tests taken at different stages within any given cycle so that the doctors can 'track' the levels of hormones which they know from experience should be at particular levels according to the stage of your cycle. In all cases of repeated abortions most specialists routinely test for antibodies for tixoplasmosis, brucella abortus and other brucellosis.

Testicular biopsy This is a simple procedure which is sometimes done in those men in whom the sperms are seen to be of poor quality or are too few on semen analysis. The biopsy is carried out under general anaesthesia. A small piece of testicular tissue is taken from each testis so as to see if there is any difference. If this shows that perfectly normal sperms are being produced, then the answer to the man's problem may be that there is a blockage in the vasa deferentia. This can be finally diagnosed at vasography.

Vasography This is an X-ray study of the vasa deferentia. A radio-opaque fluid is passed into each vas so as to detect any blockages. It is used only if a testicular biopsy has shown normal sperm-producing tissue yet there are no sperms in the man's semen. The procedure is carried out under general anaesthesia.

Immunological testing Some women produce antibodies to their partner's sperms and some men even produce antibodies to their own sperms. We shall consider this whole subject later (see page 155) but suffice it to say that antibodies can be detected, if present, in the serum of the blood. Those in favour of such testing feel that any couple with a poor post-coital test should have their blood examined for sperm antibodies and that any couple persistently resistant to treatment and in whom no other cause can be found should be tested for antibodies. If the problem is an immunological one, there are treatments that have been shown to work in some couples (see page 88).

Most couples will not need any of these 'other tests' as they will have been diagnosed before this stage.

* * *

As the tests are undergone, many people experience several emotional stages. At first, with everything ahead of you, you hope that the problem is caused by something simple, preferably (according to most women) something wrong with their basic 'plumbing' at worst and ideally something even simpler. As the tests progress and if no reason is found, you'll hope that each new test will come up with the answer until it gets to the stage where you'll be deeply disappointed when the doctor tells you that a test is normal. The trouble is that you know that you're not normal even if they haven't been able to find anything wrong. It's at this stage that the tests become frustrating because you feel there is nothing else you can do and the doctors feel similarly powerless. There comes a time though when you have to call a halt to your search for an answer because after a while, once the tests have been properly done in a specialist centre, you may have to accept that they can't find anything wrong. This doesn't mean there *is* nothing wrong with either of you – it simply means that with the tests available today whatever it is can't be found.

At this stage it's tempting to go away from the hospital assuming that the whole of your trouble is in the mind. Some doctors may even tell you to 'relax' and all will be well. This may be very well-meant advice but doesn't help the couple involved, especially when you consider that as recently as twenty years ago 40-50 per cent of infertile couples were thought to have psychological or emotional causes for their condition. Today, as we shall see in Chapter 6, most experts seriously doubt the existence of psychogenic infertility and at most 5 per cent of infertility is thought to be caused solely by emotional or psychological factors.

If all the tests are normal, and you still can't conceive, you'll have to think seriously about alternatives. You won't be alone – well over a third of all infertile couples end up after all their tests *and* treatments still unable to conceive. For a discussion of possible alternatives to having your own child, turn to Chapter 10.

CHAPTER 6

All in the Mind?

There are two main ways in which the mind can affect the sexual functioning of a couple and so reduce their fertility. The first prevents sexual intercourse and the second affects the physiological balance of the body by acting through the highest centres of the brain.

Let's look at the sexual dysfunctions first because they have been treated in depth elsewhere (see page 47). Psychological upsets and emotional disturbances (not to mention true mental illness such as depression) can all affect sexual drive.

A couple can get away with quite a low female sexual libido (from an infertility point of view, anyway) because a woman doesn't have to be sexually aroused to become pregnant – at least if she's highly fertile this is the case. A lowly fertile woman with some marginal problem of fertility might well only get pregnant on increasing her pleasure in sex (see page 47). But the real problems arise if the man's sexual urge is very poor, because he may not be able to obtain or sustain an erection. Overwork, trivial diseases, serious diseases and a host of other more reversible factors (a bad patch in the marital relationship, excessive pressures to 'perform' sexually, undue concentration on producing orgasms in the woman, money worries, physical exhaustion and so on) can all produce a temporarily low sex drive. All these things start 'in the mind' but there is a perfectly logical explanation for them and with help they can often be overcome. Other causes of impotence are considered on page 52 as is the treatment. Other sexual problems such as premature ejaculation, vaginismus in the woman and so-called 'frigidity' have been discussed elsewhere (see pages 47–54). Many of these problems can be overcome by a couple themselves within their marriage but if you're in any doubt, get professional help.

The main point of this chapter though is to look at the possible role of the mind in infertility. Many couples have told me that they have repeatedly been instructed to 'relax'. This they find infuriating because they don't feel relaxed and don't want to be told to relax as if this would suddenly produce a miracle cure. This is not an easy area to deal with because there is no doubt that increased anxiety does lead to a reduced chance of conceiving but the ways around it are not simple. Some couples find that by working at their sex techniques they enjoy sex more, have sex more often, have orgasms more often and that this results in a pregnancy. Others find that the relaxation of a holiday seems to do the trick but it's important to arrange the holiday around ovulation time or it'll be of no use.

It has been postulated over many years that emotional factors can exert an effect on things seemingly as different as the functioning of the fallopian tubes, the desire for sex at certain times of the month, the rapid expulsion of semen from the vagina, the nature of cervical mucus and, of course, the timing of ovulation.

As we have already seen, fallopian tubal spasm is now no longer accepted as a cause of infertility even if, as seems possible, the emotions can indeed cause the tubes to go into spasm. These spasms are usually short-lived and anyway disappear during sleep.

The question of psychogenic infertility is a vexed one. As recently as twenty years ago, 40-50 per cent of infertile couples were thought to have emotional causes for their trouble. Today the accepted figure is around 5 per cent.

Of all the questions surrounding infertility the role of the mind and the emotions is by far the most difficult to elucidate, yet it is one that infertile couples really want answered. 'Should I stop working, doctor?' is a very common question from an infertile woman. 'Could it be that things are getting worse because I'm worrying so much?' 'Might I simply be a non-maternal person deep down?' These and a host of other questions dog every doctor who's trying to help infertile couples because he doesn't have the answers.

The whole picture is further complicated because of social changes that have occurred since the early sixties. The upheaval of sexual values, the women's liberation movement, the new sexual demands being put on men to perform and produce orgasms in their women, a new insecurity among men as women become more assertive (more women instigate divorce proceedings in the US than do men, for example), a change in attitude to those who remain child-free by choice and the questioning of modern family structure all help to produce a psychological backdrop for us all, whether we're infertile or not. It is against this backdrop that we have to live and love and these changes have deep unconscious effects on us every day of our lives. As the years go by, what will the effect be of these newly liberated mothers on their daughters? Will infertility increase at an even greater rate than now and will male sexual performance continue to fall short of what some women say they want? It's certainly a possibility that as child-free couples become more commonplace and more accepted, being childless will be less of a stigma socially and this might lead to increased infertility levels simply because many couples won't bother to seek help. Today, the social pressures to conform are enormous and this undoubtedly pushes a lot of women especially on to the merry-go-round of medical investigations and treatment.

A basic question that has to be asked is whether the drive to procreate is built in us. Is it reasonable to assume that deep down we all have an urge as basic as that which makes us eat and have sex, to procreate? There can only be opinions on such a subject but it's an important question to ask because the inhibition of this supposed drive could produce psychological symptoms of anxiety, tension and stress which could in turn, through well-proven hormonal mechanisms, produce infertility. Perhaps, as much good research seems to show, the basic urge is to have intercourse which naturally results in a pregnancy. It is only since the adoption of contraceptive methods that we have been able to separate intercourse from producing babies and it is this very choice that has increased the dilemma for the infertile couple. Hélène Deutsch said 'that for every psychologically mature woman, the imminence of motherhood is the satisfaction of an old wish, the consummation of an old desire, which destiny and her peers have accorded her once she has recognized and accepted her femininity'. The role of sexuality in our culture, coupled with the pressures to have children, seems so strong that it might reasonably be assumed that there's a drive to reproduce – but this can't be proved. On the other side of the coin, parenthood in a world with effective contraception could be seen as simply an acceptable norm forced upon most of us by the pressures of society rather than coming from some deeper, inner source.

Biologists, ethologists and philosophers debate endlessly the whole subject of evolution and survival of the fittest. It has been argued that on purely biological grounds infertile individuals should *not* be helped because they are intrinsically 'weak' from a reproductive view point and will only produce more genetically weak individuals. Such an argument holds no appeal for me if only because so many infertile individuals have a relatively simple 'plumbing' problem that cannot honestly be said to be ordained by their genetic blueprint. The argument that the 'incurably' infertile should not be encouraged or allowed to adopt or foster children on the grounds that Nature clearly marked them out to be non-parents is also fallacious because the concept of 'curable' infertility is a relative one and because these very same individuals might well have been able to have children had they been married to other partners. To suggest that partner mis-choice (in this reproductive respect) should rule one out of being able to adopt or foster (or even to be helped in other ways to overcome infertility) is cruel and totally unacceptable. Yet it is the sort of argument that comes from the lips of many an intelligent (fertile) person. There are no studies of which I am aware that look at how 'good' a parent a treated infertile person becomes but my experience and intuition would suggest that rather than being poorer parents (as the purist biologist might claim) they in fact make very good parents, partly as a *result* of their initial setback. Research along these lines would make fascinating reading but first we'd have to decide as a society on ways of measuring successful parenting.

The role of the mind

Surprisingly, there are very few good studies that really help answer the questions about the role of the mind in infertility. For years, doctors have made the diagnosis of psychogenic infertility by the exclusion of physical causes but this is nonsense because every year we get better at finding physical causes which then relegate more of the previously 'psychogenically' infertile to new organic categories. It's fair to say that a reasonable proportion of those infertile couples who have no detectable physical cause also have no discernible psychological cause for their problem. But women attending infertility clinics with, for example, perfectly regular periods, often become irregular (so pointing to ovulatory dysfunction) as time goes by and because of this no results are obtained.

So there is no doubt that the problem of infertility and its investigation and treatment can in itself make matters worse and that most of this downhill trend comes from emotional rather than physical causes. That emotions and certain severe mental illnesses can affect the body's reproductive hormones is not in doubt. The highest centres of the brain influence the hypothalamus, which in turn undoubtedly affects the function of the pituitary gland. Since this gland controls ovulation and is responsible for the majority of the hormonal control of all the body's organs, it seems reasonable to assume that brain changes can affect the most unlikely organs via the body's hormone systems.

It has been known for a long time that fear and other stressful situations produce amenorrhoea (a cessation of menstruation). Concentration camp and wartime amenorrhoea are well documented and ECT treatment for depression sometimes causes it. Genital tract secretions generally are suppressed by anger, fear or anxiety as is saliva production in other women.

The heart of the matter seems to be an area in the brain called the limbic system. It is a very old (in evolutionary terms) part of the brain and is that part where instinctive drives, taboos and so on are located. The limbic system is intricately linked with the hypothalamus and we have seen how this affects the rest of the body. People who are depressed have a decreased sexual drive and if the depression is profound enough, a woman will not menstruate at all. The brain of the depressed person contains altered neuro-transmitter amines and stress produces changes in these same amines. The hormonal stress may be trivial (as in 'first-kiss' amenorrhoea in young girls) or very serious, as in anorexia nervosa.

Studies of stress and reproductive functioning have been done in animals but are very much more difficult to do in humans because of the ethics of stressing humans under laboratory conditions and the problems that could arise if the offspring were abnormal. Research in Germany suggests that rats whose mothers were severely stressed throughout pregnancy stand a very much greater chance of becoming homosexual later in life. Other research has proved in both animals and humans that the production of breast-milk depends on psychological factors. Farmers have used soothing music to increase milk yield in their herds and anyone who has milked cows will know how they can be put off producing milk if a dog frightens them or someone shouts at or hits them. Women who are lactating often spurt milk at orgasm and emotional stress can reduce their milk supply.

So all in all, it looks highly likely that emotional and stress factors play a part in controlling our reproductive functions and that while they are unlikely to play much of a part in a man (except if the conditions make him unable to obtain or maintain an erection) they certainly play a very important role in women. It has been postulated that stress depresses sperm production but this is extremely difficult to prove in humans.

A book on infertility is no place to go into detail about the links between mind and matter but western medicine is now beginning to realize that the links are far closer than was ever thought. It's impossible to separate mind and matter, as most of the eastern religions have been saying for thousands of years. One major study found that most patients with emotionally determined infertility also had organic problems and suggested that the medical profession should stop trying to separate the two.

The difficulties of separating the two become even more apparent when we consider whether the psychological conditions that are supposedly the cause of infertility might just not be the result of it. Several surveys, as we shall soon see, have tried to draw up psychological or emotional profiles of infertile men and women but this seems to me to prove (if indeed it proves anything) that human beings tend to react in the same way when faced with the undisputed mental trauma of being unable to reproduce themselves. It is my contention that psychological factors ought to be searched for along with cervical, seminal and tubal factors and that the *whole* patient should be treated from day one. That reassurance and caring alone works wonders is proved by the fact that more than a third of women get pregnant after even very long periods of infertility simply after having seen an expert at a clinic and before investigations and treatment begin. Yet others get pregnant while they are being investigated.

Emotional disorders seen with infertility

Studies of the personality types of the infertile abound. The findings vary enormously but repeatedly mention such things as the couple seeing themselves as less similar to their ideal selves than control couples. The females, it is claimed, often show more anxiety, neuroticism and emotional disturbances, but these factors are not found in the men. Sandler, one of the most distinguished workers in this field, suggests that infertility is a manifestation of a total personality disturbance and several workers have carried out research to try to substantiate this claim. One survey found that suicide was twice as common in the childless when compared with those with children.

Many studies have shown that infertile women have more emotional difficulties than fertile ones. This poses two questions. Do infertile women in fact have more psychiatric disease and are infertile women more likely to have psychosexual and personality disorders? Research seems to suggest that the latter is true but not the former. Hysterical and aggressive personality disorders were definitely more often seen in infertile women in some surveys and one team pointed out that fertile women tended to use more varied sex positions, which in their opinion showed a more relaxed attitude to sex generally. They found no difference in marital sexual adjustment, however. The sex lives of both groups seemed the same, satisfaction with sex seemed the same and the frequency of intercourse was the same for both the fertile and the infertile. These same studies showed that attitudes towards children were more ambivalent among the childless. Previous homosexual contacts were the same in both groups. There was also no obvious difference between the groups when it came to childhood disturbances or disturbed parent-child relationships.

Studies of this subject generally though are inconclusive. There doesn't seem to be any way of predicting what sort of woman is going to become infertile, simply because there is no common psychological factor linking them all.

Psychoanalysts have had a field day trying to link infertility to the functions of the ego and superego, for example, but with little success. Women during the oestrogenic phase of the menstrual cycle are much more outgoing, according to Benedek, a leader in this area of research. They are also more likely to want sex. After ovulation a woman wants more food, is calmer and more receptive and turns inwards towards her body. He postulates that during this 'turning inward' phase a woman who is psychosexually inadequate might resolve this threatening experience by becoming infertile. He draws a link between the way a woman's hormones make her feel towards her spouse and her ability to seek sex at a time when she is likely to become pregnant. Hélène Deutsch believed that the most common cause of emotional infertility is a fear of pregnancy and other workers have found that women's conscious and unconscious desires are often completely at variance with each other on such subjects. These conflicts arise because the woman's view of herself today is so different from the unconscious image that was built up during her childhood. Today's woman also has many ambitions and aspirations which are not child-orientated and this makes treatment difficult. Some psychoanalysts feel that whilst the infertile woman consciously and obviously yearns for a child, she unconsciously rejects intercourse, pregnancy and childbirth. These women, they argue, have an unconscious fear of sexual intercourse: 'I will be torn, ripped apart' and that birth is seen as the ultimate in self-destruction. Some analysts have found a previous conflict with their mothers to be an important feature of infertile women and some of these women, they claim, are still very hostile towards their mothers.

Infertility then is seen by many psychoanalysts as a defence mechanism against a pregnancy which, if it occurred, would bring out all the woman's unconscious conflicts with very serious results. It could be, they argue, that many of the psychological disturbances seen in infertile women are their unconscious attempts to maintain their psychological equilibrium.

All of these psychoanalytic approaches at explaining infertility assume that the basic tenets of the discipline are valid and many would question this.

Tests for psychological abnormalities

Most studies show that on psychological testing the vast majority of infertile couples are perfectly normal. Various personality tests have shown that fertile women seem to be better adjusted sexually, less neurotic and less anxious than their infertile counterparts but not all workers agree that this is the case. In fact results generally show that the similarities between infertile women and control groups are greater than are the differences. Psychological testing is therefore of very little value in assessing infertile women.

* * *

A few final thoughts. The mind can undoubtedly play a vital role in infertility, in three major ways: (1) men, under increasing pressure sexually, are suffering from more sexual dysfunction than ever before and this leads to an inability to get sperms to the right place; (2) the influence of upbringing affects the psychosexual maturity of both partners and so determines their liking for and ability to have regular intercourse (which will make conception more likely); and (3) a woman unable to conceive as quickly as she feels she should can become anxious, which in turn affects her ovulatory pattern, so reducing her fertility. In my opinion all the other psychological findings in infertile couples are the *outcome* of their condition and not the *cause* of it.

CHAPTER 7

Miscarriage

It might seem strange to have a chapter on miscarriage in a book about infertility but it is not as strange as it at first seems. In as many as 50 per cent of couples in which the woman has trouble in conceiving the woman suffers a miscarriage (according to some surveys) and because the baby is especially precious to these couples, the loss is even more tragic than to a more fertile couple.

Strictly speaking, the term miscarriage is not a medical one. Doctors speak of abortions. They call them 'induced' if they are brought about artificially (what the public calls an abortion) and 'spontaneous' if they just happen. This chapter deals with the latter group and I'll call them miscarriages so as not to confuse the two groups.

Bleeding from the vagina during a pregnancy is abnormal and may be serious or not. You won't be able to tell whether the bleeding you're having is important or not and will need medical advice. The first sign of a miscarriage is often bleeding and any blood loss must be taken seriously because it may be possible to prevent a miscarriage.

By definition a miscarriage is the loss of a fetus before 28 weeks of pregnancy. After that age the fetus is deemed to be legally viable. If such a loss after 28 weeks results in the death of a fetus it is called a stillbirth but the child could, of course, be born alive.

The spontaneous loss of a fetus is very common indeed.

MISCARRIAGE

About one in five or six of all pregnancies ends in a miscarriage and threequarters of these occur in the first 12 weeks of pregnancy. Having said this though, only a few women miscarry repeatedly. It has been calculated that the risk of miscarrying after one miscarriage is 20 per cent; after two miscarriages, 25 per cent, and after three miscarriages, 30 per cent. A woman who has lost three or more fetuses at about the same stage of pregnancy is known as a 'habitual aborter' to doctors and has about one-in-three chance of losing her next baby. Because of this, these women are defined as being 'at risk' and are looked after even more carefully than a normal pregnant woman would be.

There are several types of miscarriage, which are described in detail here.

A threatened miscarriage

This is where there is vaginal bleeding which may or may not be accompanied by pain. If ever you have any vaginal bleeding, go to bed and if necessary ask your doctor to come to you. The bleeding in this type of spontaneous abortion may be slight and may or may not be mixed with mucus. On the other hand, it may be very heavy. Some women complain of backache before and during the bleeding and there may be a dull ache low down in the abdomen. This type of miscarriage usually occurs at the time of the first, second or third missed period (at 4, 8 or 12 weeks of pregnancy) and can also occur at the 14th week as the placenta takes over hormone production from the corpus luteum in the ovary. On occasions the placenta may not be quite ready for this role and the resulting hormone deficiency produces a threatened abortion. Bed rest usually results in a 'cure' but while you are resting be sure not to use tampons and be sure to save used sanitary towels for the doctor to see. It makes sense to ensure that around the time of your next missed period you rest as much as possible because a threatened abortion points to the possibility that the pregnancy may be unstable. For this reason too, it is probably wise not to have intercourse after a threatened abortion at least until the baby can be felt to move. Some doctors feel it is essential to offer a woman who is threatening to miscarry a simple non-invasive test called an ultrasound scan. This can tell the doctor whether the baby is likely to live and saves the woman unnecessary days in bed only to find she is carrying a dead baby later. A threatened miscarriage may go on to:

An inevitable miscarriage

This is associated with pain like a period pain. The bleeding increases in amount and once again the thing to do is to go straight to bed. Your doctor will decide if you need to go into hospital. This type is called inevitable because if the cervix is open and the uterus is contracting it is inevitable that its contents will be lost. This loss can be complete or incomplete.

A complete miscarriage

This is a situation where all the products of conception are expelled. It may take only one hour from the onset of bleeding and there may be little pain. On the other hand the pain may be considerable and the process may take many hours. It all depends upon the stage of the pregnancy at which the miscarriage occurs. Once all the uterine contents are gone, the pain subsides and the bleeding stops or at least diminishes. Keep anything you expel for the doctor to see. Hopefully all the uterine contents will have come away but if they haven't further medical attention will be required because the miscarriage is then said to be incomplete.

An incomplete miscarriage

This leaves part of the fetus or placenta inside the uterus. It is the only type of miscarriage that is dangerous because it lays the woman open to further haemorrhage and to infection. If you think you are bleeding too much or for too long after a miscarriage, tell your doctor. He will stop the bleeding by giving you an injection that makes the uterus contract and then he'll have you admitted to hospital for a dilatation and curettage (D and C) so that the contents of the womb can be cleaned out.

A 'missed miscarriage'

This occurs when the fetus dies in the womb but isn't expelled. The woman has none of the other signs of a miscarriage but notices that her abdomen isn't swelling and that she doesn't feel pregnant any more. Carrying a dead baby around is very distressing and most women are very keen to go into hospital to have the fetus removed as soon as possible. Some doctors advice an immediate D and C, while others feel that the uterus should be given a chance to contract and empty itself.

Recurrent miscarriages

As we have seen, these are uncommon in general but are more common in those who have had other miscarriages. The causes are often complex and what makes any given woman lose a fetus may not be the same the next time around. Women who repeatedly lose babies will be investigated very fully (as may their husbands) to try to find a cause. Some husbands of women who repeatedly abort are found to have larger than normal numbers of abnormal and dead sperms.

What causes miscarriages?

In many cases the answer is that no one knows. Among habitual aborters, a causes will never be found in as many as 66 per cent. Very little is known about what causes fetuses to abort spontaneously but certain possibilities are coming to light. About one thing we can be sure: it is *not* the mother's surroundings. There is no evidence that frights, shocks, a fall, overwork or any other environmental hazards make a woman more likely to abort. Let's look then at some possible causes and what could be done to prevent and cure them.

BLIGHTED OVUM
Any pregnancy in which the fetus fails to develop properly is called a blighted one. This is a common cause of a miscarriage in the first 12 weeks of pregnancy. The pregnancy starts to develop normally but the mass of cells never develops into a baby. The first signs of trouble may occur at about the 8th week. There may be a small amount of vaginal bleeding and because the hormone-producing tissues aren't forming properly, the woman begins to feel 'less pregnant'. This type of pregnancy can't be saved and should be aborted artificially as soon as possible.

Just why blighted ova occur isn't entirely clear but it is thought that they arise when an abnormal sperm fertilizes a normal ovum. This theory can only be 'proved' by inference as it has been found that women with blighted ova have husbands with a larger proportion of abnormal sperms than usual. Such semen, if frozen in a sperm bank, when unfrozen will contain few, if any, poor-quality sperms and can then be given by artificial insemination. In many couples though, no such abnormality is found and they simply need reassurance that a normal pregnancy will occur one day.

It's all too easy to blame the doctor for not having 'done more' to save a blighted ovum and many couples become very angry because of this. However, it's basically unfair because there is no fetus.

TROUBLE WITH THE CERVIX
About 20 per cent of all miscarriages are thought to come about because of an abnormality of the cervix. This is the commonest cause for miscarriages in the second and third trimesters of pregnancy. Most women with an incompetent cervix miscarry at about 20 weeks. The normal cervix is about one inch long and while the uterus enlarges in pregnancy, the cervix stays tight, so ensuring that the baby doesn't fall out into the vagina. If the cervix is too loose, the baby can be lost. There are several reasons for this looseness or 'incompetence', as the doctors call it. A previous difficult or rapid labour in which the muscles of the cervix were damaged, a previous therapeutic abortion, or repeated stretching of the cervix (as in a D and C) can all be the cause.

Fortunately, as this is a mechanical problem the solution is simple and the results are good. Very few women who suffer from this condition are without a previous history of operations or pregnancy and very few cannot be treated. The diagnosis can only be made with certainty after one miscarriage because until then the doctors won't necessarily think of this as the most likely cause. The treatment consists of the doctor inserting a stitch around the cervix either before or during pregnancy. This is usually done under a general anaesthetic at about the 14th week of pregnancy, by which stage the baby is growing well and the pregnancy is least likely to be disturbed. This Shirodkar suture is named after the Indian gynaecologist who first used it. It is successful in 75 per cent of cases. The stitch is removed at the 38th week (or earlier if the woman goes into labour before this) and labour is quite normal.

HORMONE DEFICIENCIES

These probably play a part in a very large number of miscarriages. We don't know why the hormones should fail but perhaps there's a link with the higher centres in the brain that control the stimulating and releasing factors (hormones) that affect the ovary. As we saw in Chapter 1, an egg, once fertilized, needs hormones from the corpus luteum until the placenta is sufficiently developed (at about 14 weeks) to take over. Even then, the ovaries still continue to supply some hormones throughout pregnancy.

Some miscarriages occur at the take-over point, sometimes because the placenta isn't quite mature enough and the corpus luteum is failing too soon. Once the problem is diagnosed, or alternatively in those women known to be at risk, vaginal cells can be studied to check hormonal functioning. In centres where blood tests are available, the hormones themselves can be measured in the woman's blood. Once you've started bleeding, there's probably no point in having hormone treatment because the fetus will almost certainly be dead and progestogens only prolong the agony. Oestrogens are not now given since it was found that the female child of a woman so treated may develop cancer of the genital tract when she herself reaches puberty.

TROUBLE WITH THE UTERUS

Some women are born with an abnormally shaped uterus. A bicornuate uterus (one with a partition down the middle) may mean that there simply isn't enough room for the fetus to develop normally. If this is the case, a miscarriage results. Fibroids of the uterine wall can also so distort the cavity of the organ that they too can cause a woman to miscarry. Operations may be necessary to correct these problems which can be detected with X-rays once the fetus has been lost and the uterus is back to its normal, non-pregnant state.

INCOMPATIBLE BLOOD GROUPS

Incompatibility of the ABO blood group system can cause miscarriage. Because the mechanisms behind rhesus incompatibility are so well documented and because the same mechanisms are at work in all blood group incompatibilities, let's look at how a miscarriage occurs with rhesus trouble.

Trouble can only arise when a rhesus-negative woman is carrying a rhesus-positive child. In the latter months of preg-

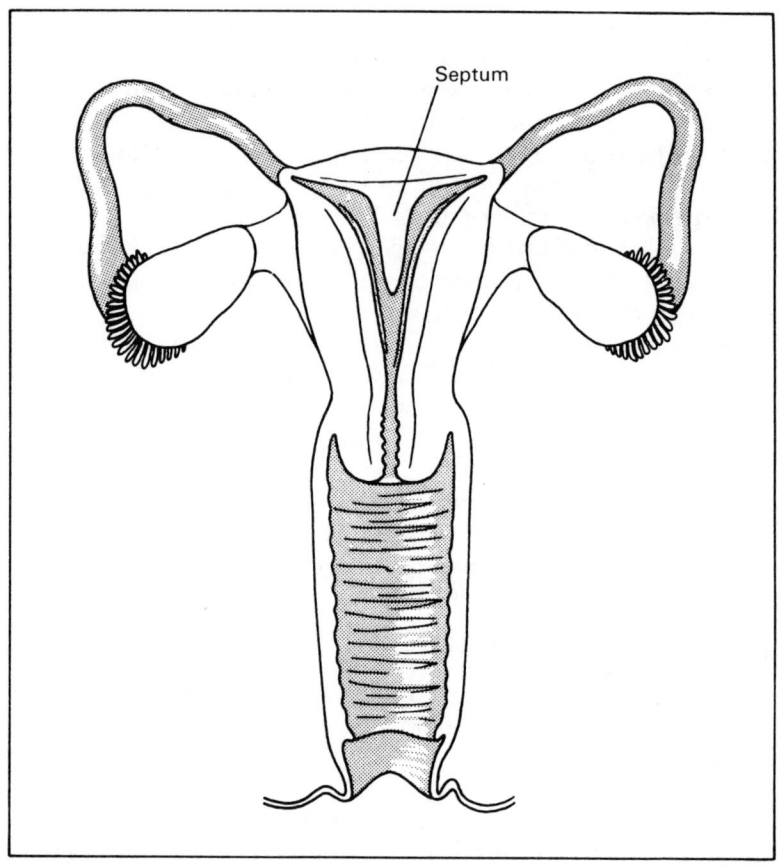

A uterus with a septum.

nancy and especially at birth, rhesus-positive blood cells escape from the baby into the mother's circulation. The mother's body recognizes these cells as 'foreign' and is primed (sensitized) to produce antibodies against them next time it encounters such cells. The antibodies don't form at once though, so it isn't until she has her second rhesus-positive baby that the trouble starts. Unfortunately, this sensitization can occur from a previous mismatched blood transfusion, a previous forgotten (or unrecognized) miscarriage and a previous (unmentioned) procured abortion.

When the second rhesus-positive baby releases cells into the mother's circulation, they meet circulating antibodies produced previously. Antibodies also cross the placenta and enter the baby's body where they start destroying red cells.

This massive destruction of red cells produces severe anaemia and heart failure which may kill the baby. Fortunately, this is a problem that is much less common today than even ten years ago because protective gamma globulin can be given to a newly delivered rhesus-negative mother (if she has a rhesus-positive baby) who might otherwise develop antibodies. If it is given within seventy-two hours of birth and provided that antibodies aren't already present, the woman doesn't produce rhesus antibodies and her present baby and future babies will be safe. Today, the gamma globulin is given to all 'at risk' women if they have a pregnancy terminated (aborted), suffer a miscarriage, or after birth as we have seen.

CHROMOSOMAL ABNORMALITIES
Because couples who don't conceive readily seem to have more spontaneous abortions (miscarriages) than do normal couples, researchers have tried to find out if there is a link between infertility and anything that could produce increased fetal rejection early in pregnancy. It had been thought for some time that eggs or sperms containing chromosomal abnormalities might lead to fetuses that are rejected by the body and one major survey in Scotland examined more than 1,500 infertile men to look for chromosomal abnormalities in their blood's white cells. Normal men were found to have chromosomal abnormalities at a rate of about four per 1,000 men whereas the infertile men's rate of abnormalities was twenty-two per 1,000. Further analysis showed that normal men had on average 107 million sperms per millilitre and that men with chromosomal abnormalities had only 31.5 million sperms per millilitre. In men with sperm counts of under 20 million per millilitre, 8.2 per cent had chromosomal abnormalities. They also found that the morphology (shape and form) of the sperms of men with abnormal chromosomes was poor.

However, most of this and other related research tends to suggest that chromosomal abnormalities produce poor-quality sperms that aren't good enough to fertilize an egg anyway and so probably don't contribute to a miscarriage in this way.

The whole subject is very complex and almost impossible to research into because many women may be having what they think is a late or heavy period when in fact they are miscarrying *very* early. The world's leading authorities in the field are

M. Boué and his wife, working in Paris. They have estimated that 50 per cent of all conceptions in normal people are chromosomally abnormal and that of all fetuses aborted spontaneously in the first 12 weeks, 60 per cent have provable chromosomal abnormalities. These abnormalities usually amount to one more or less chromosome than there should be and the signs are that these abnormalities occur when the sperms or eggs are being formed. This rejection rate of human conceptions is extraordinarily high compared with other animals. In the mouse, for example, it has been found that only 1 per cent of all conceptions are chromosomally abnormal. Why we as a species seem to have so many chromosome problems when our sex cells combine is not known but perhaps there are environmental causes.

PSYCHOLOGICAL CAUSES
It has been suggested by many experts that some women miscarry because of psychological factors. Whether these act through the effects of the higher brain centres by shutting off or reducing pituitary hormones is not known but the subject is one that arouses considerable hostility, especially among those women who are labelled as 'psychological aborters'. The evidence for psychological disturbances causing miscarriage is confused but the most experienced worker in this field, Helene Michel-Wolfromm, maintained that even though she herself was at first a sceptic, she became convinced by the available evidence.

One group of workers looked at two groups of habitual aborters. To the first group they gave superficial, supportive psychotherapy and to the second group, nothing. Three times as many women receiving the psychotherapy gave birth to babies, compared with the control group. Another study used thirty-nine pregnant women who had been habitual aborters in the past. Although 93 per cent of their previous pregnancies had terminated before twenty-eight weeks, this was reduced to 20 per cent after they received simple psychotherapy.

Some experts believe that certain women unconsciously affect their own bodies in such a way as to reject their babies as a protetive mechanism against otherwise certain mental conflict over the birth of the child. In one rather unusual study nine habitual aborters had a stitch put around their cervix to ensure that the baby would not be lost. All nine gave birth at full term but five developed a serious mental disturbance after the birth and of the other four, three received psychotherapy. Of a control group of normal women receiving the same treatment who were not habitual aborters, all but one delivered a baby at term with no psychological ill effects at all.

The best study of this subject involved the close observation of 60 women who were claimed to be spontaneous aborters for psychological reasons. Michel-Wolfromm, the woman doctor who organized the survey, found that an acute, disturbing experience had precipitated the miscarriage in 13 cases. She thought that 43 of the women were 'markedly neurotic' and that close questioning showed a fear of pregnancy in many. Thirty-three of the women didn't get on well with their husbands and in 44 women there was a poor maternal urge. This researcher concluded that despite strong assertions to the contrary, these latter women really didn't want the baby. In conclusion, she claimed that emotional factors are rarely the sole cause of a miscarriage but play a part in about 20 per cent of cases.

Having said this though, it's impossible to be dogmatic about the role of the mind (see Chapter 6). The fact that psychotherapy produces positive results in from 45 to 84 per cent of women (depending on the survey) cannot be ignored but whether this should be used in a preventive way is not yet clear.

It's interesting that women who have had a miscarriage 'feel' instinctively if something is wrong in a subsequent pregnancy. The pregnancy feels 'good' or 'bad' to them and they are rarely wrong.

OTHER CAUSES
Because repeated miscarriages are so traumatic for the couple a great deal of research is under way to try to find other causes that might be treatable. Recent work in Sweden has found that an asymptomatic infection with a large virus called T-mycoplasma is a cause of miscarriage, although many people with the infection seem to produce babies quite normally. The encouraging thing about this, if indeed it is a cause of miscarriage, is that a course of antibiotics can cure it.

Congenital malformations of the fetus are relatively common. About 5 per cent of early abortions have neural-tube defects (spina bifida or anencephaly – a related condition) and these women, once they have had one miscarriage, are more likely to have another similarly affected baby. It's also interesting that women who have had babies with a neural-tube defect have a higher incidence of miscarriage.

No doubt speculation will continue for years but real, positive steps are being made to try to predict which women might miscarry so that they can be helped before trouble sets in.

The other pain of a miscarriage

The loss of a fetus is a sad and terrible blow to any couple but is even more so to the infertile couple who have been trying so hard and to whom the baby is especially precious. Whether the physical loss is over a few minutes (early in pregnancy) or whether there is a real labour (later in pregnancy) the woman still knows she has lost what she most wanted. The knowledge that an early or mid-trimester fetus would not have lived anyway does nothing to take away the real emotional pain. Whenever the loss occurs the couple will need to grieve. Grief isn't all negative though – it's a normal and valuable way of overcoming the problem. Everyone thinks of the woman after a miscarriage, and so they should, but the man suffers too. Although he hasn't physically lost his baby, he certainly has lost it emotionally and will often put on a brave face to support his wife when deep down he too wants someone to put an arm around him and recognize the fact that it's equally his loss.

This state of affairs is often made all the worse because if the woman is in hospital, she's a 'patient' and so removed physically from her husband's comforting role and her comforting role on him. This is a time when a couple need to share their feelings and help each other through the quite natural grief they're experiencing. At this time the couple need caring for themselves and a close relative or friend can perform an invaluable role. Unfortunately, those who haven't been through a miscarriage have no real appreciation of the sense of loss, so even quite well-meaning and helpful friends and relatives shy away, because, they wrongly assume, the couple can easily have another baby. This is particularly poignant when, as is often the case, the parents and in-laws don't know about the infertility problem (because the couple have kept it from them) and so assume that 'another baby will come along'.

Many women are particularly worried and even panicky about a miscarriage because they imagine it means the end of their chances of having a child at all. This isn't true. A miscarriage means you've lost *this* baby but doesn't necessarily mean you'll lose another. On the contrary, if you're infertile the doctors helping you will tend to be even more vigilant about your future pregnancies, so the chances of losing another baby should be reduced. You'll always feel guilty about what you might have done or should not have done in order to have prevented the miscarriage, but the truth is that environmental or behavioural factors play so small a part in causing miscarriages that the chances are that whatever you did, you would still have lost the baby. Grieve by all means, but don't blame yourselves.

CHAPTER 8

The Impact on the Couple

Anyone who has been infertile or who has worked closely with those who are involuntarily childless will known that probably the greatest problem facing the couple is the group of conditions that could be called psychosocial. Historically, in many cultures a barren woman was a freak or an outcast. Society has deep-seated ideas and preconceptions about fertility and the infertile couple has to bear the brunt of these whether they like it or not. Public opinion still holds children as valuable and dotes on large families while at the same time preaching zero population growth. We live in confusing times but things are changing for the better from the infertile couple's point of view.

Personal and emotional problems

Infertility is a major crisis in life as you will know if you are infertile. If you are not you'll soon get the message when reading what infertile couples say (see pages 18–22). The inability to achieve any major goal in life always causes tensions or even more serious disturbances, depending on the importance of the goal. When the goal is regeneration, self-replication, the experience of parenthood or the opportunity to give to your children something of the good things your parents gave to you, then the crisis assumes major proportions. As with any crisis there are stages that the infertile

THE IMPACT ON THE COUPLE

couple goes through. No one can remain in a crisis state for ever, though people's reactions to and speed of recovery from any crisis depend greatly on what they had going for them in the first place. The duration and type of marriage you have, your personality types, your educational level and thus your expectations from life, your family back-up and your previous views of family life all influence the way you will react to childlessness. In response to the infertility crisis, couples tend to go one of several ways. They may come through with a stronger bond between them; they may find the whole thing too much and break up over it, though this is rare; or one or the other of them may become permanently affected by the problem in a way which endangers their interpersonal relationship, though not enough to break it up. There can be little doubt that over the centuries discreet infidelity has been one method of resolving the crisis (if the man is 'at fault') and there is no reason to suppose that this is less common today than it has ever been. Several women have told me how they have seriously considered (or actually entered into) an extra-marital affair simply to save their husband's feelings. This previously unthinkable behaviour is just one example of the lengths to which people will go to prevent the crisis from ruining their lives.

The personal and emotional problems associated with infertility usually emerge rather slowly which is in itself a blessing because it gives the couple time to come to terms with their feelings. Infertility has been compared with the actual loss of a child but I don't think this is a fair comparison because if your child is killed or dies quickly, you have no period of adjustment, you sense the loss very quickly, and you grieve. Also, hope is reborn from time to time in many an infertile couple and the dashing of these hopes causes another burst of mourning. We shall look at the grief suffered by infertile couples in more detail soon.

When a baby doesn't come along when you expect one, you quite naturally begin to wonder if you are going to be able to have one. Most couples assume that there's some temporary hold-up somewhere and that eventually all will be well. As the months go by though, the subject becomes more sensitive and the woman begins to dread the coming of her periods because when they appear it means she's not pregnant – again. After several months of this the couple starts wondering whether there might be any truth in the old wives' tales they hear and in all the advice that is offered so liberally by friends and relatives. But all this time they're not yet 'infertile' in their own eyes – the woman simply can't get pregnant.

The next big step involves taking the matter out of your own hands and putting it in the hands of the doctors. The vast majority of couples are represented only by the woman at this first contact with the medical profession and most women seeking help go first to their family doctors. How long the average couple waits and what happens once they see their doctor is discussed in Chapter 4.

Once you have committed yourself to the medical profession's care and attention you'll have entered phase two of the emotional conflicts. From now on you are 'patients' whereas previously you were a healthy couple that simply couldn't have a baby when you wanted to. At this stage the feelings begin to get more mixed and emotions to run high. Few people like consulting doctors, especially for something as personal as their inability to have children. Couples repeatedly tell me that they felt inadequate at this stage and that however nice the medical and other staff were, they worried whether deep down the staff were wondering if they really knew 'where to put it' and no one, especially in this sexually enlightened age, likes to think that people might see him or her as sexually inadequate or ignorant. However, infertility isn't usually a disorder of sexual performance, of course, and the vast majority of those attending infertility clinics are having intercourse perfectly normally, though some may be having it too infrequently to ensure a pregnancy within a reasonable time.

The merry-go-round of tests brings with it its own emotional traumas. 'What will the tests be like?' is a very common question I am asked but, amazingly, even very intelligent and outgoing people don't ask their doctors the simplest questions and as a result go home and worry, often unnecessarily, about what might happen to them. As we saw in Chapter 4, most of the tests are simple and painless. A very few involve a stay in hospital and only a tiny proportion of infertile couples ever have an operation in the real sense of the word. As each test is ordered, the couple (and especially the woman) looks forward to the results, half dreading, half longing for the next visit to the clinic to get the answers. A normal set of tests fills that partner with pleasure for a moment, only to have the joy dashed to pieces at the realization that it's their partner who's at fault.

Those of us who have children know how we suffer for them when they injure themselves or have an operation, for example, and infertile couples express the same kinds of feelings. 'I only hope he's normal', is a common remark women make or 'I couldn't bear to think of there being anything wrong with my husband'. Women, partly because of their conditioning and, I believe, partly because of their instincts, are much more protective towards their husbands in this way than their husbands are to them. There's also, of course, the natural, unspoken desire to have a normal, fertile husband and the tiny, inner voice that tells the woman she might have chosen a dud. Most men dislike the investigations more than their wives do, attend the clinics as infrequently as possible and are loath to undergo investigations and treatment unless they can't get out of it. This is ironic as the simplest investigation of all − a semen analysis − involves the man in so little and yet can be so valuable.

Slowly, as the tests prove to be negative and the treatments fail to produce results, the impact of being infertile hits the couple. The first reaction is usually one of surprise. Many couples, even after quite extensive medical attention, still feel sure that they'll conceive somehow, sometime, so to be told that the woman's tubes are irreversibly blocked or that her husband has poor sperms actually does come as a surprise. This reaction is very short-lived though and soon gives way to denial. 'It can't be right − they must have mixed up the specimens'; 'Let's try another doctor/clinic'; they must have got it wrong'. This period of incredulity gives a few days' respite, allowing the mind and spirit to recover from the shock − it is self-protection against the unendurable.

The next phase is that in which real emotional trouble sets in. The sense of denial gives way to desperation and anger, coupled with a sense of isolation from 'normal' people.

'Why us?' is the question couples ask now. 'What have we done to deserve it?' Religious women, especially, often experience self-recrimination for previous sexual misdemeanours and ask God if this is some kind of punishment for their evil ways. Both men and women who have had extramarital affairs wonder whether something could have arisen as a result of these experiences that has made them infertile. At this stage the couple has to make the decision as to whether to tell their friends and relatives and, if so, how. Even in today's so-called enlightened age people find it difficult to discuss infertility and the couple will be plied with platitudes about miracle babies and given straws to clutch at in the shape of better (often private) medical care in the hopes of overturning a stone that has not been previously touched. Most of the couple's friends will deal almost exclusively with the woman since they'll assume it is her fault. This is a time though when the couple needs comfort, sympathy and love to help them through their pain.

At this stage couples who have not already done so will start isolating themselves from situations in which children or babies feature. Some women can't even walk past an infant school without bursting into tears; will cross the road to avoid a woman with a pram; and can't bear to see the pregnant women at the hospital when they go for tests or treatment. The pain is especially acute at christenings and in other people's homes where there are children, and even living on a housing estate with lots of children can become unbearable. In the presence of all of these experiences many couples change their lifestyle - moving into an area where there are lots of people without children, changing jobs if they involve children (and for some reason many women attending infertility clinics seem to be teachers) or even refusing to go out much at all. The couple become isolated in their own house; the woman may have no one to turn to except her husband and he has enough problems of his own. They possibly get on each other's nerves and the relationship can suffer very seriously at this stage. It is around this time that the partner who is 'at fault' might embark on an extra-marital affair to prove to him or herself that he or she is still desirable, as sex between the partners may reach an all-time low at this stage.

The next phase is anger. 'Why us?' as a general sort of question may become 'why US?' in tones of resentment. The sense of having no control over what's going on is extremely frustrating and anger is soon aimed like grapeshot at all and sundry. Anger at doctors who are 'useless'; anger at the health service which is a dead loss; anger at parents who are horrible for putting the pressures on them; anger at people who tell them to 'pull themselves together and learn to live with it'; anger at the neighbours' children who are even more unbearable than usual; anger at the spouse's habits and idiosyncrasies; and so it goes on. A lot of the anger is against oneself if one is the 'guilty' party and against the sympathetic, understanding partner simply because (s)he *is* sympathetic and understanding. The way to get rid of this anger is to verbalize it with a third person. Best of all is to go to a self-help group – they'll all have been through it and will know exactly how you feel. The main thing at this stage is to get it all off your chest. Don't bottle up your feelings or you'll become depressed.

As the days or weeks go by (and the rate at which people work their way through all these quite normal stages of the crisis varies enormously), you'll be left with a sense of loss as your main emotion. For the outsider it's difficult to see how you can feel a sense of loss over something you've never had but the truth is rather different. We have all experienced 'family' even if we haven't experienced parenting and once we make the decision to have children we've committed ourselves implicitly to wanting to be parents. We do this either to give our proposed children all the things we had or alternatively those we didn't have but, either way, infertility robs us of this opportunity and so it's a deep sense of loss that overwhelms the infertile couple. This loss produces a sense of disorientation (because you'd always assumed your life would run along quite another course), deprivation, sadness, jealousy and personal hopelessness.

All of these feelings are exactly parallel to the feelings of those who have recently been bereaved and it's at this stage that infertile couples are often the least well understood. Outsiders can understand all the stages this far and can even sympathize, but they have great difficulty in understanding that the infertile couple is grieving for the death of their unborn child. This grief has been called 'unfocused' by Peter Houghton, Director of the National Association for the Childless in Britain, because the infertile sufferers, unlike the couple who have lost an actual child, have nothing to bury. When an actual child is lost, everyone rallies around and the grief is shared. The infertile couple, however, often grieves alone and that makes it all the harder to bear. It's even worse when the infertility can be 'blamed' on one partner because as well as bearing the grief, that person has all the additional fears of being left, being blamed for ever, being a failure in the eyes of the one they love most and so on.

Infertility is usually a blameless matter, of course, but this is of little consolation to the one whose 'fault' it is. Not only does the 'guilty' party grieve but the fertile one does too. After all, he or she has been deprived of parenthood too, and knowing that you're fertile, but not with the one you want to be, can be even more hurtful than being the one with a medical diagnosis to cling on to. As one infertile man put it, 'the trouble is doubled by my wife's reaction. Not only is she barren through no fault of her own. In addition to the burden of knowing that I am less than a man, my wife's suffering, her mourning, is attributable to something for which I am to blame. It is almost as if I have betrayed her in some subtle but very final way.'

But grief after the diagnosis of infertility has to be worked through just as does grief at any other time. The trouble with childlessness is that it's the loss of an *experience* that you're mourning. Normal bereavement isn't one's fault but childlessness is seen by some outsiders to be so and that makes the grieving all the harder. Add to all of this the fact that the childless person has never really been 'normal' (unlike the man who has lost his wife, for example) in the eyes of society and it's easy to see why society finds it hard to mourn with the infertile. Grief is normal and essential and runs to a classical pattern, although it's hard for those in the throes of it to see it at the time. Denial and disbelief, anxiety, restlessness, anger and guilt all become intermingled and may never be completely forgotten for the remainder of the person's life.

It's encouraging to know that everyone in the same position experiences identical feelings and that after the tears, the suffering and the repeated chewing-over of the problem the grief subsides over weeks and months depending on the individual and his environment. Eventually, recovery sets in and life seems brighter. The couple starts going out again, makes new friendships, starts new jobs and the man and woman try to brace themselves for the periodic reminders at birthdays, family gatherings and other occasions when their own loss seems most painful. Some people, especially men, say that they never really come to terms with their infertility – indeed there is no treatment for the long-term pain. Only when you have come through this recovery stage should you ever start considering adopting or fostering because until then you won't be ready to embark on such a major step, even though you may think you are.

Finally, the conflicts resolve and the couple accepts its new status. The man and woman then get on with life and apart from the few times when external situations trigger off the pain again their lives can proceed on an even keel. Eventually, all the negative feelings about life and their own loss of esteem are lost and life begins to have a purpose again. The 'pain' of infertility can't be cured by drugs yet the number of people who take anti-depressants, tranquillizers or other drugs during their grief period is enormous. This may not necessarily be the best way of handling the grief because the final cure must lie in coming to terms with the pain and dealing with it in the context of one's personality. If you have a good, sympathetic family doctor, work through this trying time with his help and only use drugs if you are absolutely sure you have to. Drugs are only a crutch and you won't want to have to go around on crutches for long – after all, you're not a cripple.

The effects on your sex life

Although some couples say that their shared emotions and troubles bring them closer together in every way and improve their sex lives, this is not the norm. Most couples undergoing investigations and treatment and the stages of emotional reaction along to the final diagnosis of infertility suffer a body blow to their sexual relationship. This is hardly surprising since infertility is all about sex and however much we may kid ourselves that sex is for pleasure, when infertility arises it brings home the realization that sex is really for something much deeper – self-replication and continuity.

One of the earliest knocks to the couple is that which assaults their sexuality. The way boys are brought up is to believe that men are expected to behave in a certain way to women and vice versa. This expectation is enhanced at puberty as we develop our physical and genital masculinity and feminity. One of the major concepts that we carry into adult life is that we'll form some sort of pair bond and that the woman will bear children. Many infertile women express a deep sense of failure *as women* and parallel feelings are, of course, expressed by men. As one woman put it, 'From that moment, I was neuter, I wasn't a woman with a valid role. I was an IT.' This blow to the person's sexuality is reflected in his or her whole view of him/herself. Some people already have a very poor view of themselves even before the revelation of their infertility and this discovery simply adds another nail to their coffin of poor self-esteem. It's quite normal for even healthy, well-balanced couples to go through a stage of feeling that they are useless for anything and some people lose all confidence in their looks, sexual attraction and even their ability to do *anything* right.

All of these negative feelings are reflected in the bedroom, which is, after all, where all the 'trouble' started. As we saw earlier, problems begin with the keeping of a temperature chart. However important this is seen to be by the couple it soon attains the dimensions of a bogey because after a very few months of 'hitting the jackpot' on the most fertile night, the game loses its lustre and the chart begins to rule your life. I mentioned a way of overcoming this to some degree on page 119 and that is by taking your temperature in the evening, so enabling you to be able to use the evenings for sex rather than the time before breakfast when the act is usually rushed and it is certainly not convenient to lie in bed for half an hour afterwards (for the woman) or for the husband to go to sleep after sex. But even this doesn't take away the fact that you have to declare publicly on the chart every time you make love and for most of us this takes a bit of getting used to. 'Will the doctor tell us off for not having sex on such and such a night?', 'We just didn't feel like it on D-day' and 'My wife spends so much time charting her temperature that I dread the nights around ovulation, because however good sex may be all the rest of the month I often don't feel like it on the right nights and I feel as though I'm performing to order' are just some of the many heartfelt comments one hears. Even after the doctor has learned all he needs to know from the temperature chart, the woman will often keep a mental chart in her head and by subterfuge 'encourage' her husband on certain specific nights of the month. Once the man gets wind of this it often leads to fights and a further deterioration in their sexual relationship.

There is no doubt that it's best to follow your normal sexual urges if you want to prevent a steady decline in your sex life. Be guided by how you feel at the time and don't save up sperms; it does very little good. If you feel like making love, do so, whatever the time of the month. Just because you're trying to get pregnant doesn't mean that you have to lose sight of what sex has been for up until then – pleasure. There's probably more sexual disturbance caused by couples trying to separate 'getting pregnant' sex from 'for pleasure' sex than from anything else in this area of infertility. The more concerned you become, the less you'll enjoy sex, the more likely the woman's ovulation is to fail, the more difficult it'll be for the man to obtain and sustain an erection and eventually he might well even become incapable of one.

Many men find it difficult to 'do their stuff' for post-coital tests and for producing semen specimens but these difficulties are not permanent. The higher levels of the brain are delicately set and have such powerful control over how we perform sexually (especially in the case of men) that it doesn't take much to get the balance slightly wrong and so produce temporary sexual dysfunctions. Small amounts of alcohol can help at these times as they tend to reduce inhibitions and so enable the couple to relax more.

But all these temporary and annoying problems can be further heightened once a final diagnosis of infertility has been made. Some infertile women describe themselves as feeling 'barren', 'dead' and so on and some men are very sensitive about 'firing blanks', as it were. Many couples feel cheated as they had previously taken so much care over contraception for many years and now realize what a mockery it all was. Many couples go off sex completely for weeks and then say how sad, negative and empty they feel when they eventually resume intercourse. Normal, enjoyable, spontaneous sex may take months to come back and you have to guide each other as to when to restart. The fertile partner often offers sex as a softener to the infertile partner but the recipient can't cope with this gesture until a reasonable time has elapsed and (s)he has worked through her or his grief.

It sometimes helps to reorganize your sex life if making love in bed reminds you too much of your failed efforts to conceive. Try other places as a way of getting back into the swing of your old sex life. Some people find oral sex and mutual masturbation are a good way to get started again because they have no obvious connections with 'baby making' and are purely sex for sex's sake. And this is probably the sign that you're on the mend. If you can come to terms with sex for sex's sake, which is after all exactly what you'd been doing for years before starting to try to conceive, then you're on the way to a normal sex life again.

Infertility is a crisis but the grief it produces isn't a terminal illness. It's a body blow at the most vigorous, healthy and optimistic time of our lives and at a time when we least expect trouble. But life must go on. Give in to your emotions and work through the terrible times. Get help from others who understand the pains and then start to rebuild your life – you enjoyed it before and you will again.

CHAPTER 9

Artificial Insemination (AI)

'Insemination' literally means to sow seed into something. The normal way in which human seed is 'sown' is, of course, by intercourse. Some infertile couples though, even after all the relevant tests, are still judged to have no chance of having a baby other than by artificial insemination (AI).

There are several groups of infertile couples who'll benefit from AI. Obviously if for some reason the man can't place his sperms inside the woman's vagina (see page 46) he's not going to get her pregnant and will need help to get the sperms to the right place. A few women have a normal uterus and tubes yet have vaginal abnormalities that prevent normal intercourse. Some men with poor sperm counts can have their semen spun down at a high speed in a centrifuge and the 'concentrated sperms' given by AI. Some of these men will also stand a better chance of impregnating their partners if the first few spurts of ejaculate only are used because it has been found that in certain men this early fluid is richer in fertile sperms. (For more details of this so-called split-ejaculate method, which need not involve AI, see page 56.) AI can be used in couples in whom there are proven sperm antibodies which, if washed off, leave the sperms more fertile (see page 88). Clearly such sperms can only then be given by AI. But the biggest group of couples who eventually end up in AID clinics are those where the husband produces too few or even no sperms at all, yet has a normal wife.

ARTIFICIAL INSEMINATION

Having said all this though, only about 2,000 couples in the UK are currently being treated using AI. There are thought to be 4,000 couples awaiting artificial insemination by donor in the UK today. It's impossible to estimate how many babies are born by AI because of the confidentiality of the records but it is estimated that 15,000 babies are born by this method in the US each year, and the UK figure is probably around 2,000.

What *is* certain is that the number of babies born as a result of AID is rising substantially as more infertile couples turn to this method as a way out of their dilemma. This has been encouraged at least to some extent, by the appearance of commercial AID clinics on both sides of the Atlantic.

Before any infertility expert suggests AI, whether the sperms will eventually come from the husband (in which case it's called AIH) or a donor (AID), he'll want to be sure that the basic tests indicate that it is necessary. The couple will have been examined carefully and a full history taken. The woman will have had her tubes checked to see that they are normal and her ovulation time ascertained using a temperature chart or the cervical mucus method or both. She may well also have had an endometrial biopsy or her blood progesterone checked to ensure that she is actually ovulating. There's little point in going through the lengthy and emotionally fraught experience of AI if you aren't ovulating and therefore stand no chance of conceiving anyway.

If the husband is to be the donor of the sperms he'll have to be examined for a varicocele (page 82), have a batch of hormone blood tests done (page 138), two or more semen analyses and even perhaps a biopsy of his testes. Should any or all of these tests prove that he is unlikely to be fertile, then the couple will have to decide whether or not they want to proceed to AID.

Artificial insemination isn't a new procedure – it has been practised in animal husbandry for centuries. At the end of the last century secret experiments were perfomed in humans for the first time but it wasn't until very recently that the subject became popular within and outside the medical world. Today, increasing numbers of infertile couples seek AID as an easy way out of their problems. This isn't a good idea, as we shall see. AID should remain a last choice and not a first choice, for all kinds of reasons.

How it's done

There are two main ways of using semen for artificial insemination, either of which can be used whether the sperms come from the husband or a donor.

In the first method, the man ejaculates into a container and the semen is drawn up into a plastic syringe. The contents are then placed on to or in the cervix. In the second, the semen is placed in a cap which is held against the cervix. This is the method especially suitable for use at home for AIH (see below).

There is conflicting evidence as to which is the better but some experts feel that if there is thought to be a hostile factor in the woman's cervical mucus, then the direct placing of the semen into the uterus probably gives her a better chance of conceiving. This is not as easy as it sounds because semen injected into the cavity of the uterus irritates it and induces the production of naturally occurring substances called prostaglandins. These make the uterus contract and expel the semen so you might not achieve anything. Those in favour of the technique argue that it at least gives a few sperms the chance of finding their way into the woman's tubes before expulsion occurs and that this might be the only hope in a woman with hostile mucus and a sub-fertile husband.

Most doctors simply place the semen on the cervix and in either case the woman is asked to remain lying down on the couch where the insemination took place for about half an hour. Both these procedures are painless and are no more distressing than having a manual internal examination.

Artificial Insemination by Husband (AIH)

If you're going to try AIH you should be aware of the disadvantages in order to help you overcome them. First, the husband has to be able and willing to masturbate into a container and second, the wife has to be sure that she is ovulating and then take her husband's specimen along to the clinic or hospital. This can involve quite a feat of timing and understandably a number of husbands find they are reluctant or can't perform 'on demand'. This may mean putting the whole thing off a month, to the dismay of the woman and often of her doctor too.

One way of overcoming these problems is to do it yourself at home. This isn't difficult, once you've been shown how and has been made possible by the invention of a special cap (Davidson's cap) that fits snugly over the cervix. Any woman who can use a contraceptive diaphragm will be able to use this type of cap easily and a woman who can't can learn in about five minutes. Some women have the cap inserted by a doctor.

The device is a plastic diaphragm with a fine tube in its centre. The tube is about four inches long and projects down the vaginal cavity (outside the vulva) when the cap is in place. The man should abstain from ejaculating for four days. At the appointed time (usually on alternate days twice a cycle, starting before ovulation; days 11 and 13 or 12 and 14 are best) the husband then ejaculates into a jar provided by the clinic and after drawing up the semen into a plastic syringe, injects it down the tube with the cervical cap in place in his wife's vagina and clamps it off. This places the sperms right up against the cervix where they stay until the cap is removed. This method can be used in a clinic or hospital but is especially easy for domestic use. It's particularly useful and liable to result in a pregnancy if the husband's semen volume is low or if he has a low sperm count. It has been known for several years now that the first few spurts of semen in an ejaculation are richer in fertile sperms than the rest of a man's ejaculate, so if after trying the method outlined above for a few months you still get no results, try the split-ejaculate method and use only the early-emitted fluid in the cap.

In this method the man prepares two jars and ejaculates the first few spurts into the first and the rest into the other – the contents of the second jar are discarded and those of the first used for injecting into the cap.

Clearly there are no legal or moral problems associated with this method, except perhaps for orthodox Jews or Roman Catholics, to whom masturbation is unacceptable. Increasing numbers of Catholics are getting permission to use AIH if a doctor says that the method is their best or only chance of conceiving. Most Jewish rabbis will give a dispensation for this method because the importance of having children is judged to be greater than the sin involved in masturbation.

Whether or not AIH actually works is a matter of debate. A survey published in 1976 followed 158 couples who used the method and found that only about one in ten women became pregnant. There were fifteen pregnancies. Of those who did conceive, more than half did so within two cycles and fifteen women had conceived within five months. However, 113 of the 158 had stopped treatment by the end of the fifth month. The pregnancy rates were the same whether the couple were using the cap or having semen placed in the cervix. The researchers concluded that the pregnancy rates using these two methods were no better than those they would have expected with normal intercourse in the couples studied.

Having said this though many couples find that once they get used to the 'plumbing' aspects of these methods they relax more and some even report getting pregnant on holiday after leaving their cap behind by mistake. AIH remains a minority treatment for infertility and probably offers very few advantages over normal intercourse. This cannot, of course, be said for AID.

Artificial Insemination by Donor (AID)

AID is an increasingly popular way of overcoming infertility that is caused by the inability of the man to produce enough good-quality sperms to impregnate his partner. However, there are moral, religious and philosophical problems as we shall see.

In spite of this, about 2,000 children are born each year in the UK as a result of AID. Just how many are born as a result of discreet infidelity on the wife's part (often to save her husband's feelings) will never be known.

AID involves the insemination of a donor's semen into the vagina of a fertile woman. As with AIH, it is essential to know when the woman is ovulating so that the insemination can be timed to coincide with ovulation and so increase the chances of a pregnancy. Perhaps it should be stressed that AID is not a treatment for the infertile *man*. This is a method that by-passes the man in order to enable his wife to get pregnant.

SELECTING SUITABLE COUPLES
Most couples for AID select themselves after all other doors seem closed to them. It appears that AID is of greatest appeal to the middle classes as nearly half of all couples come from the highest socio-economic groups. Once the couple has come forward and expressed an interest, the doctors involved take care to satisfy themselves that they are suitable for AID. Three main questions have to be answered. Does the couple have a

real infertility problem likely to be helped by AID; is the woman potentially fertile; and is the couple sufficiently well informed to be able to accept the implications of AID?

On the first point, men are assessed as being good candidates if (1) they have very low sperm counts or no sperms at all on repeated analyses; (2) if they have a high sperm density with no other abnormalities; (3) if their sperms are abnormal; (4) if they are carriers of lethal or harmful genes; and (5) if they are ejaculating into their bladders yet retrieved sperms do not produce a pregnancy after AIH. The majority of candidates for AID fall into the first category.

Counselling and careful discussion is needed to establish whether the couple really understand what AID is and what they are getting involved in. It is generally felt that the couple should have a stable, mature relationship and be able to discuss the matter freely. There is no point in having AID 'to save a marriage' – in fact it can have the opposite effect if the couple is not prepared. The wife's health is screened to ensure that a pregnancy wouldn't harm her and that she wouldn't stand a greater than average chance of having an abnormal or ill baby. The man should ideally have come to terms with his infertility by the time AID is embarked on or otherwise he might well resent the baby once it is born. The woman for her part has to accept deep down that the baby will be at least partly hers genetically but never her husband's, and this can prove difficult. Some women use AID as a revenge against their husband's inability to give them a baby.

The couple should have cleared any moral, religious or philosophical doubts they may have had and lastly, they shouldn't be too concerned about donor selection. This seems rather a list but if you can honestly say you're happy on all of these points, then you're ready for AID. If you can't, you need more time, more advice, more information and lots more discussion with your partner. AID is not something to be gone into lightly.

WHERE DO THE SPERMS COME FROM?
Donors are carefully selected and screened for good intelligence, physical and mental fitness and freedom from familial diseases. In many centres medical students are used. The semen is analysed for its quality and then used fresh, or deep frozen and put into a sperm bank. Technology has come along way since semen was first frozen in 1938 and the current

freezing techniques do nothing to harm normal sperms. Abnormal ones are killed off by the freezing and thawing process but this can only be an advantage. The number of live births produced by using fresh or frozen semen is exactly the same.

Some people feel that the donor should have proven his fertility before being accepted but this is not necessary in fact because semen analysis is at least as good a predictor of fertility in healthy males as is previous paternity. Many centres pay their donors but some people feel this is undesirable in case, as has occurred in the US with blood donors, certain undesirable individuals simply 'do it for the money'. The screening and control of the whole system is so meticulous in the UK that this argument doesn't apply and most experts feel that donors should be paid. At the moment, they receive about £8 per donation.

Two things are important when selecting donors. The first is the selection of the right men to be donors and the second is the matching of the right donor to the right woman. Obviously the first procedure must ensure that the men selected are very fertile and have a minimal chance of producing physically or mentally abnormal children. Highly intelligent men are not necessarily desirable as donors because although an intelligent child is an advantage to intelligent parents he can be the cause of real unhappiness in a dull family. Blood grouping and certain other specialized screening tests are performed on all donors and some centres even look at their chromosomes. The risk of the birth of genetically abnormal children to AID mothers has been calculated to be one to two per thousand, which is what one would expect in normal marriages so it doesn't seem justifiable to perform expensive chromosomal testing on otherwise normal donors with no family history of genetic disorders.

The number of donations that any one donor makes is also regulated because it is feared that, in theory at least, a single donor impregnating many women could cause problems of inbreeding if people of his genetic stock were to meet and marry. This is a tiny risk in practice but is increasing as AID becomes more popular. It has been calcuated by an expert committee set up to examine AID that with 2,000 children a year being born in the UK by this method, if each donor were responsible for five children the chances of a subsequent incestuous marriage occurring are about once in fifty to a hundred years. It has also been reported that a survey of the blood groups of the families of rhesus-negative women in a London suburb revealed that no less than 30 per cent of babies could not have been the children of the father named in the birth register. So clearly the problems of this kind produced by AID are likely to be infinitely smaller than those produced by irregular unions in the general population.

It is not difficult to match the donor father for race, height, eye colour, build and hair colour and any good centre will do at least this. A very small panel of donors can in fact supply all the sperms that are needed in the vast majority of cases.

CONFIDENTIALITY
Infertility clinics and especially those carrying out AID are organized to maintain strict confidentiality. The name of the donor is kept secret from the recipient and that of the recipient from the donor. However, because of the way that society is evolving, this may not always be the case in the future. We are more open than ever about such matters and look like becoming increasingly so. The common policy in adoption today is early sympathetic disclosure of the child's origin and this has evolved in a very few years from a previous policy of complete secrecy. In the future children and adults will undoubtedly assert their right to know who their parents really were, particularly as AID becomes more widespread, and people begin to question what they have until now considered their assumed parentage. How can one deny a person that knowledge as an adult? Lastly there can be a crisis of confidentiality between the donor and his future (or even present) wife. If a married man intends donating semen he must ensure that his wife can cope with the implications. The problems are more difficult for the (more commonly) unmarried donor. He has to gamble that his future wife will be able to accept his past actions and some women have difficulty in doing so.

THE TREATMENT ITSELF
AID is straightforward and painless. The woman first ensures that she is ovulating and that she knows when this occurs each month (see page 113). This is almost essential because the success rates of AID rise enormously if ovulation is certain at the time. In fact, in some clinics, if the woman's cycle is not regular and the timing of ovulation is difficult to predict she'll be given clomiphene with or without a gonadotrophin to

produce definite ovulation. She phones the clinic a day or two before ovulation to arrange an appointment at which fresh or previously deep-frozen semen is instilled into her vagina. (There are several methods of doing this, as outlined above on page 174.) She then remains lying down for about half an hour before going home. It is important not to bathe or douche after the treatment for at least twelve hours, and some doctors advise making love on the same day so that should the woman become pregnant it'll be impossible to know whether it was by the husband or by the donor. It is very uncommon for a woman to conceive in the first cycle, three to five cycles being the average time it takes. About 70 per cent of women are pregnant three months after AID. If after six months of trying the woman is still not pregnant, other tests may have to be done to search for an overlooked cause of infertility although it has been found that the stress of the procedure renders some women anovulatory and that they need to have their ovulation encouraged.

If donor inseminations are performed several times per cycle the cost begins to mount up but most couples feel it well worth while. The emotional and other costs of repeated, timed visits to the clinic can be tedious but by this stage the woman is usually so determined to succeed that these are easily accepted.

THE PREGNANCY

Once you conceive by AID your pregnancy will run exactly as it would have done had you conceived by intercourse. However, every pregnancy carries some risks and AID won't protect you from these. You may miscarry or have a baby with a defect but the chances are no higher than had you conceived a baby the usual way.

THE LAW

Legally AID is still in a confused state worldwide. Only fourteen states in the US have accepted it and one actually deems it to be adultery. In the UK there are no laws against AID and provided it is carried out with the husband's consent it cannot constitute grounds for divorce on the basis of adultery or unreasonable conduct.

Strictly speaking an AID baby should be registered at birth in its mother's name only, the father's name being left blank. The full birth certificate would therefore imply that the child was illegitimate though the shortened form would conceal this. Technically the child should then be adopted by the couple. However, in practice babies born within a marriage are deemed to be legitimate and provided that there has been intercourse while the treatment was taking place there is no way of knowing whether it is the husband's child or not. In strict legal terms the couple is breaking the law by entering the husband's name as the father but if you are worried about this you should discuss it with your solicitor, especially if you foresee any problems about inheritance in the future. You'll need to think about inheritance in the event of your ever having children of your own. There can also be problems if you ever seek advice in the future on your own behalf or that of your child on matters of genetic counselling.

With the passing of the Children Act in 1975 the adoption register must now be opened to disclose to an adopted child his natural mother's name and a similar legal change will probably come about to clarify the position on AID babies. As the law stands now, your child will never know that you are not both his parents unless you choose to tell him. Many clinics even go so far as to burn their AID clinic notes as soon as the woman becomes pregnant.

ARE THERE DANGERS?
We've discussed the dangers of abnormal babies and seen that the chances are no higher than for other births. Many couples are worried about sexually transmitted diseases but there is almost no danger of this because all donors are carefully screened and each semen sample is checked before use. In the unlikely event of an infection occurring, treatment with antibiotics is effective.

THE MORAL PROBLEM
For those who worry about such things, the moral questions raised by AID are numerous. They are summarized in this brief extract from a leading theological expert at a Ciba Foundation Symposium on AID held in London in 1972. He said, 'It is a matter for serious concern that a new medical practice, grounded upon scientific research and so upon a high value put upon truth, should in fact result in, and to some extent require, deceit and uncertainty. The secrecy involved in AID obliges the practitioner, the husband and wife, and the donor to conspire together to deceive the child and society as to the

child's true parentage and his genetic identity. Trust is violated, credibility is undermined, and this is a serious ethical matter.'

In addition to the morals that relate to the child there are those relating to the couple and their marriage. Most of us in the western world agree that the link between marriage and begetting children is extremely close – and most of us want to keep it that way. Today, even though conception can occur without genital contact (AID), some people still see AID as basically adulterous *in principle* if not in fact. If you accept AID you have to accept that the exclusive sexual bond between husband and wife excludes only actual intercourse with another and that the sperms from the donor are simply a sort of fertilizing treatment supplied by a doctor. In practice many couples can only come to terms with AID by considering it as a kind of medical treatment and so ignoring the deeper moral dilemmas.

None of these moral questions is easy and each one of us has to answer them according to his own conscience. The Roman Catholic Church and orthodox Judaism both forbid the use of AID though the Jews, because procreation is considered so important, accept the offspring as legitimate whilst the Catholics see the children as illegitimate and the act itself as adultery.

EMOTIONAL REACTIONS

Emotionally AID can often be the icing on a cake already made of dynamite. In a survey of AID couples carried out in 1976 it was found that 80 per cent of the husbands had guilt feelings. They also felt self-accusatory because their wives were the victims of their (male) inadequacy. Most of the wives had considerable guilt feelings because they didn't share their husband's failure in reproduction. The researchers found, however, that the women's guilt feelings could be reduced if their husbands went to the clinic with them, if they talked a lot to the doctors and if they found the surroundings congenial and confidential. All of the people studied wanted to have AID rather than to adopt so that the child would at least be like the wife. All of those questioned felt the child would be more 'ours' as compared with an adopted one.

Their interest in the donors was almost all on a simple level. They all wanted to know about his mental and physical attributes, and because they were paying indirectly they had no resentment towards the donor.

Reactions to the prospect of AID vary enormously. Some couples get cold feet at the last moment and find they can't go through with the whole thing and put off the appointment. It's so final after all, and the chances of getting pregnant are so relatively high that most women want to give their husband 'one last chance' to make it *his* baby. This often leads to their repeatedly delaying the final act.

Once the procedure has been effected and a pregnancy doesn't materialize it's common for the woman to start wondering if it's her husband who is at fault after all. She may start to panic – the definite cure-all might not work; could this mean permanent childlessness? Once conception occurs, most women are so pleased with the positive outcome that they soon forget the negative thoughts they may have had and start to wonder what the baby will be like. Many mothers tell of their fears that the baby won't look at all like either of them and that people will say 'where did you get that?' or make snide remarks about the milkman! As the birth approaches the going gets more difficult for many husbands. At last the whole business is coming to a satisfactory end point with the woman fulfilled and involved with the new arrival, but it's a difficult time for some of the 'non-fathers' because here is living proof that they themselves can't father a child. Other infertile men, of course, enter into the spirit of the event and are genuinely joyful, not only for their wives' sake but for their own. After all, as one husband put it, 'We may not have sown the seed together but we've certainly reaped the harvest and it's wonderful!'

It's interesting to note that couples who have an AID baby have far more stable marriages than those who have children normally. In one US survey a follow-up study of 800 couples who had AID showed only one divorce and that couple had applied for AID and had been turned down. Experts believe that AID marriages are more stable because (1) the couple are still together after years of unhappiness and disappointment over the infertility itself with its tests and treatments; (2) they have come to terms with the husband's sterility and have decided to have another man's child; and (3) the husband wants desperately to make things up to his wife as the trouble is his 'fault'. As one expert put it, 'for the man, social fatherhood is more important than genetic fatherhood'.

AID, for those who can accept it, is a very real and

increasingly popular alternative to childlessness. It can produce a baby which resembles one of the partners, enables the woman to experience pregnancy and birth and, if regulated ethically, should present no hazard to society as a whole. The fact that people come back again for AID and even sometimes ask for the same donor speaks for itself.

CHAPTER 10

What If All Else Fails?

It has been estimated in the US that about 60 per cent of all those seeking aid for infertility are helped and eventually have a child. There is no reason to believe that the UK figure is substantially different and there are indications that it might even be higher. Even allowing for those who are subsequently successful when using AID, there still remains a core of infertile couples (about 35 per cent) that remain involuntarily childless for no apparent reason. A tiny fraction of these eventually adopt or foster but the majority will have to come to terms with remaining childless. In this chapter we're going to look at all three alternatives.

There are basically two options open to you if you've been through the tests and treatments generally available and still can't have a child of your own. You can consider becoming parents to someone else's child or you can come to terms with child-free living. There are two ways of parenting children not born to you – adoption and fostering. The decision as to which to go for is often very difficult but there are signs that the second option is growing in popularity – if only because the first cannot supply the growing need.

Adoption and fostering are not primarily ways of supplying babies to couples who think they want them. On the contrary, they are ways in which children who are in need of care can get it in the best possible way. The first duty of the agencies involved in adoption or fostering is to the child – not to the prospective parents. Because of this, the screening methods are rigorous and are procedures that we as a society have decided upon and wish to see implemented. No one wants to see children dragged from one unsuitable home to the next, so clearly the preparatory work has to be meticulous. This very careful selection, made all the more poignant because there are so few babies to adopt, may put you off thinking about adoption or fostering. Don't let it. Someone has to be chosen and it might well be you.

The first choice of most childless couples is adoption because this provides a child which is 'theirs' both legally and in practice. Unfortunately, far fewer infertile couples end up adopting than would like to, so fostering must now be seen as a realistic alternative.

Adoption

Adoption first became legal in this country in 1926 when it was mostly arranged on a private basis and over the intervening years about half a million children have been adopted in the UK. The peak year for adoptions was 1968 when nearly 27,000 children were placed in families. Since then the numbers have declined to 9,284 in 1981. But within this figure there have been substantial changes. Whereas the number of children adopted by people unrelated to them has dropped, the number being adopted within their own family has gone up. The numbers of parents adopting step-children or illegitimate children of their own have increased dramatically as more marriages end in divorce and remarriage and increasing numbers of young girls decide to keep their illegitimate babies. In 1981, 54 per cent of all adoptions were by one or both of the natural parents.

The trouble is that most childless couples are under the impression that there are lots of babies around to adopt. This was so until the late 1960s but is no longer the case. Because of abortion law reforms, better contraception and the fall in numbers of single mothers placing their babies with adoption agencies (there's been a sustained decline and a 70 per cent fall in the US in the last decade) there were only about 2,000 babies needing new parents in the whole of England and Wales in 1978. Unfortunately, even doctors and other professionals working in this field don't realize just how few of these babies there actually are and so still give a falsely rosy

WHAT IF ALL ELSE FAILS?

picture to childless couples. This is further compounded by the relatives and friends of the couples who, having the 1950s and 1960s memories in front of them, assume that the supply of babies is as it was then. This is absolutely not so.

To be horribly blunt about adopting a baby, the position today is that unless you are under thirty-three years of age, reasonably conventional, and prepared to accept a coloured or handicapped baby, there's a very slim chance of your adopting at all.

If you're thinking about adoption, there are two things you ought to bear in mind from day one. First, adoption lasts a lifetime and isn't something to be undertaken lightly; second, there are far more would-be adopters than babies to adopt. For every healthy baby there is a queue of would-be parents and this means that the adoption process can be frustrating and time-consuming. Having said this though, there are lots of school-age children and young children with physical or mental handicaps who desperately need good parents.

WHY ADOPT?
The childless couple, perhaps frustrated, amazed and bitter, often turns to adoption as an 'easy' way out of their dilemma. This is unwise for several reasons. As we saw in Chapter 8 it's perfectly normal for a couple who have been told they can't have children to mourn. The deep sense of their loss, their lost hopes and expectations for their children and their lost place in posterity all weigh heavily in the early weeks and months. This is a time when the infertile spouse feels intensely guilty at having let his or her partner down; at which marital relationships are often at their worst; at which anger is let loose at the most convenient person; at which the couple's envy of friends is at its highest; and so on. The 'innocent' party in the couple feels desperately let down and often dares not discuss the problem with anyone. This is no time to think about venturing forth into the adoption world. Adoption is no way to ease the pain and bring yourselves closer together. Normal child/parent relationships can't occur when a couple is still mourning and in fact adoption under these circumstances has been found to lead to failure in far too many cases.

If you go into adoption in this frame of mind you'll find yourself ending up blaming the child for everything that goes wrong. You may also feel that the child isn't right for you, which will lead to your rejecting it. Some couples interpret the child's behaviour as a deliberate attack on them as a couple and counselling and therapy very often don't work at this stage. The timing of adoption is absolutely crucial for infertile couples. Unfortunately, relatives, doctors and other professional workers, unaware of the depth of the feelings surrounding the diagnosis of infertility, keep up the pressure to adopt and many couples enter the system too early. They then get bitter when they are 'rejected' but in all honesty many look back and see that they simply weren't ready.

You'll know you're ready to embark on the long road to adoption if you can discuss your infertility easily and in a relaxed way; if you can sort out your motives for adoption clearly; if you know what sort of child you'd like (realizing that you'll have to be flexible); if you have thought about the implications of the child being joined by one of yours (should you eventually become pregnant); and if you are rational and open in dealing with adoption workers. Unless you have sorted yourself out in these areas, you'd be better off waiting before making an application to adopt.

HOW TO GO ABOUT IT
Once you've decided to apply to adopt, the first thing to do is to write or telephone the British Agencies for Adoption and Fostering, 11 Southwark St., London SE1 1RQ (Tel 01-407 8800) and ask them for their booklet *Adopting a Child*. This contains a list of all the adoption agencies in this country. As with many social services, the placing of children by adoption was formalized by voluntary agencies. Today, more and more work in this area is being done by local authorities but the forty-six voluntary agencies still place many adopted children. The societies range from large national bodies like Dr Barnardo's to church-based ones covering one religion or even a single diocese. Clearly if one of them only accepts Catholic applicants and you are not a Catholic there's no point in applying, but at this stage you should contact all the suitable agencies direct and ask what the situation is. Some will say that their lists are closed (because they have too many applicants for too few babies) and others will take you on their books and start off the screening process.

Remember, adoption agencies supply parents for children and not the other way round, so the agency has to find out if you are going to be right for the child for whom they have a statutory and moral responsibility. They'll also want to be sure that adoption is right for you. Doing this job of sorting out who'll be the best parent for any given child is almost impossibly difficult. At times it'll seem as though you're being interrogated but the demand is so great and the supply so small that the agencies simply don't have to take all comers and have to draw lines somewhere.

You'll be asked to go through several interviews and to have a thorough medical examination to ensure that you're basically healthy. After all, the child has already lost one set of parents so it's only fair to ensure that his adoptive parents are healthy. Because teenage children are physically and emotionally so taxing, all adoption agencies place an upper age limit on those would-be parents of babies they accept so that they'll still be young and healthy when the child is in his teens. In practice this means that if you're over forty you stand very little chance and many agencies have lowered their age limit to thirty-five and even thirty-three. By law you have to be over twenty-one and if your ages are very different this could go against you. The age qualifications can be a real hardship for the infertile couple because most of them aren't through their tests and treatment much before the age of thirty-three, by which time they often find they're too old to adopt.

If an agency doesn't accept your application, don't get angry that they are criticizing you and your marriage – after all, they know what sort of children they have available and you may simply not be right for them. Whilst on this subject, there's very little point in writing off to adoption agencies miles away if you're turned down locally. The chances are extremely small that you'll fare any better, because adoption is a complex business involving preparation and follow-up and it's not possible either physically or financially to follow up adopted children who live hundreds of miles away from the agency involved. If you live outside the agency's boundaries you might be considred for a special child (one who is older, difficult or handicapped) but otherwise the chances are slim.

It's best to get your ideas about adopting a handicapped or coloured child sorted out *before* you start on all the interviews. If the agency sees that you're only open to a very narrow range of acceptable children, they'll quite understandably view you less favourably. You should also be very sure that you're using the same terms that they use. If when you say you wouldn't mind having an 'older child' you mean an eighteen-month-old baby, beware. Remember that however much you'd like to have a baby, babyhood lasts only a short time but parenthood lasts a lifetime.

The same applies to black or 'mixed race' babies. Nowadays, agencies are increasingly realizing that the child needs cultural security wherever possible and are trying hard to place children in families of the same ethnic origin. However, there still tend to be more black children than there are black parents coming forward to adopt, and so white parents will continue to have black children placed with them. But the parents who take on these children are expected actively to encourage their sense of racial identity and not attempt to convince them that they are 'white in everything but colour'.

In recent years many agencies have started group meetings for people considering adoption. These are good because they provide the opportunity of finding out about adoptions generally and about that agency in particular. Some people, after hearing about adoption at such a session realize it isn't for them and others perceive that that particular agency wouldn't suit them and so try another.

If you're determined to adopt, keep writing to the agencies in your area every three to six months to remind them that you're still interested and to ask them to notify you when they reopen their lists. All this can take months or even years but the agency must do lots of checking and research to make sure that the match of child to parent is the best possible. Because the adoption agency's responsibility includes doing a thorough study of each child they place, they amass a lot of detail about his background, his family and its health history, their appearance, skills, achievements and their reasons for releasing him for adoption. By going into such depth with both parties they can ensure that the needs of the child and the future family are met in the best possible way; that prospective adopters can know as much as possible about the child before making the decision to go ahead; and that the adopted child can in the future know all he needs to about his origins. Since the 1975 Children Act, adopted children can, on reaching the age of eighteen, obtain a copy of their original birth certificate so that their real parents' names are disclosed to them. Up until that age, it's up to you how and when you tell your child that he's adopted but its important that the child is told.

THE PROBATIONARY PERIOD

Once you have the child in your home you'll treat him as if you were his natural parents but you will not legally be his parents until after a probationary period of at least three months. During this time you as prospective adopters have no legal rights and the child's natural parents can take him back at any time. This rarely happens in practice – only about 2 to 3 per cent of babies are reclaimed by their parents during this interval. Towards the end of the three-month period you can lodge adoption papers at court but the actual adoption order cannot be made in under three months. If the child comes to you before the age of six weeks, the probationary period cannot start until he is six weeks old. Early in the probationary period you'll be visited by a social worker and he or she will keep in close contact with you until the adoption is legalized. Once you have lodged your application in the court, you will be visited by a court's officer who may or may not be the same person as the local authority's social worker.

The adoption agency will also be in close contact during this time and it's important that you're completely happy with the child and he with you. If you think you've made a mistake, do say so. The agency will respect your decision and would rather that the child was found a more suitable home than see you or him unhappy. They will suggest another child for you at a later date, if you're still interested. During this probationary period, Child Benefit and income-tax relief can be claimed for that child, just as for any other child of the family.

MAKING IT LEGAL

Only courts can legalize adoption and the adoption agency will sort all this out for you. In Scotland, adoptions usually go through the sheriff's court and legal representation is normal. In England and Wales a solicitor is generally not needed, court hearings are brief and simple and the adoption order is usually granted with a minimum of red tape. Once the order is granted the child becomes a member of your family and is in line for your inheritance exactly as are your natural children. If you are childless you'll have to think about this carefully because your first child (adopted) will have an equal standing in law with any other children you may subsequently have of your own. All the rights of the child's natural parents cease to exist and he may not inherit from his natural family. It's a good idea to make a new will and to name your newly adopted child in it.

PRIVATE ADOPTIONS
It is now illegal to arrange private adoptions because the Children Act of 1975 outlaws these adoptions unless the proposed adopter is a relative of the child.

WHAT IT COSTS
The cost of adopting is very small. Local authorities and many agencies make no charge at all and even those agencies that do charge seek only to recover their expenses; they may not by law make a charge for arranging the adoption itself. If legal representation is necessary, as in Scotland, the price can rise a little and medical examinations and certificates add at least another £20 to the bill as these are not covered by the NHS. You may be asked to pay for the pre-placement medical examination and court medical certificate but the most you're likely to have to pay is £86 overall. This is a small enough cost for most couples to have to bear, but it's interesting to note that in the US the giant IBM Company gives its employees a payment of up to $1,000 (about £600) for each child that has been placed in an employee's family. This Adoption Assistance Plan brings adoptive parents who work for the company in line with other employees who get help with their medical and maternity fees when they have a baby. Who knows, UK companies might take up the idea in time.

ONCE YOU'VE ADOPTED
An adopted child is, as we've seen, legally a member of your family and once he's yours, the official questioning and form filling is over. He's all yours although the agency you got him from will often take trouble to keep in touch with you and even to offer an ongoing service to support you. As your child grows older he'll have questions to ask about his real parents and these can often be difficult to handle. It's at times like these that other people with similar experiences can be helpful and your agency will help you meet them. Telling your child he's adopted is one of the problems you'll have to come to terms with even before you adopt and it's never very easy.

There's a common belief that infertile couples who adopt are subsequently more likely to conceive than those who do not adopt. Several studies have been carried out on this and most of them show that adoption has no effect on subsequent conception rates. If you are going to conceive then you will do so whether or not you adopt.

Last, do remember that adoption, however rewarding and enjoyable an experience, is not a cure for infertility. Adoption eases the pain of childlessness but the infertility is still there. Having said that, adoption gives a couple a chance to be parents, a chance that is usually welcome and challenging.

Fostering

WHAT IS IT?
Fostering is a form of child care in which a child is looked after in a family other than its own. There are many different types of fostering, ranging from day fostering (a sort of child minding) to permanent arrangements which are virtually as permanent as adoption except that the foster parents are not the legal parents of the child. Fostering isn't a single method of child care but a whole host of methods which vary from place to place in the country. Clearly, because fostering means so many different things, we have to be sure what we are discussing or confusion may arise.

When considering what fostering is, one soon comes across the problem produced by a kind of care that doesn't give the 'parents' the absolute responsibility for the child in their care. Foster parents usually see themselves as substitute parents whilst the child-care agencies see them as caretakers or therapists. The confusion is further compounded because not only is there a child-welfare agency involved but the natural parents are often still in the picture too. This produces a situation in which the child is cared for by three sets of people of which the foster parents must, almost by definition, have the fewest rights. This is the irony that has to be accepted if you're thinking of fostering – you'll be in effect the day-to-day parents of the child but his natural parents or the social-work agency can terminate your relationship at any time. If you can grasp this nettle, you're ready to consider fostering. From the child's point of view, this three party care can be very unsatisfactory because there will often be gaps in certain areas and overlaps in others.

It's not easy for foster parents to 'share' a child with others but it's even more difficult for the child who is being 'shared'. Having put the pessimistic side of the picture though, this situation often works out more smoothly than you'd imagine, especially in the long term because, according to most studies, only about 10 per cent of natural parents visit their children in foster homes even once a month and the majority seldom or never see them. This in effect leaves the foster parents and the child-care agencies to manage the situation and if all is going well, the latter might only keep a watching brief and let you get on with it.

BACKGROUND
Modern fostering practice as we know it probably dates back to the 1948 Children Act but fostering was practised in the nineteenth century when children of workhouse parents were 'boarded out'. The 1950s and early 1960s saw an enormous enthusiasm for fostering but this changed in the late sixties and the seventies. This was partly due to the reorganization of the health and social services which diluted specialist skills and promoted some of the most able and active people from practical to management posts.

In the past few years though there has been an upsurge of interest in fostering again with the result that in England and Wales in 1977, 34,000 children were placed in foster homes. All the parties involved are now working on new fostering schemes which provide maximum flexibility and there is great interest in training foster parents and research into methods of parent selection and support. The 'tug-of-love' cases so widely publicized in the popular press, and the Children Act of 1975, which increased the legal rights of children through their foster parents, have led to an upsurge of professional interest in fostering – an interest which was never as strong as that in adoption. Adoption has attracted many good researchers over the years and most facets of the subject have been carefully studied. Fostering has always been seen as something of a poor relation by health and social-science workers but there are signs that this is changing.

TYPES OF FOSTERING
Children who need fostering are of all ages, from babies (who often need very short-term care before being returned to their natural mothers) to teenagers who stay with their foster families for years. In 1981, 39 per cent of the 96,900 children in local authority care in England and Wales were boarded out and at least another 115,000 were estimated to be in

private foster homes. Strange as it may seem, national figures of how many children are fostered under the various methods are scanty or frankly unavailable but it's probably fair to say that the infertile couple stands a much better chance of fostering than adopting.

Traditionally, foster parents have been paid an allowance to cover the cost of looking after someone else's child in their home. The rates of payment vary according to area, age of child and the type of problem the child presents the foster parents with. New schemes give enhanced allowances for those who take especially difficult or disturbed children and some foster-care authorities offer further financial reward in special circumstances.

The most ususal type of foster parents though are a couple who have children of their own and who feel that they can offer a child (or children) a good home for an unspecified length of time with no legal strings attatched. The length of time the child will stay is very variable but there are three broad time-scale categories, which tend to attract different kinds of children – and parents.

Short-stay foster homes These are really alternatives to residential nurseries, short-stay children's homes and reception and assessment centres. The type of children who need this short-term care (usually up to eight weeks) are those whose parents are ill, whose mothers are having a baby or whose family is going through a domestic crisis. Short-term fostering also gives the authorities a chance to see the child in a normal home environment and so allows them a breathing space to make more suitable long-term plans. Other children that need short-term fostering are those who need pre-adoption care and preparation, those whose parents can't look after them during the week and those children who have committed offences and are awaiting a court decision. Almost all of these children maintain very close links with their families and the foster parents don't see themselves as substitute parents at all. After three months, the position has by law to be reviewed so you can't drift into the long-term care of such a child.

Increasingly, foster parents are being asked to look at the task not primarily as one of substitute parenting but as a treatment, positively keeping the child's background alive, even if he may hardly have known any other way of life. There is, of course, an element of substitute parenting but current thinking encourages this to be seen as part of the whole task and not the prime responsibility.

Medium-term foster homes These provide care for anything from a few months to a few years. When child-care agencies are involved in these cases, they try to keep the natural parents in touch but, as we have seen, most parents do not in practice visit. The role of the foster parents is obviously different here compared with that in the short-term situation because the child will stay long enough for them to feel that they have at least some parental role. If the child is placed in such a family while his parent's health, marital problems or other troubles are overcome, then clearly the natural parents will be kept involved. Most people imagine that these medium-term situations are the majority in the fostering scene but this is not so. Studies have shown that if children don't go back home within a few months they are likely to remain in care for a very long time. About one quarter of all children seeking foster homes are thought to need permanent homes. A detailed study in one local authority showed that 88 per cent were expected to remain in care until their eighteenth birthday. This sort of fostering is probably the most difficult if only because, unlike short- and long-stay types, you don't know where you stand nearly so well, because it's difficult to keep unattached and 'professional' for a long period.

Long-stay fostering These foster parents form by far the largest group. This might seem surprising in the light of better and more effective social work but as we have just seen, a very large percentage of children in foster homes are expected still to be there at the age of eighteen. One study found that maintaining a child in his foster home was rated as top priority by social workers in 92 per cent of cases, while in only 3·4 per cent returning the child to its natural family was cited as the top priority.

Obviously long-term fostering is the best way of giving a child a permanent substitute home if the natural parents want to stay in the picture and so allow him to grow up as normally as possible. Even if the natural parents do keep in touch their role diminishes as time passes and the child sees his future with his new parents.

Foster parents of all kinds get paid a subsistence allowance by the local authority but money is not the reason that foster parents go into fostering. The vast majority of them are long-term non-professionals who simply like looking after children. Their only need is for a reasonable allowance that reflects the real costs of looking after a child. At the moment the average rate is £20-£40 per week, depending on the age of the child and in which part of the country you live.

Once you've decided to foster or if you would like to discuss it further, you should contact the National Foster Care Association, Francis House, Francis Street, London, SW1 (Tel. 01-828 6266). You can also contact your local social services department direct.

Fostering though has one complication that adoption does not. As I have pointed out, once you have an adoption order the child is legally yours but with fostering the child is never yours (although if you have fostered a child for five years you have a right to an adoption hearing). This leads to the concept of inclusive and exclusive fostering. Inclusive fostering is a term used to describe the situation when the natural parents, social workers and the child's past are all integrated into the care of the child in its foster home whilst the term 'exclusive' describes the situation in which the child is completely taken into the new family as one of them and everyone else is shut out. Both systems have advantages. The former has the advantage of being honest and open; the latter provides continuity and total commitment. A mixture of both may well be needed according to the child's stage in the fostering situation.

In either an inclusive or exclusive setting the child's natural parents may well want to visit and this can produce considerable heartache for all concerned. The parents have a legal right of access but the law is really beside the point when it comes to such emotions. Unless the parents visit regularly, there'll be no continuity of their parent-child relationship, which must suffer as a result. Parents who genuinely feel they'll be able to have the child back visit more often than those who see no such chance. Natural parents often find visiting difficult, quite understandably, and the foster parents tend to discourage it because it disrupts their relationship with the child which may well have taken a lot of building up in the first place. To be fair though, increasing numbers of foster parents have contact and good relationships with the child's natural parents.

The future looks brighter for fostering as it becomes part of a unified child-care system which offers many different types of care for the children who need them. From the point of view of the infertile couple, fostering can be a fulfilling and realistic alternative to adoption. Until about ten years ago, most agencies favoured as foster parents those couples who already had children, but today more and more are offering children to childless couples. There is a serious hazard with fostering if you're infertile though, and that is the ever-present possibility that the child might have to go. This loss can more easily be borne by those who have a family of their own than by a childless couple to whom the child has become very important, but clearly it varies from child to child. If you think you could cope with this potential hazard of fostering, then it may be right for you.

Child-free living

When, if all your tests and treatments have proved unsuccessful, you rethink the whole subject and try to find the best way forward, it won't be long before you find yourself seriously considering whether to make a positive thing of remaining child-free. Some couples come to this decision easily but most have to go through all the stages described in Chapter 8 and only arrive at this solution as a last resort. I think this is a shame because they become obsessed with the next test, the next treatment and the next period. I personally feel that there is a good case to be made for seriously re-assessing the position once the tests and treatments are over (assuming they're normal). It's never easy actively to bring things to a halt and the natural human response is to carry on grasping at every straw. People who have worked in this field for years tell how destructive and disappointing this is to the couple, their friends and relatives and their professional helpers.

So at some stage, which I feel should be sooner rather than later, it's probably worth coming to terms with not having any children and reorganizing your life accordingly. This very defusing of the situation results in a pregnancy in a small proportion of couples and the peace of mind it can bring is remarkable. Once you make the decision you change from being child*less* (a negative state) to being child-*free* (a positive state of mind in which you accept that life doesn't revolve around children and that you can have a happy, fulfilled and meaningful life as a couple).

The long fight to get pregnant, the mechanical sex and the

anguish and bitterness that have dominated the last few years of your life as a couple may have dulled your relationship and may even have killed many of the good things you used to enjoy. This has got to change because you didn't marry each other solely to have babies, and you were probably very happily married for several years before you started trying. At this stage you really have to recapture all that you used to have together and this may not be easy. Once you relax about it you may find you've simply got caught up in a web of medical, parental, peer group and social pressures and that left to yourselves you're not that concerned about children after all. Also, over the years you've been trying for a baby and going through the medical hoops you've gained a few years in age and hopefully some wisdom. Maybe your attitudes to life are different now compared with what they were when you first started trying for a baby and perhaps there are new openings for you both that you'd closed your eyes to while a baby was still a possibility. After all, a couple surrounded by friends and family can still be a viable family unit – they don't have to have the statutory 2·2 children.

Having said this though, many women in particular can't get over not having contact with children – simply because they like them. Experts give very different advice about what should be done in this situation. Some say 'keep away from children or you'll feel broody and this will maintain your negative feelings about your infertility' whilst others advise a lot of contact with children as the next best thing to having your own. Clearly there is no glib answer because we are all made so differently. To one woman the answer may be to get a job working as a child minder, running a toddler group or training as a nursery nurse, whilst for many, child avoidance is the only way they can cope.

Whatever you do will not cure your infertility – nothing can make that go away, except having your own baby. And that might happen at any time, unless you have one of the few completely irreversible causes of infertility. We have no rights to have children – only rights to ourselves as human beings. What we do have though is a right to try to change society so that the increasing numbers of infertile couples in the future won't be made to feel abnormal and unacceptable. Perhaps as more couples choose to be child-free and as more childless, infertile couples are seen to have come to terms with the problem, society will become less sensitive about infertility and will accept that some couples will have children and others will not.

CHAPTER 11

The Future

The future for research into infertility is the most exciting and controversial that it has ever been. Trends in society mean that infertility is on the increase and for this and other reasons, the population of the western world may fall alarmingly within the next twenty-five years.

The Henley Institute of Forecasting in England has predicted that the population of this country will fall from its present 54 million to about 52·1 million or less by the year 2002 and others have forecast similar falls in the US and the USSR by the year 2015. This will be accounted for by a sharply decreasing birth rate. At present we need seventy births per thousand women in order to maintain the population, but the most optimistic forecast for 2002 is fifty births per thousand. This fall in the birth rate will occur because of the increasing trend for couples to postpone having children until they are past their most fertile stage, because of the growth of infertility-producing factors outlined in the Introduction, and because increasing material expectations will mean that couples will find it unacceptable to have more than one or two children, if indeed they have any at all.

Although this is unlikely to produce a national crisis in the near future, it is highly likely that a situation in which nearly one-quarter of the population cannot reproduce itself (which is the forecast of one American expert in this field) within the next decade or so, will be unacceptable to governments and public alike. Either pressure groups acting on behalf of the childless millions or the economic problems created by too small a population (such as those which recently led the French to introduce tax incentives to increase the population) will force governments to do something about population control. Ironically this may not be solely a dilemma of the western world in the future because many of the same causes of infertility and population decline are increasingly to be seen in the Third World. There is nothing like affluence to bring the birth rate down and this, coupled with effective contraceptives and vast epidemics of venereal disease in much of emergent Africa, for example, could well affect the pundits' estimates of overpopulation there in the next twenty-five years.

Whatever happens in the rest of the world though, it seems likely that we in the West are on the brink of some major, legal, moral and philosophical dilemmas surrounding the management of infertility. These will come about because of the realization of Huxley's science fiction in his book *Brave New World*. What seemed like a faint possibility a generation ago is now just around the corner. Of course, new synthetic fertility drugs will be invented and new surgical techniques developed but these will be as nothing compared with the possibilities and problems posed by 'test-tube babies' and cloning.

First let's look at what these are and then examine the dilemmas they present.

Test-tube babies (*In vitro* fertilization, IVF)

'Test-tube babies' is a science-fiction term that emotively conjures up the image of government-run baby farms producing quality controlled citizens for a brave new world. For this reason alone, most people involved in infertility research would like to see the term abandoned, if only because it doesn't even accurately describe what happens. The babies are, after all, grown in a woman's uterus and not in a test-tube as the term implies – yet even this possibility is not all that far away. When I wrote the first edition of this book IVF was very much an experimental procedure in the hands of a few gifted experts. Today there are more than 160 clinics offering IVF in the USA alone and there are others in the UK and Australia where the technique was pioneered. More than 2,500 babies have now been born worldwide using this method. One reason why it has caught on (apart from the pure commercial one) is that IVF results in pregnancies in well over 40 per cent of women receiving the right hormones to induce ovulation. This is a far better success rate than that with normal intercourse.

More properly, test-tube babies should be called *in vitro* fertilizations or embryo-transplant babies. *In vitro* technically means 'in glass' and is a scientific term to describe the laboratory-based nature of the procedure. What happens is this. Eggs are obtained from a woman's ovaries by laparoscopy and then mixed with her husband's sperms in a glass vessel in a laboratory. Any eggs that start to develop into early embryos are nurtured and one is selected to be injected into the uterine cavity of the woman. This is easy as the embryo is very tiny (only a handful of cells) and is done via the cervix. The intention is to place the embryo on the wall of the womb so that it will implant there and develop as a normally conceived baby does.

This may sound like simple plumbing but it isn't, for three main reasons. First, most women produce only one egg a month from one or other ovary and the chances of being able to catch this at laparoscopy are very small. To get over this problem, these women are given gonadotrophins which, as we saw earlier, make the ovaries produce several eggs at once. This gives the gynaecologist a much better chance of ending up with one fertilized egg to implant into the womb.

The second difficulty with this procedure (and this took Dr Edwards of the Edwards and Steptoe team in England, who pioneered the method, most of a professional lifetime to overcome) is to produce a receptive environment in a non-pregnant uterus so that it can support the embryo for the next nine months. Under normal circumstances a woman's womb is influenced by hormones to produce exactly the right environment for the embryo to grow. This is triggered by the presence of the fertilized egg in the fallopian tube. Women whose eggs have been fertilized in a laboratory have obviously missed out on this stage, so it becomes an essential part of the procedure to determine exactly the right mixture of hormones each particular woman should receive and this is not easy.

Lastly, sperms, which naturally undergo (capacitation) changes as they pass through the female genital system – changes which mature them so that they can penetrate an egg and fertilize it, don't get a chance to do this and so aren't able to do their job. This meant an enormous amount of research into the 'ripening' of sperms and the development of optimum fluids in which this delicate procedure could occur. Remember that so little was known of the importance of subtle influences on the developing embryo that it was quite possible that slightly inaccurate chemical concentrations or temperatures could have brought about tiny changes in the embryo that could have resulted in an abnormal child. But after more than fifteen years of painstaking research and many failures in humans, Edwards and Steptoe passed into the history books in 1978 with the birth of a normal baby to Mrs Lesley Brown. A second baby was born in Edinburgh, six months later and the technique is now reproducible in good hands elsewhere.

Here then is a method which, although it started out as a way for a woman with irreparably blocked tubes to have a baby of her own, can now be applied to other infertile (or fertile) women – even if they have normal tubes.

The most obvious application of this work (other than that for which it was designed, which was to enable women with irreparably blocked tubes to have a baby) is that of producing babies for women who don't want to submit to the inconvenience of and risk of going through a pregnancy themselves. After all, the embryo conceived in a 'test-tube' doesn't have to grow in any particular mother's womb, as work with cows has shown. Valuable Charolais cows produce eggs which are then fertilized and implanted in ordinary cows and these cows act as foster mothers pre-natally, finally giving birth to Charolais calves. This is especially advantageous when the Charolais calves are destined for export because it's clearly a lot cheaper and easier to fly embryos to host mothers abroad than to fly the cows themselves.

Once the human method is refined, it is possible that clinics will start to offer surrogate mothers to carry the fertilized egg of a woman who doesn't want to get pregnant herself. Conversely, it would also be possible for a woman who doesn't ovulate to receive a donor egg (fertilized by her own husband) in the laboratory) which would enable her to experience the pregnancy she so wants. This is a fairly unlikely development though because ovulation-inducing drugs are now so effective. As a technique this is, after all, much like AID today but has the disadvantage that whereas it's easy for a man to supply sperms to give away, it would mean the woman donor undergoing a minor operation (laparoscopy) so that the eggs could be collected. This would probably mean that she would have to be highly motivated, highly paid or both.

The next logical step is clearly to do away with the human uterus altogether and considerable research is underway on this right now. So far, results are very poor and success has only been recorded with quite lowly animals. However, if society really wanted it, the technology is there and success is simply a matter of enough manpower and money being applied. The cost would be minute in terms of cancer research or the space race but at the moment the will isn't there to make the investment on a sufficiently large scale. Perhaps as populations begin to fall, more money will be spent as public pressure mounts.

'Helper' embryos

The next exciting development in this field will probably be the division of single fertilized eggs. They can now be divided into two and even four, giving twins and quadruplets. The replacement of more than two embryos seems to help the implantation of one embryo. The subsequent embryos are now known as 'helper' embryos. These may not themselves all survive, but do apparently help one to survive. The theory is that these helper embryos replace the absent signals that are normally sent by an embryo while in the fallopian tube to the uterus to become more receptive.

Cloning

If embryo transplants make you feel uneasy (except within the strict confines of their current usage) then cloning will keep you awake at night. To understand what cloning is, we need to go back to some basic principles from Chapter 1.

An egg contains only half the total number of chromosomes of a body cell, the other half coming from the sperm. When an egg is fertilized in the normal way, the entry of a sperm triggers off a series of events involving the coming together of the two half-sets of chromosomes, followed by division of the egg and growth to form an embryo and ultimately a mature baby.

In cloning, an egg is collected after being released from the ovary and the nucleus is destroyed by ultra-violet irradiation. A nucleus from a cell of the same species is implanted into the egg with the destroyed nucleus which then behaves as though it had been fertilized and starts to grow and divide. The embryo that is produced is exactly similar in every way to the adult from which the donor nucleus came – it is a replica produced in the laboratory.

Rather as with embryo transplants, describing it simply makes it sound easy but it's extremely difficult. So far the work has mostly been done in frogs whose eggs are about 1 millimetre in diameter so it is not difficult to imagine the feat of micro-dissection needed to implant the nucleus of one cell into another. Mammalian eggs are many times smaller and so present even greater problems. Then there are the problems of the host mother's womb, just as with embryo transplants. Successful experiments in this area are rare and one of the world's leading experts, Dr Derek Bromhall in Oxford, reckons on a 99 per cent failure rate, even after many years of intensive work. He is working with small, warm-blooded mammals and has come out very firmly against experimenting with humans. 'No one in his right mind would clone humans,' he has said.

It's not difficult to see how tempting these two procedures would be to desperate, childless couples (even though cloning does not produce a genetically 'shared' child as does an embryo transplant) but the legal and moral issues they raise are enormous. Cloning is certainly the more horrific method, if only because it would be possible to breed 'Mozarts', 'Hitlers', 'Einsteins' and slaves by the thousand and at either end of the scale the implications for humanity are too unpleasant to countenance.

Embryo transplants look much more hopeful for the infertile – and remember that we're talking about a great many people. Estimates in America and the UK show that about 60 per cent of infertile couples are helped by existing technology. This leaves 4 million people in the US and about 1 million in the UK at any one time who aren't. Of these, an estimated 20,000 in the US find success with AID and another 80,000 adopt each year. (In the UK these figures are 2,000 and 12,000 respectively.) This still leaves $3\frac{1}{2}$ million Americans and nearly a million in the UK who remain involuntarily childless. These people have made a decision to have a family and are wide open to any reasonable way of achieving this.

Nineteen seventy-nine was the Year of the Child, and a great number of people asked why it was that with so many would-be parents hoping for children we couldn't pair up children and potential parents across the world. Unfortunately it's not that easy, for all kinds of reasons. Mostly they're based on racial prejudice, bureaucracy and national pride. It takes a very loving and stable couple successfully to adopt children of a completely different race, especially if the children are malnourished, ill, handicapped or past infancy. Many people feel that these children are better off in their own countries anyway and point out that some countries don't allow adoption and consider children a valuable asset even if they are poorly nourished and likely to die young. It's easy to understand how valuable a live baby must seem in societies where infant mortality is high. Having said all this, Third World adoption *is* on the increase.

So, all in all, a redistribution of children around the world from those that have to those that have not seems highly unlikely – after all, we don't seem to be able to move much-needed food around to our mutual advantage, let alone human beings.

But if we're years away from being able to sort out this approach to the problem, we're even further away from solving the legal, moral and philosophical problems raised by the technology-based solutions.

Would a child conceived after a father's death (perhaps from his banked deep-frozen sperm) be legitimate? Supposing a child conceived in the normal way were followed by one from a sperm banked years before, which would be the elder and who would inherit what? Would a mother who carried a baby for someone be able to claim it was hers after the birth, when in fact all she had supplied was the uterus for it to live in? What would be the legal status of a host mother? What are the implications of lesbians wanting babies by AID? These and many other questions are going to press on us with increasing urgency as time goes by. For a world that can't even agree about legal status of babies conceived by AID (a well-proven procedure) and lets them fall by default into a legal no-man's land, the outlook doesn't look too hopeful. It has been suggested that there will have to be an entirely new category of legal relationship between parent and child and between both the state – that of the 'accepted' child. So long as the child were accepted by the parents it would be legally theirs with all that that implies.

Last, it's worth considering a more unlikely option but one

which still raises legal issues – the buying and selling of babies. At present it is illegal to buy and sell babies but it nevertheless happens. When I was researching this book I asked every finally infertile couple whether they would, if given a chance, buy a baby, even in the knowledge that it is illegal. Almost all of them from every social class and racial origin said they would and many mentioned the thousands of pounds which they would be prepared to spend. There is no way of knowing how typical this finding is, but I suspect that it is a very widespread desire in this group of infertile people. There is no doubt that a few women like being pregnant *and* would be prepared to give up their baby to a childless couple for a fee – indeed, most couples who offer babies do so almost entirely for the money. This seems heartless to most of us, especially if we have personally experienced the bond that can occur between a mother and her baby, but many thousands of women give up their children to be adopted under the current situation, so this could simply be seen to be a logical next step. I am not making a case for mothers to sell their babies and realize that the whole subject is extremely sensitive, but it is the opinion of certain people working in this field that it might be an answer to the finally childless which they would find more acceptable than any other. The law it seems becomes an insignificant barrier if you're really desperate to have a baby after many years of trying and trailing around hospitals for tests. There comes a stage of desperation in many infertile couples at which they'll consider anything and at which buying a baby seems a perfectly acceptable way out. The after-effects in the donor mother cannot be pleasant and there is the ever-present danger of blackmail as long as it is illegal, but it is easy to see that these would scarcely be the main concerns of the parents who had bought their precious child.

There is no easy way out for the finally infertile (except of course to accept their infertility and alter their lifestyle accordingly) and the near future doesn't hold out any great hopes. Embryo transplantation is unlikely to become widely available this decade because of the cost and the scarcity of resources and there are few other major developments in the pipeline that look as hopeful although lots of research is going on worldwide.

The final answer must lie in prevention. Society must change somehow to encourage earlier childbearing; improved detection of venereal diseases and better treatment will prevent many of the blocked tubes we now see; we must change the way we live so as to reduce stress and so encourage normal hormone production and thus normal ovulation; better methods of contraception must be found that have no long-term unwanted effects on fertility and greater control of environmental toxins and drugs will ensure that sperms have as great a chance as possible of developing normally. But to be realistic, even with all of these changes there'd still be millions who couldn't have the child they so desperately want.

Infertility isn't going to go away — in fact all the signs are that whatever we do in the near future, the problem is going to get worse in spite of recent advances in treatment. It's up to all of us who spend most of our reproductive lives trying *not* to have children to do all we can to change our attitudes and so help those who *can't*.

Glossary

(For more details of any term, see Index and then follow text. Some of the words are not used in this book.)

Abortion – the premature ending of a pregnancy before the twenty-eighth week either spontaneously or because of operative intervention.
Adhesion – an abnormal sticking together of surfaces (usually of the peritoneal surface inside the abdomen) by bands or masses of fibrous connective tissue.
Afterbirth – the placenta – the organ which is attached to the uterine wall, supplies the baby with all its oxygen and nutrients and removes waste products (via the umbilical cord) whilst it is in the uterus. It also makes pregnancy hormones.
Agglutination (of sperms) – the sticking together (clumping) of sperms.
AID – artificial insemination using donor semen.
AIH – artificial insemination using husband's semen.
Amenorrhoea – the absence of menstruation.
Ampulla – a widening of the upper end of the vas deferens in which some sperms are stored prior to ejaculation.
Androgen – a male sex hormone.
Andrology – the study of diseases specific to men.
Anovulation – no ovulation. Menstrual cycles in which no ovulation occurs are called anovulatory. A woman can still have periods yet not be ovulating.
Antibody – a specific protein produced by the body in response to a challenge from a foreign substance. Men and women may produce antibodies to sperms, for example.
Artificial insemination – the placing of semen into a

woman's reproductive tract artificially as opposed to using a penis.

Aspermia – a total absence of sperms in semen.

Asthenospermia – poor motility of sperms in semen.

Azoospermia – an absence of living sperms in the semen (often used in the same sense as aspermia).

Basal temperature – the body temperature (taken orally or rectally) usually in the morning before any activity.

Bicornuate uterus – a congenital abnormality of the uterus in which it is divided internally in varying degrees to form two 'horns'.

Biopsy – the taking of a small piece of tissue from the body for microscopic study.

Capacitation – a process that occurs in sperms as they pass through the female genital tract which gives them the ability to penetrate and fertilize an ovum.

Cervical – pertaining to the uterine cervix.

Cervix – the neck or opening of the womb into the vagina.

Chromosomes – structures within every body cell that carry the genes or hereditary characteristics.

Clomiphene (Clomid) – an oestrogen-like infertility drug that stimulates the normal production of follicle stimulating hormone and produces ovulation.

Coitus – sexual relations; making love; intercourse.

Conception – the joining together of the ovum and sperm – fertilization.

Condom – contraceptive sheath; French letter; rubber.

Congenital – a characteristic or defect present at birth.

Contraception – the prevention of pregnancy.

Corpus luteum – a small yellow body developing within the ruptured ovarian follicle after the egg has been released.

Cryptorchidism – undescended testis.

Culdoscopy – the direct visualization of the pelvic organs by inserting a special instrument through the top end of the vagina into the abdominal cavity. Of diagnostic use in infertility.

Curettage – the scraping of the lining of the womb with a special instrument (a curette).

Cytology – the study of the body's cells.

D and C – dilatation and curettage. A widening of the cervical canal to allow the introduction of a curette to take a sample of womb lining; used as a diagnostic and therapeutic measure in infertility and as a means of aborting a fetus.

GLOSSARY

Douching – the use of fluids to irrigate the vagina.
Dysgenesis – faulty formation of a body organ.
Dysmenorrhoea – painful menstruation.
Dyspareunia – painful or difficult intercourse.
Ectopic pregnancy – a pregnancy that occurs anywhere other than in the uterus. This can occur in the fallopian tubes, in the ovaries or in the abdomen.
Ejaculation – the ejecting of semen from the penis; male orgasm.
Embryo – the earliest stages of development of a baby in the womb.
Endocrine – pertaining to hormones. Endocrine glands produce hormones which are passed into the bloodstream and affect parts of the body which are often distant from the gland itself.
Endocrinologist – a doctor who specializes in disorders of the endocrine glands.
Endometrial biopsy – the taking of a small sample of endometrium for examination. Usually done in infertile women to confirm ovulation.
Endometriosis – the presence of endometrium anywhere but inside the womb. It can occur in the fallopian tubes, the ovaries or inside the abdominal cavity. A cause of infertility.
Endometrium – the internal lining of the womb.
Endoscopy – the visualization of the interior of the body using instruments such as a laparoscope, culdoscope or hysteroscope.
Enzymes – chemicals produced by cells in the body but capable of acting independently of the cells. They are complex substances capable of inducing and hastening chemical changes in the body.
Epididymis – the organ above the testis in which sperms mature for several months.
Epispadias – a congenital abnormality of the penis in which the opening (usually the tip) is situated on top of the organ.
Erection – the state of the penis when it is enlarged and rigid, usually prior to ejaculation.
Fallopian tubes – a pair of tubes that carry ova from the ovaries to the uterus and in which fertilization occurs.
Fertilization – the penetration of an ovum by a sperm; conception.
Fetus – the product of conception; a baby in the uterus.
Fibroids – masses of fibrous tissue in the walls of the uterus.

Fimbriae – the wafting tentacle-like ends of each fallopian tube that 'collect' the ovum and guide it into the tube.
Frigidity – a poor term used to describe the inability of a woman to become sexually aroused.
FSH – follicle stimulating hormone. A hormone produced by the pituitary gland (near the brain) which in women stimulates the ovaries to produce ripe ova and the hormone oestrogen. In men it stimulates sperm production.
Gametes – male and female reproductive cells – sperms and ova.
Genes – parts of the chromosomes that control the inheritance of specific hereditary characteristics.
Genetic – pertaining to hereditary characteristics.
Gland – a cell or group of cells in the body which produces secretions.
Glans – the bulbous tip of the penis.
Gonadotrophins – hormones that stimulate the gonads.
Gonads – the sex glands that make sex cells. These are the testes in the male and the ovaries in the female.
Gynaecologist – a doctor who specializes in diseases of the female reproductive organs.
HCG – human chorionic gonadotrophins. The gonadotrophic hormones produced by the chorion of the developing embryo early in pregnancy. Sometimes given therapeutically in certain types of infertility.
Hermaphroditism – a condition in which the person has characteristics of both the male and female sex.
Hormone – a naturally occurring chemical, produced by endocrine glands in the body, that circulates in the blood to have an effect on a distant organ or organs.
Hostility factor – a term used to describe a situation in which sperms cannot survive in the female genital system. It can be caused by many conditions, the commonest of which is probably too acid a mucus or the presence of antibodies to sperms.
Hühner test – see post-coital test.
Hydrocele – a swelling of the scrotum caused by an accumulation of fluid.
Hydrosalpinx – a swelling of one or both fallopian tubes containing fluid.
Hydrotubation – a washing or flushing through of the fallopian tubes with a sterile solution which may sometimes contain medication. Used to clear a blockage or treat

GLOSSARY

disease in the fallopian tubes.

Hymen – a membrane of skin that partially covers the vaginal opening in virgins.

Hyperplasia – an abnormal enlargement of tissues or organs of the body.

Hypospadias – a congenital abnormality of the penis in which the opening (usually at the end) opens on the under side of the organ.

Hypothalamus – a part of the brain that serves as a link between the higher centres of the brain and the pituitary gland. It controls the activity of the pituitary gland.

Hysterectomy – removal of the uterus.

Hysterosalpingogram – an X-ray study in which a radio-opaque fluid is injected into the uterus so that doctors can see the inside of the womb and the fallopian tubes. Also called a tubogram.

Hysteroscopy – the use of a very fine telescope to view the inside of the uterus.

Hysterotomy – an opening up of the uterus to perform a surgical procedure (often an abortion). The uterus is stitched closed and remains in place.

Immunological response – the formation of antibodies in a woman to her husband's sperms which are then immobilized or clumped together when they enter her body.

Implantation – the embedding of a fertilized ovum in the endometrium of the uterus.

Impotence – the inability to achieve or maintain an erection for successful intercourse. Can be caused by emotional or physical problems, or both.

Infertility – arbitrarily defined as the inability of a couple to produce a pregnancy after one year of intercourse with no contraception.

Insufflation of the tubes – the blowing of carbon dioxide into the uterus under pressure as a diagnostic (and sometimes a therapeutic) test of infertility caused by blocked fallopian tubes.

Interstitial cells (Leydig cells) – the cells between the seminiferous tubules of the testes that produce the male hormone testosterone.

IUD (IUCD) – intra-uterine contraceptive device. Used for contraception and a possible cause of infertility in some women.

Klinfelter's syndrome – a congenital abnormality of men in which there is one X chromosome too many. Most men with this condition are sterile.

Laparoscopy – a technique by which the internal abdominal organs can be visualized directly using an instrument which is introduced through a small incision in the abdominal wall below the navel.

LH – luteinizing hormone. A pituitary gonadotrophic hormone which stimulates both the rupture of the follicle and ovulation in women. It reaches its peak level just before ovulation. This hormone is called interstitial cell stimulating hormone (ICSH) in men.

Libido – the desire for sexual intercourse.

Masturbation – obtaining an orgasm and ejaculation in men or simply an orgasm in women. Usually self-induced but one partner can masturbate the other.

Menarche – the beginning of menstrual periods in girls.

Menopause – the cessation of menstruation that occurs around the age of fifty; 'the change of life'.

Menstruation – the monthly period of bleeding that normally occurs throughout a woman's reproductive life unless she is pregnant or breast feeding.

Miscarriage – a spontaneous abortion before the fetus is twenty-eight weeks old.

Mittelschmerz – a German term used to describe the 'middle pain' which occurs in some women when they ovulate in the middle of each menstrual cycle.

Motility – the power of movement. Usually used to describe sperms which move under their own power.

Mucus – slimy fluid produced by specialized cells to lubricate body surfaces. Mucus produced by the cervix changes greatly under hormonal influences.

Necrospermia – a condition in which the semen contains only dead sperms.

Nidation – implantation of a fertilized egg in the endometrium.

Obstetrician – a doctor who specializes in the supervision of pregnancy and childbirth.

Oestrogens – the female sex hormones oestriol, oestrone, oestradiol and the synthetic equivalents having the same physiological actions.

Oligospermia – a condition in which there are fewer sperms in the ejaculate than there should be.

GLOSSARY

Orgasm – sexual climax. In men this is accompanied by an ejaculation of semen.
Ovaries – the female sex glands that produce eggs (ova). There are two, one each side of the body, situated at the ends of the fallopian tubes and resting in the pelvis.
Ovulation – the shedding of an egg cell each month.
Ovum – the egg cell produced by the ovary.
Pap (Papanicolaou) test – a simple test involving the taking of a swab or a smear of the cervix to see if there are any cancerous cells present.
Penis – the male organ of intercourse and urination.
Pergonal – human menopausal gonadotrophin – a natural hormone used to treat infertility. It is extracted from the urine of post-menopausal women.
Pituitary gland – an endocrine gland at the base of the brain that produces several hormones. It is the master gland of the endocrine system of the body.
Polyp – a nodule or small non-cancerous growth found on mucous membranes. Can occur in the cervix or uterus.
Post-coital test – a diagnostic test for infertility in which vaginal and/or cervical secretions are examined in the presence of sperms removed from the cervix after normal intercourse.
Progesterone – a hormone produced by the corpus luteum after ovulation has occurred. It is also produced by the placenta in pregnancy.
Prostate – a gland, found only in men, that surrounds the first part of the urethra after it leaves the base of the bladder. It produces an alkaline fluid essential to the survival of sperms.
Pseudocyesis – false pregnancy, a condition in which the woman believes herself to be and may even have some of the signs of being pregnant, but isn't.
Puberty – the stage of life during which boys and girls become capable of reproduction.
Salpingitis – inflammation of the fallopian tubes.
Salpingogram – *see* Hysterosalpingogram.
Salpingolysis – surgery to unblock the fallopian tubes.
Scrotum – the bag of skin that lies between a man's legs below his penis. It holds the testes, epididymes and the first parts of the vasa deferentia.
Secondary infertility – a condition in which a woman cannot conceive after having already successfully conceived in the past.

Semen – the fluid ejaculated from the penis at orgasm. Only a fraction of semen is composed of sperms.

Semen analysis – the study of a fresh ejaculate under the microscope to count the number of sperms per cubic millilitre, to check their shape and size and to assess their motility.

Seminal vesicles – a pair of glands above the prostate in the male that produce a thick, alkaline solution which is added to the sperms on ejaculation.

Seminiferous tubules – the long tubes in the testes in which sperms are formed.

Seminology – the study of semen.

Spermatocele – a cyst containing sperms that grows from the upper part of the epididymis.

Spermatogenesis – the process by which sperms are produced in the seminiferous tubules.

Spermatozoa – the medical name for sperms – the male reproductive cells.

Split ejaculate – a method of collecting semen so that the first half of the ejaculate is caught in one container and the rest in a second. The first half is richer in fertile sperms and can then be used to inseminate a woman.

Spontaneous abortion – *see* Miscarriage.

Stein-Leventhal syndrome – a condition characterized by cystic ovaries which responds to removal of part of the ovaries or to fertility pills.

Syndrome – a set of symptoms and clinical signs which, taken together, constitute a particular disease or condition.

Testicle – the testis. An organ (one each side of the body) situated in the scrotum that produces sperms and some male hormones.

Testis – the medical term for testicle.

Testosterone – the main male sex hormone produced by the testes.

Test-tube baby – a baby that has come from an egg fertilized outside the body and reimplanted into the mother's womb where it grows until normal birth. An unfortunate term. Better called embryo transplantation.

Thyroid gland – a two-lobed gland at the base of the front of the neck, which produces hormones that, among other things, are thought to be essential for fertility.

Thyroxine – a hormone produced by the thyroid gland.

Tubal insufflation – *see* Insufflation.

GLOSSARY

Turner's syndrome – a congenital condition of some women in which there is a chromosomal abnormality which renders them sterile.

Urethra – the narrow passage that takes urine from the bladder to the outside. In men it also carries semen during ejaculation.

Urologist – a doctor who specializes in disorders of the urinary system. He also often has an interest in male genital disorders.

Uterus – a small, hollow, muscular organ that carries the fertilized ovum through the nine months of pregnancy, enlarging to accommodate it as it grows.

Vagina – 'front passage' or 'birth canal' – the tube that leads from a woman's uterine cervix to the outside (vulva).

Vaginismus – a spasm of the muscles surrounding the vaginal opening which can make intercourse difficult or impossible.

Varicocele – a varicose vein of the testis (normally the left). A major cause of male infertility.

Vasa deferentia – a pair of thick-walled muscular tubes in the male that lead from the epididymis to the prostatic section of the urethra.

Vasectomy – a minor operation, usually carried out under local anaesthesia, to interrupt the vas deferens so as to render the man sterile.

Vasography – an X-ray technique for visualizing the vas deferens when looking for an obstruction.

Venereal disease (VD) – any infection transmitted by sexual activity. VD is a major cause of infertility in both sexes but especially in women.

Useful Addresses

National Association for the Childless
318 Summer Lane
Birmingham B19 3RL
(Tel. 021-359 4887)

National Foster Care Association
Francis House
Francis Street
London SW1
(Tel. 01-828 6266)

British Agencies for Adoption and Fostering
11 Southwark Street
London SE1 1RQ
(Tel. 01-407 8800)

Index

abortion, 13
  pelvic infections from, 66
acrosome, 40
adoption, 185-193
  agencies, 188-90, 192
  age qualifications for, 189
  cost of, 192
  legalizing, 191-2
  motives for, 187-8
  private adoptions, 192
  probationary period, 191
  procedure, 188-90
  small supply of babies for, 186-7
  your adopted child, 189-90
age and incidence of infertility, 12-13, 38, 92, 102
alcohol consumption, 55, 107
Alexander, Prof. Nancy, 75
amenorrhoea, 60, 62, 64, 145
ampullae, 36
anorexia nervosa, 60, 79
appendix, perforated, infection from, 66, 104
artificial insemination
  methods, 174
  numbers of babies born by, 173
artificial insemination by donor (AID), 172, 173, 176-84
  confidentiality surrounding, 179
  emotional reactions to, 182-3
  legal implications, 180-1
  method, 179-80
  moral problems, 181-2
  pregnancy following, 180
  selection of donors, 177-8
  selection of suitable couples for, 176-7
  worries concerning, 181
artificial insemination by husband (AIH), 54, 172, 173, 174-6

Bartholin's glands, 111
basal body temperature recording test, 60, 113-118, 170
Benedek, 148
birth rate, decline in, 200-1
blood groups
  incompatibility, 155-7
  and male infertility, 95
blood tests, 138
Boué, M. and Mme, 157-8
breast feeding, 17, 30, 59
breasts, presence of milk, 62, 110
British Agencies for Adoption and Fostering, 188
Bromhall, Dr Derek, 205
bromocriptine, 62, 64
Brown, Mrs Lesley, 203
buying and selling of babies, 206-7

capacitation, 30, 40
cervical cap, 75, 76
cervical mucus
  causing infertility, 73-7
  method of determining ovulation, 119-22
  post-coital test, 127-9, 73-4
cervix, 13, 27, 29, 45
  abnormalities, 75, 154

infection of, 73, 76
childfree living, coming to terms with, 198-9
childless people
  attitudes towards, 16, 143-4, 162, 168
  numbers of in UK and US, 205
  views and feelings of, 18-22, 44, 147
Children Acts: 1948, 194; 1975, 181, 190, 192, 194
chlamydia trachomatis, 65, 91
chromosomal abnormalities, 78, 157-8
clitoris, 24-7
clomiphene citrate (clomid), 61, 62, 63, 78, 97
cloning, 204-5
conception
  basic necessities for, 38-9, 42
  time to, 38, 43, 103
condoms
  and reduction of fallopian tube infection, 67
  in treatment of sperm antibody problems, 76
contraception, study of linked with infertility research, 97 see also Pill
corpora cavernosa, 32-3
corpus luteum, 32, 124, 155
corpus spongiosum, 33
Cowper's glands, 37
culdoscopy, 137
cycle of the female body, 30-1
cystic fibrosis and male infertility, 94

danazol (danol), 70
Davidson's cap, 175
depression and female infertility, 79
Deutsche, Hélène, 143-4, 148
diabetes, 53, 79, 87
dietary fibre, 82
dilatation and curettage, 123-4

doctor's role in dilemma of infertility, 15, 17-18, 99-100
douches, 47, 76, 105
doxycycline, 67, 72, 73
drugs, 13, 55, 87
  immunosuppressive, in treatment of sperm antibodies, 77, 89
  and male infertility, 92, 95, 108
drug treatment of female infertility, 62-5, 70

e. coli, 71
ECT, 145
Edwards and Steptoe team, 202, 203
ejaculation disturbances, 86-7 (see also premature ejaculation)
embryo transplants, 201-4
emotional disorders, 147-8
emotional factors
  in female infertility, 107
  surrounding AID, 182-3
emotional impact of infertility, 162-71
endocrine problems
  in female infertility, 79
  in male infertility, 84
endometrial biopsy, 123-4
endometriosis, 29, 68-71
endometrium, 32
epididymis, 83-86

Fallopian tubes, 30
  menstrual back flow into, 79
  problems concerning, 65-8
  spasms of, 142
  surgery to repair, 68
family doctor, seeking help from, 98-100
female infertility
  main reasons for, 59
  specialist clinics, formal questioning at, 104-7
  spontaneous recover from, 62
  treatment of, 58-80

INDEX

'fertility' drugs, 62-5
fertility rates, decline of 12-14, 143
fibroids, 78, 155
fimbriated ends (of fallopian tubes), 30
follicle stimulating hormone (FSH), 31, 37-8, 61-2, 97, 119
food additives, exposure to, 13
fostering
  background of system, 194
  definition of, 193-4
  exclusive system, 197
  inclusive system, 197
  long-term, 196
  medium-term, 196
  natural parents, access to child, 197
  payment for, 196-7
  short-term, 195-6
  types of, 194-8
fractional post-coital test, 130
frenulum, 52
frigidity, 48-9
fructose, 36, 128

G-spot, 26
general practitioner, seeking help from, 98-100
genito-urinary infections
  female, 71-3
  male, 90-1
glandular problems, male, 84
gonadotrophins, 63-4, 78, 84, 86, 202
gonorrhoea, 13, 65-6, 67, 85
Graafian follicles, 69
gynaecological examination, 110-13

heat, adverse effect on tests, 34-6, 55, 93-4, 107
'helper' embryos, 204
Homosexuality, 48, 146, 147
hormonal treatment of
  endometriosis, 70
  female infertility, 76

male infertility, 90, 96-7
sperm antibody problems, 90
hormones, female, 30, 38, 202
  deficiencies causing miscarriage, 155
  and ovulation, 31-2, 61
hormones, male, 36, 37-8, 70, 84
human chorionic gonadotrophin (HCG), 63, 84, 97
human menopausal gonadotrophin (HMG) (Pergonal), 63, 64, 97
hymen, 27, 49
hypothalamus, 31, 60, 61, 92-3
hysterosalpingogram (HSG), 68, 131-4
hysteroscopy, 134

IBM Company, 192
illness, and male infertility, 94-95
immunological testing, 139
impotence, 43, 49, 52-4, 85
infectious illness, and temporary female infertility, 79
intercourse, 25-7
  douching, 47, 76, 106-7
  female attitude to, 106
  frequency of, 42-5, 85, 104-5
  orgasm, *see that heading*
  pain associated with, 42, 49-50, 69
  positions, 45, 52, 106
  procedure following, 47. 106
  timing of, 42, 105, 118-19
intra-uterine device (IUD), 13, 66, 67
in vitro fertilization, 201-4

kidney failure, long-term, 94
Klinefelter's syndrome, 83

Laparoscopy, 69, 134-7
legal and moral problems of technological solutions, 206
Leydig cells, 36
Libido, drugs affecting male, 95
Limbic system, 145

liver disease, effect on sperms of, 128
Luteinizing hormone (LH), 31, 38, 61-2

Male infertility, 32, 38
  drugs and, 108
  main reasons for, 81-2
  questions asked at specialist clinic, 107-8
  treatment, 81-97
marital relationship, 15-16, 44-6, 50-1, 162-71
Masters and Johnson, 26, 41, 50, 51
masturbation, 102, 106, 171, 175
menopause, 59-60
menstrual back-flow, 79
menstruation, 31, 60, 69
methylprednisolone, 77
Michel-Wolfromm, Helene, 158, 159
mind, role of, in infertility, 141-9
Miscarriage, 150-61
  complete, 152
  grief caused by, 160-1
  incomplete, 152
  inevitable, 152
  'missed miscarriage', 152-3
  recurrent, 153
  threatened, 151
miscarriages, causes, 153-60
  blighted ovum, 153-4
  cervix abnormality, 154
  chromosomal abnormalities, 157-8
  congenital malformation of foetus, 159
  hormone deficiencies, 155
  incompatible blood groups, 155-6
  psychological causes, 158-9
  T-mycoplasma, 159
  uterus abnormality, 155
moniliasis (candida albicans), 72
moral and legal problems of technological solutions, 206
mucus, see cervical mucus
multiple births, 63, 64
mumps, and testicular inflammation, 83-4
myotonic muscular dystrophy and male infertility, 94

necrospermia, 90
nitrofurantoin (furadantin), 73
nutrition and infertility, 13, 79

obesity, 55, 79, 93
occupation, affect on fertility of, 44, 53, 107, 108
oestrogen, 32, 62, 64, 75, 76, 96
orgasm, 24-7, 45, 46-7, 106
ovaries, 30
  absence of, 78
  polycystic, 78
ovulation, 29, 30, 31-2, 42
  methods for confirmation, 113-25
  problems, 59-62
ovum
  blighted, 153-4
  lifespan of, 42, 118
  size of, 40

pelvic inflammatory disease and female infertility, 29, 66-7
penis, 32-4
  foreskin, 109
  frenulum, 52
  size of, 34, 46, 53
pergonal, 63, 64, 97
pernicious anemia and female infertility, 79
physical examination
  female, 110-13
  male, 109-10
Pill, the, 67, 72
  as cure for endometriosis, 70
  and ovulation, 60, 61
  prolonged use of, 13
pituitary gland, 31, 60, 61, 62, 92-3, 145

INDEX

pituitary gonadotrophins, 63
placebos, 62
pollution, exposure to, 13, 92, 107
population, zero growth rate, 14
post-coital test (PCT), 73-4, 129-30
pregnanediol, 124
premature ejaculation, 43, 50-2
prepuce, 34
primary infertility, 11-12
progesterone levels in the blood, 32, 60, 124
prolactin levels, and female infertility, 61-2, 64, 80
prostaglandins, 27, 31
prostate gland, 36
  inflammation, 91
  surgery, and retrograde ejaculation, 87
psychogenic infertility, 142-7
'psychological aborters', 158-9
psychological and emotional factors in infertility, 38, 49, 61, 141-9
psychological testing, 149

radiation, 93
religion, problems associated with the solution of infertility problems, 48, 49, 53, 102-3, 125, 175, 182
remedies for infertility, 14
reproductive system
  females, 24-32, 59
  ignorance of, 23-4, 41
  male, 32-8
retrograde ejaculation, 86-7
rhesus incompatibility, 155-7
Rubin test, 131

Sandler, 147
Science, 75
Scientific American, 14
scrotum, 34, 55
secondary infertility, 11-12, 15, 103

seeking medical help, 14-15, 44, 98-101, 164-5
self-help, 17, 41-57
semen
  alkalinity of, 36-7
  colour and consistency, 37
  high viscosity, 90
  volume, 37, 46, 86, 126
seminal fructose, 36, 128
seminal vesicles, 36
sex life, effects on infertility on, 166, 169-71
sexual dysfunction, 43, 47-54, 87
sexual technique, 25-6, 41-6, 121-2
Shirodkar suture, 154
smoking, 55
social pressures, 143, 162
specialist clinic
  female physical examination, 110-13
  first visit to, 18, 100-1
  formal questioning of the couple, 101-3
  male physical examination, 109-10
  questions addressed to the man, 107-8
  questions addressed to the woman, 104-7
  seeking help from, 101-13
specialists in the problems of infertility, 18
sperm agglutination, 74, 76, 88-90
sperm antibodies, 74-5, 76, 86, 88-90, 91, 139
sperms
  analysis, 125-7
  counts, 44, 125-7
  drugs affecting production of, 95
  formation of, 34, 39
  function, 71
  high counts, 90
  'hostile' cervical mucus, effect of on, 74-6

lifespan of, 42
liquefaction, 128
morphology, 128
motility, 36, 56, 127-8
'saving up' technique, 44
sensitivity to radiation, 93
size, 40
sperm invasion test (SIT), 74
tests on, 125-9
transport of inside the female body, 26-7, 39, 40
volume, 46, 126
washing of, 76-7, 89
split-ejaculate technique, 56, 86
squeeze technique, 51-2
Stein-Leventhal syndrome, 78
sterilization (female), reversal of, 68
steroids, 77, 89
stress, 55-6, 79-80, 92-3, 108, 145-6
'survival of the fittest', 144
syphilis, 66

temperature, basal body recording test, 60, 113-18, 170
testes, 34, 55, 83-4
 cancer of, 88
 examination of, 109
 sensitivity to heat, 34-6, 54-5, 93-4
 twisting, 84
 undescended, 87-8
 varicocele, 82-3
testicular biopsy, 85, 139
testosterone, 36, 96
tests and investigations, 113-140
 emotional effect of, 164-5
 for psychological abnormalities, 149
'test tube' babies, 201-4
thrush, see moniliasis
thyroid gland, 84, 96
T-mycoplasma, 67, 71-2, 159
tranquillizers, and ovulation, 61
trichomonas vaginalis, 71, 72
tubal insufflation (Rubin test), 131

tuberculosis, 67, 79, 85, 91
Turner's syndrome, 78

ultrasound, 69, 151
urethra, 27, 33
urinary and genital systems (female), infections of, 71-3
urinary pregnanediol estimation, 124-5
uterus, 26, 29
 abnormalities, 78, 155
 examination of, 111-12
 retroverted, 29, 45
 tests on, 130-7

vabra catheter, 123
vagina, 27-9, 34
 infections, 71-2
 lubrication, 47, 107
 physical examination of, 110-13
 problems of, 49
vaginal cytology, 138
vaginal orgasms, 26
vaginismus, 42, 49-50
varicocele, 82, 109-10
varicose veins, 82
vasa deferentia, 34, 36, 138-9
 obstruction to, 85, 91
vasectomy, 36, 75, 85-6, 89
vasography, 138-9
veneral disease, 13, 65-6, 85
virgin wives, reasons for, 42, 111
vitamins, role of, 79, 90, 93
vulva, 24, 26

weight change, 60-1
 see also obesity
womb, see uterus

X-rays
 damage from, 78-9, 93
 in infertility testing, 131-3, 138-9

zinc, presence in the human body, significance of, 91-2